Anti-Colonial Solidarity

EXPLORATIONS IN CONTEMPORARY SOCIAL-POLITICAL PHILOSOPHY (ECSPP)

Series Editors: Naomi Zack (Lehman College, CUNY) and Laurie Shrage (Florida International University)

As our world continues to be buffeted by extreme changes in society and politics, philosophers can help navigate these disruptions. Rowman & Littlefield's ECSPP series books are intended for supplementary classroom use in intermediate to advanced college-level courses to introduce philosophy students and scholars in related fields to the latest research in social-political philosophy. This philosophical series has multidisciplinary applications and the potential to reach a broad audience of students, scholars, and general readers.

Beyond Blood Oil: Philosophy, Policy, and the Future, by Leif Wenar, Anna Stilz, Michael Blake, Christopher Kutz, Aaron James, and Nazrin Mehdiyeva

Reviving the Social Compact: Inclusive Citizenship in an Age of Extreme Politics, by Naomi Zack

Making and Unmaking Disability: The Three-Body Approach, by Julie Maybee

Comparative Just War Theory: An Introduction to International Perspectives, edited by Luís Cordeiro-Rodrigues and Danny Singh

Living with Animals: Rights, Responsibilities, and Respect, by Erin McKenna

The American Tragedy of COVID-19: Social and Political Crises of 2020, by Naomi Zack

Anti-Colonial Solidarity: Race, Reconciliation, and MENA Liberation, by George N. Fourlas

Anti-Colonial Solidarity

Race, Reconciliation, and MENA Liberation

George N. Fourlas

ROWMAN & LITTLEFIELD
Lanham • Boulder • New York • London

Published by Rowman & Littlefield
An imprint of The Rowman & Littlefield Publishing Group, Inc.
4501 Forbes Boulevard, Suite 200, Lanham, Maryland 20706
www.rowman.com

86-90 Paul Street, London EC2A 4NE, United Kingdom

We gratefully acknowledge permission to reprint the following chapters:

Chapter 1, "The 'Unknown' Middle Easterner: Post-Racial Anxieties and Anti-MENA Racism throughout Colonized Space-Time," originally appeared in *Critical Philosophy of Race* 9, no. 1 (2021): 48–70. Copyright © 2021 by The Pennsylvania State University. This article is used by permission of The Pennsylvania State University Press.

Chapter 3, "Calling in MENA Nationalists: Why Recent Geopolitical Boundaries Fail to Account for MENA Subjectivity," appeared in an earlier version as "Being a Target: On the Racialization of Middle Eastern Americans," in *Critical Philosophy of Race* 3, no. 1 (2015): 101–123. Copyright © 2015 by The Pennsylvania State University. This article is used by permission of The Pennsylvania State University Press.

Copyright © 2022 by The Rowman & Littlefield Publishing Group, Inc.

All rights reserved. No part of this book may be reproduced in any form or by any electronic or mechanical means, including information storage and retrieval systems, without written permission from the publisher, except by a reviewer who may quote passages in a review.

British Library Cataloguing in Publication Information Available

Library of Congress Cataloging-in-Publication Data Is Available

ISBN: 978-1-5381-4145-8 (cloth)
ISBN: 978-1-5381-4146-5 (pbk)
ISBN: 978-1-5381-4147-2 (electronic)

For Niketas and Felix

The classification of society into categories and terms following a certain pattern is produced artificially by capitalist monopolies. Such societies do not exist. Their propaganda does. However, societies are essentially political and moral. Economic, political, ideological, and military monopolies are constructions which contradict the nature of society by merely striving for the accumulation of surplus. They do not create values. Nor can a revolution create a new society. It can only play a positive role in restoring the moral and political fabric of the society that has been eroded. The rest is determined by the free will of moral and political society.

—Abdullah Öcalan, The Political Thought of Abdullah Öcalan

Devastating events can help us overcome our desconocimientos, which dehumanize other people and deny their suffering, prompting us to realize our common humanity. As we see beyond what divides us to what connects us, we're compelled to reach out beyond our walls of distrust, extend our hands to others, and share information and resources. The human species' survival depends on each one of us connecting to our vecinos (neighbors), whether they live across the street, across national borders, or across oceans. A calamity of the magnitude of 9/11 can compel us to think not in terms of "my" country or "your" nation but "our" planet.

—Gloria Anzaldúa, Light in the Dark = Luz En Lo Oscuro

One particularly dangerous dimension of the imperialist aspect of European civilization is its ideological hegemony. Without challenging it, we shall never be able to enter an independent path of political and economic development and share in a sustainable and just world order.

—Abdullah Öcalan, Prison Writings

"... the longing for unity cannot be indefinitely frustrated, whether by outside intervention or by domestic suppression, with impunity. To the degree to which such legitimate, vital, and popularly-appealing aspirations are obstructed, to that degree the indignation and wrath of the peoples concerned is incurred, and the counsel of moderation is resultantly discarded in favor of extremism and fanaticism.

—Fayez A. Sayegh, Arab Unity

Contents

Preface and Acknowledgments ... ix

Introduction: Beginning with Ends ... 1

1 The "Unknown" Middle Easterner: Post-Racial Anxieties and Anti-MENA Racism throughout Colonized Space-Time ... 19

2 Changing Lenses: Anti-Racist Posturing versus Praxis, an Enactivist Critique ... 35

3 Calling in MENA Nationalists: Why Recent Geopolitical Boundaries Fail to Account for MENA Subjectivity ... 55

4 Decolonizing the Ancients: Or, The Known West and the Anti-Colonial Principle ... 73

5 Flip the Script: Myth and Example from the Shores of Shinar ... 93

6 Be Ready: Lessons from Cyprus and Rojava ... 115

Conclusion: MENA America and the Future ... 131

Notes ... 135

Bibliography ... 155

Index ... 171

About the Author ... 181

Preface and Acknowledgments

I am responding to a problem. The general problem is the ongoing domination of the majority of the earth's people, with a focus on those dispersed populations from the broader world that have most recently been objectified as the Middle East and North Africa (MENA). I am trained as a philosopher, but I will appeal to any means that seem useful for addressing this general problem and bringing about a liberatory end. Hence, I think of my work and methods through those resources, people, and experiences that have influenced me, such that these acknowledgments are both a reflection on method and an expression of appreciation.

Before steeping myself in philosophical works, I found and continue to find inspiration—affirmative and negative—through my immediate communities and the defensive strategies they deploy to survive. In this sense, I am moved by those various resistant creative traditions, which are not typically discussed in academic discourse (e.g., various musical and artistic forms) but nevertheless meaningfully speak to our dislocation and the violence of life in America and the extended colonized world. Similarly, my thinking and tactics have been influenced by those theorists and activists who have liberatory goals and who are sometimes objectified through categories that include Africana, Native American, Asian and Pacific Islander, or Latin American. Part of this appeal is unintentional, the result of growing up in places where the problems I wrestle with are primarily addressed by non-MENA actors. I am especially drawn to the critical traditions found throughout Latin American philosophy because the problems being addressed within that tradition are most directly connected to the problems of the MENA region and its peoples, and those texts have become more readily available in the United States in a way that other texts have not.

Put differently, the texts that were available aligned with the spoken tradition that came prior to my academic training, and I tend to work with who or what resonates. And it is not a coincidence that Latinidad thinkers resonate with post-Ottoman and more specifically anti-colonial MENA thought. As I argue throughout, the East of the West—the Americas—was similarly overdetermined by Orientalist-racist attitudes, practices, and discourses, and though there are obvious contextual differences, it remains the case that, as Ana Tijoux and Shadia Mansour put it, "Somos Sur."[1] Indeed, I remember reading Enrique Dussel for the first time and being shaken by his reoccurring, seemingly deferential reference to one of my critical heroes, Edward Said, but also longing for that reference to be extended and expanded. What did it mean for Latin American thought and MENA American thought—if that is or could be such a thing—that Said is so fundamental in Dussel's world-historical understanding?

Insofar as I am attempting to create a groundwork or reclaim an already-existing foundation that might be understood as MENA thought, I am confronted by concerns similar to those in the Latin American philosophical tradition. Namely, in this case, what does it mean to say that MENA thought is distinct from other philosophical movements? My response to the contingent character of this problem is twofold. First, as I will argue throughout the text and especially in Chapter 4, the philosophical project emerged through what is now understood as the broader MENA region, making philosophy a pre-colonial and thus indigenous MENA practice; yet that project was appropriated with a great deal of emphasis on a selective, as well as romanticized (emphasis on the *Roman*), understanding of Athens, Sparta, and Jerusalem, as they were proprietized, and then claimed as European. Like the mythical namesake of the false continent, Europa, philosophy was stolen and violently forced into a foreign modality.

With the damage done, however, MENA thought, insofar as it is distinct, must now find a way to reclaim its philosophy from its captive state. Hence, my second response follows the arguments put forward by Stephanie Rivera Berruz in her effort to answer this problem for Latin American philosophy.[2] Rivera Berruz suggests that the focus be shifted from the descriptive question to a normative one, ultimately challenging Latin American philosophers to be explicit: "What do we want Latin American philosophy to do?"[3] This challenge seems to be evenly applicable to philosophy as such, but I am not the sort of universalist who denies the significance of contextual rootedness and emergence, and I think that the question must be asked by all liberatory critics in relation to the specific set of problems being confronted. For MENA American actors, the set of problems is the dual force of external racial domination that is exacerbated by internal racialized nationalist tensions and gender norms. MENA American thought ought to be concerned with overcoming these divisions, and that is another way of framing what I take to be captured by the ideal of *anti-colonial solidarity*.

Similarly, my work is also informed and inspired by the critical traditions that emerged alongside mainstream colonial thought, often in resistance to certain elements of the Western tradition despite also being a part of the colonial canon, especially the work that stems from Marx and Nietzsche. The deployment of a genealogical critique that is driven by liberatory ideals captures this unlikely pairing. I mention this Western influence only to clarify what I take to be an obvious point about identity, which is to say that grappling with hybridity is an epistemic-material project. I remain restless. And sometimes the tensions that follow from hybridity cannot be reconciled. To paraphrase Gloria Anzaldua, to live hybridity is to tolerate and ultimately ameliorate what appears to be contradiction.[4]

Most importantly, the heart of my method is conversational and experiential. Indeed, the cultivation of *Anti-Colonial Solidarity: Race, Reconciliation, and MENA Liberation* was largely possible because of various ongoing personal and professional relationships, circumstances, and events that I recognize below. Still, much is lost while much is gained in the process of becoming, creating, and sustaining, and while I struggle to affirm my relational existence through a recognition of others, I also will certainly fail to account for everyone and everything that matters. I am not sure if a relational existence can ever be fully recognized and appreciated, but I hope that I will be forgiven for any omissions, especially because so much has happened since I began. And I hope that the spirit of appreciation mentioned above will be carried forward throughout the text.

I finished this book during a global pandemic that continues to decimate the world's least well-off; during one of the most volatile elections in United States history that culminated in a violent insurrection; while Gaza and the Palestinians were bombed with overwhelming and sadistic force; while people around the world protest for an end to violent domination, for basic dignity, and for a living wage or the freedom that presumably comes with such wages. I finished this book a year after George Floyd was publicly murdered. And these are only a few of the major events that happened in the past year, which marked my teaching at the university level and in my home—there were no readily available children's books to help make sense of a pandemic in March of 2020.

The year before the lockdown, my youngest child was born, and only a few months after his joyous emergence, my institutional home, Hampshire College, where I was on a generous sabbatical leave, was taken over by what seemed to be a hostile president who was attempting to sell the land to the

University of Massachusetts, Amherst, and presumably fire the various amazing people who define the institution. Luckily, the students, faculty, and staff at Hampshire are rebellious in the best sense of the term, and protested these efforts—successfully, I should add. The folks at Hampshire organized and resisted this neoliberal fire sale, and as of this writing, the school survives. I could go on for some time—life in the twentieth and twenty-first centuries has been defined by this accelerated dialectic of crisis and resistance—but one thing is certain: constant crisis is, at the very least, exhausting, and neither I nor this book would exist if not for the vibrant life-worlds, and the people therein, who support me even when I am not my best.

On this point, my deepest gratitude is reserved for Elena Clare Cuffari, my partner in all things, who has read all of my writing, who has attended to and challenged my ideas, and who knows me best—sometimes better than I know myself. I could not have dreamed of a greater person to enact a life alongside, multiple lives actually, and any brilliance that shines through in this writing is due to Elena's presence, support, and tolerance.

I am also deeply grateful to various comrades who have supported me and this work, in solidarity, across institutional affiliations, at various points, and sometimes under ridiculous circumstances. José Jorge Mendoza has consistently acted as one of my primary interlocutors. He has also read most of my writing, including early drafts of this book, and has helped me develop my thought since we first met in graduate school at the University of Oregon in 2008. Specifically, José invited me to give a talk at UMass Lowell in 2017, the content of which has since become Chapter 1 and an article in *Critical Philosophy of Race*, while early versions of Chapters 4 and 6 were presented on panels that he organized for the Society for Mexican American Philosophy at the APA and Philosophy Born of Struggle.

Alfred Frankowski has also remained one of my primary interlocutors since our original meeting at the UO in 2008. Al's careful and honest reading, as well as commentary, have always helped to illuminate the strongest aspects of my work, and various points of clarity in this volume are thanks to Dr. Frankowski's support. Naomi Zack has also consistently encouraged and supported me, long after I stopped being her student, and she facilitated the publication of this text, along with Laurie Shrage, as a part of their series with Rowman & Littlefield. My good friend Richard Schmitt offered invaluable grounded criticism for key chapters in this book and helped me talk through these themes over many coffee and dinner meetings. John Harfouch also provided careful and crucial commentary, and more generally reached out to me to build the solidarity I had only dreamed of, such that this text and the evolution of my thought owe much to John's friendship. Matt Yanos offered careful feedback on Chapter 1 and has also consistently acted as a critical sparring partner with whom I have honed my argumentative skills while remaining focused on the liberatory ideal.

Benjamin Stumpf and Asa Needle each acted as research assistants at earlier points in the formation of this book and have remained interlocutors, as well as friends, since graduating from Hampshire College. Maceo Whatley acted as my research assistant in the summer of 2021 and read through the nearly final draft of the manuscript with the goal of making my writing accessible to undergraduates or a general audience, and to build the index. My thought has been shaped in many ways by the amazing conversations, reading groups, and the hope that these students have somehow managed to evoke at times that otherwise seemed hopeless.

Similarly, my many colleagues and friends from Worcester, Massachusetts, where most of this book was written, helped with these ideas and also offered the far more crucial material support that is a community: Kristin Waters, Henry Theriault, Dan Shartin, Aldo Guevara, Frank Boardman, Lucy Candib, Hardeep Sidhu, Alex Tarr, Vicki Grunzynski, Dani Benavidas, Elizabeth Osborne, Dana Rognlie, Hasnaa Mokhtar, Victor Pacheco, and Melanie Gnazzo.

My appreciation also goes to Cheyney Ryan, Hugo Slim, and the Oxford Consortium for Human Rights (OCHR). I have engaged with the OCHR since its founding, and all of the meetings that I have attended have been helpful to my work. However, in 2017, I spent three difficult weeks with OCHR in Geneva and Thessaloniki, working with refugees, as well as activists, near the Greco-Turkic border. My experience during this meeting helped solidify a redirection in my work from a general focus on reconciliatory efforts to a strict focus on MENA solidarity. After seeing firsthand how often voluntourism and narcissistic personalities complicate the efforts of human rights activists, and more importantly the survival of MENA peoples who continue to flee violence, my desire for a defensive solidarity was renewed with greater adrenal focus. Many folks from this event helped me work through the experience, offered outstanding support, and gave me great feedback on the work I presented. Hence, I am especially thankful for the support of Anna Evans-Goldstein, Deen Chatterjee, Elijah Munyi, Katie Dwyer, and Elizabeth Gamara.

Another event and emergent group that has been absolutely pivotal for my work was organized by John Harfouch—the Society for Anti-Colonial Middle East and North African Thought (SAMENAT). The first meeting of SAMENAT, which took place at the University of Huntsville in the spring of 2019, was a two-day workshop that brought together voices in philosophy who are working on MENA issues. I cannot overstate how powerful this event was for me and my writing—indeed, it continues to be impactful as

John and I collaborate on future meetings as affiliates with other philosophical organizations and as an independent group. Hence, along with John, I also owe many thanks to Alia Al-Saji, Falguni Sheth, Sabeen Ahmed, Marzouq Alnusf, Seloua Boulbina, Shaila Bora, Dylan Baun, and Dunya Majeed for all of your feedback and support, and for being amazing people.

Alia Al-Saji subsequently invited me to give a talk at McGill in the fall of 2019 as a part of the Montreal Workshop in Critical Philosophy of Race. The conversation here was also pivotal for my work, especially the helpful commentary and resources that were illuminated by Alia, Naïma Hamrouni, Bryan Mukandi, Celia Edell, Muhammad Velji, Aziz Choudry, Sebastian Rodriguez Duque, José Jorge Mendoza, and Joel Reynolds—and a special thanks to Joel for getting José and me across the border safely.

In the spring of 2019, I joined the Critical Genealogies Workshop in Eugene, Oregon, and shared an early draft of what has since become Chapters 5 and 6. Here I received careful feedback from Jordan Liz and Stephanie Caron Jenkins, which ultimately shaped this writing into its present form. I also want to thank Verena Erlenbusch-Anderson, Colin Koopman, Amy Nigh, Don Deere, and Kevin Thompson for comments and conversations throughout the 2019 meeting. Verena and Colin have been regular supporters of my work, prior to and after the CGW event, and I look forward to continuing to work with them on future genealogical projects.

In 2016 David Kim invited me to present an early version of Chapter 4 for a workshop at my alma mater, the University of San Francisco. Along with David's always-excellent feedback, I also received invaluable commentary from Leah Kalmanson, Peter Park, Lewis Gordon, and Amy Donahue. Like Naomi, my mentors and dear friends from the University of San Francisco have continued to support me long since finishing my undergraduate work, and so along with David, I also want to thank Ronald Sundstrom and Manuel Vargas for remaining in solidarity as I make my way.

My sincerest thanks to the Carlton and Wilberta Ripley Savage Endowment for International Relations and Peace, Portland State University, and Harry Anastasiou for supporting my work in conflict resolution and my time in Cyprus. Many thanks to Maria Hadjipavlou for her kind and helpful feedback, and her tireless efforts to realize peace. Chapter 6 and a sharp shift in my thinking would not have been possible without Maria and Harry, as well as the work being done by Cypriots to reclaim the past and build a peaceful future.

I must also extend my gratitude to the Radical Philosophy Association, the Caribbean Philosophical Association, Philosophy Born of Struggle, the Society for Mexican American Philosophy, the North American Society for Social Philosophy, and the American Philosophical Association for consistently making space for my work. From these various conferences and the ongoing relationships these organizations help to preserve, I have received support and feedback in the production of various parts of this book from Andrea Pitts, Aaron Shepherd, Sergio A. Gallegos, Michael Monahan, Linda Martín Alcoff, Ann Ferguson, Stephanie Rivera Berruz, Mlado Ivanovic, Reese Faust, Grant Silva, Amelia Wirts, and Fulden Ibrahimhakkioglu.

I cannot begin to pinpoint the myriad ways that my amazing colleagues and friends from Hampshire College have had an incalculable impact on me and my work since joining the community in 2015, but several folks have directly influenced this project, and so I am eternally grateful to Omar Dahi, Margaret Cerullo, Flavio Risech-Ozeguera, Kimberly Chang, Laura Greenfield, April Merleaux, Jennifer Hamilton, Stephen Dillon, Roosbelinda Cardenas, Christoph Cox, Jennifer Bajorek, Susana Loza, Kara Lynch, Monique Roelofs, Daniel Altshuler, Daniel Ross, Uzma Aslam Khan, Alan Goodman, Maria Cartagena, Mary Bombardier, Chyrell George, Monsita Moorehead, and Jackie Jeffery.

Hamsphire's system is unique in many ways, not the least of which being that it attracts some of the brightest and most creative students I have ever had the pleasure of knowing. Hampshire faculty and students work together closely on research projects, especially during the senior year. I have learned a great deal from my students through these collective projects, and this monograph would not have emerged as it has without the support and feedback of Claire Saboe, Emma Gross, Madeline Miller, Desta Cantave, Haley Grey, Lexx Cespedes, Elan Goldman, Tess Greenwood, Bijan Pakdel, Helen Makkas, Eddy Ongweso, Aram Martirosyan, and Bar Kolodny. I also received a great deal of invaluable support from the Ethics and the Common Good program (ECG), including the amazing actors who make ECG happen: Javiera Benavente, Teal Van Dyck, David Bollier, and Julie and Laurie Schecter.

Finally, I have spent the pandemic year under lockdown in various places throughout Pennsylvania, and with much support from my colleagues at Franklin and Marshall College. I owe many thanks to Stephanie McNulty, Nick Kroll, Kelly Schenke, and Paulina Ayala.

Most importantly, I would not have made it through this year—or any year—without my family, who consistently models solidarity, with reciprocity and acceptance. Words fail to express my gratitude for Niketas, Felix, Elizabeth, Alethea, Kenneth (the older and Costas), and Thomas, as well as my many other relatives who have supported me throughout my life.

Introduction
Beginning with Ends

There are many aims that I envision in calling for and theorizing *anti-colonial solidarity*, and many that can only be imagined as that relational mode is increasingly realized. The general end—to transcend or overcome entrenched colonial social-institutional norms of domination and realize power that is based in reciprocity—is implicit to the name. I borrow the language of anti-coloniality from various scholars and activists, most recently from my friend John Harfouch, who forcefully defends Middle East and North African (MENA) peoples and argues for the enactment of solidarity through the counter-institutional framework exemplified by the Boycott, Divest, and Sanction (BDS) movement.[1] In his defense of BDS, I understand Harfouch to be suggesting that all anti-colonial and decolonial scholar-activists have an obligation to directly address the Israel/Palestine conflict, and thus the subjugation of Palestinian peoples, as well as anti-nationalist Israeli comrades, by the Israeli security state. I concur and I begin with Harfouch's point for two reasons: First, by way of extension insofar as we need—and in fact, as I will show, we already have the framework for—an affirmative project to accompany negative movements like BDS. On this point, John says, "an anti-colonial movement must disrupt the economics of colonialism, including practices within the university, even when such opposition makes representation difficult,"[2] and here I am extending this demand by emphasizing the development of post-state or autonomist economic systems—while we disrupt we must also build an alternative.

Second, and unfortunately of greater exigence, *Anti-Colonial Solidarity* is written in response to the Orientalist-racist understanding and justification of Israel/Palestine, as well as MENA-perceived people more generally. The colonial powers struggle to maintain a stranglehold on this narrative, the Orientalist-racist position, and this is especially evident in the weeks that I am writing this passage, May 2021, as Israel has systematically decimated Gaza with a hellfire bombing campaign and people around the world have risen in protest on behalf of Palestinian liberation. As Mohammed el-Kurd says in a special edition of the *Groundings* podcast, "Israeli politicians are kicking and screaming, they are terrified of losing the narrative. . . . They are terrified of this ability to self-articulate."[3]

The Orientalist-racist position takes as given that MENA people are naturally opposed, barbarians with a thirst for the blood of our enemies, and that we will never know peace without a leviathan to keep us in check because of our oppositional and irrational nature. Indeed, the historical fact that the vision of a Jewish homeland materialized as a militant settler-colonial state and not a pluralist coexistence as it was imagined by more ethical thinkers, specifically Martin Buber, is at least partly the result of a false naturalization of our oppositions.[4] On this point, the conservative and Machiavellian among us are especially keen to rely on this naturalized animosity in more or less explicit ways depending on who is listening. Indeed, for those MENA folks who are raised outside of the broader MENA territories—especially those who live abroad because they were displaced by genocide and other acts of primitive accumulation—the ethno-nationalisms that drive these sentiments are instilled early on. We are taught "the enemy" and who they are. I reject these naturalized oppositions, and thus one of the primary goals of this text is to offer an alternative narrative for MENA peoples, one that lends itself to *anti-colonial solidarity*. The heart of this counter-narrative is this: our oppositions are produced and maintained, often intentionally, in order to prevent our cooperative self-determination (cooperative-determination).

The force of the narrative I am countering is elucidated by the fact that there are obvious cases of MENA people—including Israeli and Palestinian actors—working together toward peace, who are largely ignored or disregarded.[5] When not glibly written off, these examples are taken as novel exceptions, and as such their relation to similar cases is nullified. From this reified perspective of the Western status quo, it seems strange to discuss Israeli and Palestinian solidarity in the same context as Armenian or Greek and Turkic, or Pakistani and Indian solidarity. Along with being treated as aberrant, solidarity among groups that are supposed to be in conflict also irks some because so little is known of the historical-material circumstances that afford the current divisions known as the Middle East and North Africa—or, for that matter, the designation of Europe as a distinct historical and continental object.[6] Indeed, the spatial limit *MENA* is a twentieth-century production, one that I hold on to for reappropriative purposes and because other names, *Arab*, for example, are misunderstood by Western ideologues as well as MENA peoples. As Abdelkebir Khatibi carefully emphasizes, "the name

'Arab' designates a war of naming and ideologies, which bring to light the active plurality of the Arab world."[7] Khatibi goes on:

> This unity is, for us, for the past, to be analyzed in its imaginary insistence. And besides, this alleged unity that is claimed so vehemently includes not only its specific margins (Berber, Coptic, Kurdish . . . and the margins of margins: the feminine), but also covers the division of the Arab world into countries, peoples, sects, and classes—and the divisions of divisions, up until the suffering of the individual, deserted by the hope of his god, forever invisible.[8]

Rather than fight over authenticity from the margins, where nothing is won, I am rearticulating the "insistence" of unity noted in the previous quote through a reappropriation of the more recent categorical attempt at our epistemicide—that is, the objectification of a MENA region and peoples, the limits of which have been overdetermined and imposed in myriad insidious ways that I address throughout.

Yet, given the reified or taken-to-be-given ways in which the MENA region is discussed by non-MENA peoples—and, occasionally, by nationalists who identify with the MENA world—with deep hesitation I grant the following: There is some truth to the claim that a hyper focus has been placed on Israel—at least in certain politically right-leaning Western discourses—such that if something is known of the MENA region then it will likely be a cursory and myopic knowledge of the Levant in the twentieth century. The claim, however, is not then that attention ought to be directed away from the crimes of the Israeli state. Rather, the point should be taken as a challenge to witness how the atrocities committed by the Israeli state are right in line with the genocidal policies and thus acts of other colonial arrangements. For example, Israel looks and acts a lot like the United States or, more pointedly, the Ottoman empire and the Young Turks in particular, who, of course, are responsible for the historical and ongoing genocide against Ottoman Christians—Armenians, Assyrians, and Greeks—which was used to justify the Shoah.[9]

Paying attention to other colonialist projects, and more importantly anti-colonial projects, in the MENA region, alongside the colonialism of the state of Israel, is necessary not just to build connections—though these sorts of epistemic bridges are crucial. Historically the divisions that currently overdetermine MENA people and that produce the MENA region as a known object result from the exploitation of tensions that existed prior to colonial influence, especially throughout the Ottoman world. Given that the current fascist regime in Turkey is attempting to create a neo-Ottoman empire, the attention to these other conflicts is also important for resisting the ongoing domination of MENA people. Hence, I focus my attention to some of these other divisions and those allegedly exceptional cases of solidarity that counter the naturalized conflict narrative, in order to bolster the more local claim that Israeli and Palestinian people, and in fact all MENA people, not only can coexist but can also flourish together when colonial force and thus the domination state is sufficiently undermined or blocked from intervening in the relational coordination of said actors. My critical opposition to the naturalized narrative about MENA peoples thus paves the way for an affirmative project: *anti-colonial solidarity*.

With all of this in mind, however, this book is most importantly written for the MENA diaspora who carry colonial divisions outside of the MENA context, while simultaneously being confronted with new and more immediate violent domination through the primary colonial powers of Western Eurasia and the United States. The MENA American experience, for example, is compounded by colonial pressures that are imported from local familial experiences and anxieties, and by the more general colonial norms of race/racism that frame and mistreat the MENA-perceived populations as a degenerate collective. Thus, the MENA-perceived actor is particularly vulnerable to violent domination from the state and from social forces that include white supremacists, as well as other MENA people, who imagine themselves as engaged in an ongoing war.[10]

Put simply then, *anti-colonial solidarity* is about envisioning and working toward the creation of a social-political modality, specifically but not exclusively among MENA people, that affords self-defense and ultimately aims to liberate from colonial power in its various insidious, as well as decadent, forms. *Anti-colonial solidarity* is both an ideal that ought to be realized and a modality that is already being enacted by MENA people throughout the world, and this fact is not an aberration but a call to action.

The enactment of an *anti-colonial solidarity* is a massive task, and by no means do I expect to have the final word on the project. Rather, I draw on already-established discourses and movements that are responding to colonial domination from around the world with a modest twofold aim: First, I work to frame the problem of coloniality—that lingering asymmetrical system described by Aníbal Quijano and Sylvia Wynter that relies on racial realist hierarchies and the objectifying framework of scientific rationality to secure some at the expense of most—in relation to the imagined Orient and more specifically MENA-perceived actors in the U.S. context.[11] Second, I am writing for a better possible future.

On this first point, as Edward Said teaches throughout his writings, too often the MENA-perceived person and the MENA world are ignored or treated with a myopic focus, through phobic or philiac fetishizations.[12] The phobic side of contemporary Orientalism is obvious insofar as most popular conversations about MENA people or the MENA region concern ridiculous polemics on terrorism, state formation, and the difficulties of Westernization in relation to degrading stereotypes of Islam and Muslim populations. The philiac fetishization of the MENA region is sometimes less obvious because the idea of the MENA, a twentieth-century construct, does not align with the actual history of MENA peoples.[13]

Indeed, the study of the ancient or pre-colonial world is often an example of the philiac fetishization of what is now sometimes thought of as the MENA world. The MENAphile pines to take a selfie in Istanbul, or to recover the library of Alexandria or the Buddhas of Bamiyan, to hold the Rosetta stone or to stand in the Parthenon, recalling an imaginary and fetishized past that does not include the MENA people who allegedly let these wonderful things disappear, fall into disarray, or intentionally destroyed the fetish objects. Along with the fetishization of historical places and things, the MENAphile can also have a hypersexual longing for the perceived MENA actor that often manifests as a desire to "liberate." Indeed, as Mehammed Amadeus Mack argues, the relationship between freedom, sexuality, and inclusion are directly linked for Muslims in France.[14] Hence, there are various micro-contributions that I hope to make to the larger anti-colonial discourse. This includes extending Said's descriptive work in relation to the racialization of MENA-perceived people and unpacking the normative ends of such critique by calling for *anti-colonial solidarity*.

Regarding my second aim, on possible futures, I am laying the groundwork for a world that I hope for, in relation to a past where such a groundwork was lacking and disallowed such that I, and others like me, are forced to deny ourselves or scavenge for meaning in fractures and schisms. I imagine my children or grandchildren having restless nights, working through the problems that I also confront, and ideally finding some direction or at least comfort in this text—even if that guidance comes only through the absolute failure of what I have written—while also avoiding the long path that I had to take to arrive where I am. I write this text in order to affirm an existence—which so many forces have tried to erase, appropriate, and degrade—and demand dignity. I write this text to emphasize that we must protect ourselves—treat our wounds and take up various forms of preventative care—and to strategize ways of enacting that self-defense that do not reproduce domination. In other words, I write for freedom and cooperative-determination, autonomy, or liberation. Hence, the path that I will take throughout this text is defined by the transformation of our oppositions (i.e., race) through collective meaning-making labor (i.e., reconciliation).

GENERAL OVERVIEW AND SPECIFIC CHAPTER REFERENCES

The overarching tryptic structure of *Anti-Colonial Solidarity* begins with race, then turns to reconciliation, and ends with the challenge of liberation. I expand on these concepts throughout, but for the sake of clarity I now offer some basic descriptions. I ask that my audience carry these basic definitions forward into the subsequent chapters on the promise that I will clarify and problematize these notions through more nuanced reflections.

The *anti-colonial* element of my title is emphasized above and is concerned with overcoming the systems, as well as habitual-cultural norms, of domination that constitute and maintain the coloniality of power. Solidarity is the possibility that comes out of anti-colonial thought and action, but it remains underdetermined in order to avoid imposing one rigid sense over and against another, which would reproduce coloniality and undermine the anti-colonial demand. The sort of solidarity that acts as the ideal of these critical reflections can be witnessed in many exemplary cases beyond those discussed in this book, such as the abolitionist work of John Brown, the recent refusal of Italian port workers to load arms shipments being sent to Israel, and in the collectivist effort of organizations like the *International Peoples' Assembly*.[15] Hence, *anti-colonial solidarity* is not a call for oneness, however, or the uniformity that is often found in militant nationalist movements. Rather, the concept that best captures what *anti-colonial solidarity* aims for is, as Danielle S. Allen puts it, wholeness.[16] Allen says:

> In fact, wholeness, not oneness, is the master term in the history of the production of democratic peoples. Indeed, the effort to make the people "one" should be seen as but a single version of the more general endeavor, necessitated by the more fundamental democratic project, to make the people "whole." The word derives from Old English and Germanic forms meaning "uninjured, sound, healthy, and complete." Now it means rather "full," "total," "complete," and "all." . . . A speaker cannot use the word "one" to mean multiplicity, but the word "whole" entails just that. The effort to make the people "one" cultivates in the citizenry a desire for homogeneity, for that is the aspiration taught to citizens by the meaning of the word "one," itself. In contrast, an effort to make the people "whole" might cultivate an aspiration to the coherence and integrity of a consolidated but complex, intricate, and differentiated body. Why does it matter how democratic citizens imagine "the people" of which they are a part? As a democracy develops an explanation of how its citizenry is a coherent body, "the people," and makes this body imaginable, it also invents customs and practices of citizenly interaction that accord with that explanation.[17]

An emphasis on solidarity that maintains multiplicity, however, involves overcoming the tactics of domination in the myriad ways that they operate. In this sense, the form wholeness can take will vary across material experience, which makes it not merely difficult but in fact a contradiction of value to envision solidarity in a fully worked-out way. Solidarity is not built from a blueprint. Rather, the positions on solidarity that align with this project focus on the conditions of the possibility of wholeness or a unity of difference, rather than the end itself. And the actual structures, systems, or institutional forces that eventually afford solidarity may be illegible to a liberal-minded person.

Put differently, the goal of the theorist is not to offer a detailed schematic for how the future social-institutional arrangement should look; rather, the philosopher should (at the very least) describe current problems, illuminate possibility from the historical-present, and challenge any future possible emergence through normative constraints. The philosophical project, at least the one that I am engaged in, is part of a tradition of critique that clarifies the conditions of possibility from the material past and present. Hence, I maintain the strong normative position that all people ought to strive toward *anticolonial solidarity* for at least three reasons, though the text itself is concerned with the more modest possibility of solidarity for MENA people, as well as other historically subjugated groups.

My first reason for maintaining a strong normative position is that, pragmatically speaking, the alternative is mass extinction. The logical end of a system that relies on colonial domination—which is the starting point, means, and end of liberal-capitalism as it has emerged throughout history—is collapse, degradation, and death.[18] Unlike other theorists, however, I do not think that the internal contradictions of capital necessarily lead to a more advanced or progressive social-institutional arrangement. There is no future for anyone without the active and intentional participation of the majority of the world's peoples coordinating our collective transition to some other world-historical arrangement.[19] We can fail to respond to the problem of coloniality, and the historical consequence of that failure is not a better arrangement for human persons; it is merely a transition to a nonhuman arrangement. The problem, then, is not at the normative level because we obviously should figure out how to collectivize and act together—our survival is at stake. The problem is that not enough has been said about how a disparate and divided people actually collectivize, such that involved parties can affirmatively act in solidarity. Or, what has been said is largely misguided and grounded in a false-secular notion of rationality.[20] It is easy to say, "If we only worked together we could change the world," and much harder to articulate how we coordinate to make that change.

This is not to say that solidarity has not and does not occur, but too often solidarity is rooted in an imagined or actual enemy *other*. This form of solidarity fails in various ways, but the most crucial for my purposes is that it reinforces the divisiveness that allows colonial structures to operate unchanged—that is, solidarity through enemies is central to the colonial project and thus not sufficiently anti-colonial. Indeed, divide and conquer is the primary tactical means of the colonizers, and the best way to divide a people is to catalyze and take control of already-existing tensions.

The rationality of coloniality is compounded in anti-colonial responses, especially those that take up arms against the oppressor either at the national or, as Darryl Li eloquently elucidates, at the transnational level.[21] Fanon clearly begins with this same concern, noting, "Decolonization is always a violent phenomenon."[22] The question that lingers in Fanon's text, and decoloniality more generally, is how violence is and ought to be directed. For Li, and the anti-colonial actors he discusses throughout his analysis, this concern with violence emerges through the language of Jihad, a concept that is most commonly deployed for the inward disciplinary struggles involved in being virtuous. I mostly avoid the *Jihadist* terminology, instead focusing on the inward and outward framework that is captured by the concept because that seems to be the more important element of the concept. What work is required, at the individual and social level? How must we navigate what Di Paolo, Cuffari, and De Jaegher describe as the primordial tension, to achieve a solidarity that does not reproduce colonial domination?[23]

Hence, my second reason for maintaining a strong anti-colonial normative position is rooted in the means by which I argue that solidarity is best achieved, which I understand to be reconciliatory in focus and intent. In my earlier writings I have argued extensively for a definition of *reconciliation* that avoids the trappings of resignation, apologetics, or eurocentrism, and for the sake of this text I rely on the distilled version of that analysis: by *reconciliation* I mean both the conditions of the possibility of cooperative meaning-making, and that same cooperative process as an ongoing meaning-making activity.[24]

Here, I understand *meaning* to include the functional or pragmatic position, which is consequences in lived experience, and the not so explicitly functional transcendence that accompanies what Martin Buber describes as an *I-You* relation. Cooperative meaning-making is then a coordinated effort to "make sense" of consequential experience, or boundary-blurring experiences like those of close friends and lovers, and simultaneously change the outcome of experience, ideally, through intentional effort (i.e., the will to change).[25] By *experience* I mean the material engagement of living beings in interaction with other living and nonliving beings. Experience, however, is never neutral, and part of the tension that I critique throughout this text is the ways our interactions both influence and also are influenced by the ecosystem wherein we are functioning, such that we gain experience through living and become habituated in various ways. Indeed, habituated experience can be the source of many social conflicts, which is why I also advocate for intentional training or conditioning work to combat said breakdowns with a specific focus on anti-racist praxis.

For the conflicted social world, as well as for proto-agential beings (e.g., young children), material conditions must be produced and sometimes carefully stewarded in such a way as to afford cooperative meaning-making encounters, while for relatively peaceful agents—those who have presumably been well-socialized in the basics of meaning-making—the social encounter presupposes the capacity and will to make sense together. Indeed, agents maintain a thin sense of trust that peers will coordinate and satisfy basic expectations for the sake of mundane meaning-making.[26] In the absence of this thin trust, basic social activities—such as safely walking through a world that includes other people—become impossible. As people cultivate relations, a more robust connection emerges that is often described as friendship or through the convoluted languages of love.

Hence, the second reason for maintaining a strong normative stance—we ought to strive for an *anti-colonial solidarity*—is that it is also a more satisfying way of being together. War, violence, conflict, or constant oppositional encounters are exhausting, tragic, and make for a generally terrible life. Framed as such, the reconciliatory reason is also a pragmatic reason, but the reconciliatory justification can also be articulated as a means to freedom.

In this sense, a third reason for defending an *anti-colonial solidarity* is that it is liberatory. *Liberation* meaning quite simply "freedom *from* domination," which is the freedom *to*—as Grant Silva nicely frames it—realize a meaningful life in, through, and with community.[27] The liberatory notion of freedom is not to be confused with the sociopathic or anti-social freedom that is central to the liberal-capitalist project, which treats the *other* as an obstacle to be navigated or used for personal gain, affording a delusional world wherein a select few position themselves beyond sociality as if they were gods.

Before arriving at reconciliation and liberation, however, I must say more about what stands in our way. The horizontal divisions that allow the coloniality of power to persist are entrenched and multiple.

Still, for the sake of analysis—not reduction—I first focus on race as the primary contradiction or that central institutionally bolstered objectified status that mediates human relations and thus undermines our capacity to work together toward a cooperatively-determined future. By *race* I mean the lingering belief that humanity is made of distinct biological kinds that exist in hierarchical and oppositional relation, and the institutional reinforcement of that lingering belief through asymmetrical and unjust power relations. Racial pseudo-science, which produced the mess that is race, was largely debunked in the twentieth century, yet the myth of racial difference persists in the arrangement of our many unreconciled institutions and in the minds of various misdirected social worlds.²⁸ Racism persists insofar as people are still treated as if they are of distinct and hierarchically situated races. Thus, when discussing race, I am also discussing racism and racialization. By *racialization* I mean an objectifying social and institutional relation that heavily relies on what Linda Alcoff calls "visible identities," or the phenotypic referent to racial myths that are used to target, denigrate, exploit, and ultimately divide to conquer.²⁹ Racialization and racism are deployed to keep the racialized in their hierarchically determined places.

I focus on race, rather than some other objectified form such as class or gender, because I think that these other objectified forms are obfuscated by racial division, such that we cannot realize the normative demands of intersectionality or creolization—that is, the belief that people ought to be engaged and understood in their hypercomplexity and not reduced to stereotypical object forms, a position that I agree with and defend throughout this book—without first working to overcome racial division and thus racism. Of course, within racialized collectives, other objectified divisions will take on different significance depending on the conditions of said groups such that solidarity is further undermined by these objectifications that are often obfuscated by or as race.³⁰

So, for example, Pauli Murray and more recently Kimberlé Crenshaw critique legal power as it operates through the formal review of discrimination cases—or the failure to review based on the type of claim being made—and demonstrate how the legal system is unwilling, as well as unable, to open the Pandora's box of human complexity.³¹ The Pandora's box, in this case, is doubly risky for legal power. On the one hand, the system depends on its bureaucratic identity forms as if they are distinct, and if the hypercomplexity of life were recognized, then the number of possible discrimination cases would certainly rise, thus creating a practical burden on the system. Besides giving legal actors far more labor than they likely are comfortable with, the recognition of a distinct race/gender experience would also be a threat to the mode of power that supports some forms of discrimination in order to block the recognition of other forms. Hence, the emphasis on the distinct race/gender form presumably threatens the formal recognition that one can be discriminated against on grounds that are not exclusive to one predefined protected class status, but in fact on contingent grounds that involve the overlapping function of multiple objectified categories (i.e., race/gender, but once the box is open, then all identity forms can be recognized as potential reasons for discrimination claims).

These rigid categories are reflective of the larger problem of coloniality—namely, that it cannot move past the epistemic limits that it creates and maintains; to do so would be to invert key aspects of the system. So, on the other hand, intersectionality becomes a normative demand, but one that is always made in response to objectified domination of the variety described by Crenshaw. On this point, I generally agree with the intersectional plea and, as Anne McClintock suggests, maintain that "race, gender, and class are not distinct realms of experience, existing in splendid isolation from each other,"[32] but the force of that position only makes sense in relation to a world where these forms are treated as distinct by people with power (i.e., guns and administrative positions) and by people who have been pitted against themselves. On this point, Tommy J. Curry emphasizes that Crenshaw's version of intersectionality seems to reobjectify Black males, claiming:

> Intersectionality relies on a conceptualization of gender that allows the reconstitution of Black female identity around sameness and difference (with Black men and white women) while requiring Black males to be theorized primarily through the sameness they share with "men" as patriarchs. Under intersectionality Black males are denied the reformulations afforded to Black females.[33]

Curry's point is crucial for how I understand the normative claim of intersectionality to make sense, which is to say deobjectification or the recognition of the hypercomplexity of life ought to be broadly granted, but the fact that life continues to be reduced to archaic categories and the naturalized myths that accompany said object forms prevents the realization of an intersectional position—perhaps, according to Curry, even within Crenshaw's work. To that end, I maintain that race too often acts as the primary contradiction or the main obstacle to cooperative action and thus intersectional, or more specifically reciprocal and open, relational modes.

For example, as I write this paragraph in mid-March 2021, eight people, six of whom were Asian women, were murdered by a white supremacist in three different spas throughout Atlanta, Georgia, and apologists are trying to claim that the killer was motivated by "sex addiction," not race, as if these things operate independently especially in relation to Asian spa workers.[34] Colonial apologists are unable and unwilling to recognize the complexity of racial domination, while at the same time securing the imagined purity of whiteness by saying that the killer was an aberration, a twisted sex addict, not representative of white supremacy as such. The normative demand is intersectional, but the descriptive problem is categorical rigidity, oversimplification, or more pointedly the sort of denial that always bolsters and drives genocidal movements. Rather than shy away from this descriptive fact, I am suggesting that solidarity emerge on the premise that genocidal denial is not likely to change on our behalf any time soon and we need to protect ourselves from violent domination. I expand on these claims throughout the chapters that make up this book.

The specific chapters therefore unfold as follows: I take up this three-part critique—race, reconciliation, and liberation—across 6 chapters, and I begin with race as the primary contradiction, with a specific focus on the complexities of MENA racial experience.

In Chapter 1, I focus on the experience of MENA-identified people in the U.S. context as racialized. Here, the claim that Middle Eastern persons are racialized is made in response to complexities that are definitive of the current post-racial situation in the United States—namely, that the language of race, racism, and racialization are antiquated and thus fail to capture MENA experiences for various reasons that have driven some critics to call for different terminology (i.e., *xenophobia* or *Islamophobia*). I argue that we ought to call racism against Middle Eastern people *racism* because to call it something else is to ground the experience in an incomplete description that affords a lighter moral responsibility and that disconnects the experience from an ongoing historical conflict.

The first section elaborates the problem of racial conflict in the United States and the specific problem of Middle Eastern racialization. I respond to this problem with a historical argument in the second section that emphasizes key genealogical markers in the co-emergence of Orientalism, colonialism, and racialization. In the last section, I contrast the idea of race with competing terms—xenophobia and Islamophobia—to emphasize why we ought to hold onto the concept for descriptive purposes. I close by reflecting on why the terminology ought to be maintained for ethical reasons, which is the primary focus of the next chapter. Chapter 1 can also be understood as setting a basic critical standard for *anti-colonial solidarity*, which is to understand race and racism within a global historical-material context.

Chapter 2 follows up with a key point of defense from the previous chapter, wherein I emphasize that the normative force of calling racism by its name is crucial because such accusations or critiques carry greater moral weight than other objectifying categories. Nevertheless, a problem remains concerning the practical force of naming race/racism/racialization. I understand this problem in two ways: (1) Generally speaking when racism is named in interaction, the common response is defensive—to deny, deflect, or double down. (2) More specifically, those who are seen as MENA by racists and subsequently mistreated generally lack the legitimacy to even declare the racist action as racist—after all, in many contexts MENA people are, in the absence of institutional recognition, categorized as white, or the experience of racialization is explained away through other terms that are less morally forceful (i.e., *Islamophobia*). In order to fully address (2), the epistemic limits of white guilt, I begin with (1) or the general problem of condemning racism.

The full implications of naming racism will vary based on the positionality of the person whose actions are being condemned; yet, recent forms of condemning racism—what I will call anti-racist posturing—have failed to appreciate the nuances of power, and the importance of social work, such that a blanket approach to moral failure has been taken that produces greater division among folks who ought to otherwise operate in and for solidarity. The mode of condemnation I am alluding to has been recently witnessed and critiqued as call-out or cancel culture. The first part of my critique is therefore focused on examples that fit these specific forms of moral failure and responsive outrage, though the claims I make here can also be extended to include other moral failures and call-out responses. I argue that calling-out racism too often reinforces racism, yet I also defend the call-out as an appropriate reaction, especially when directed at actors whose power positions them beyond sociality. My critique of call-out culture rests on a distinction between anti-racist posturing and praxis—modes with different paradigmatic starting points and thus different ends—so I begin by elaborating that split and defending a relational concept of praxis in order to create a clearing for an anti-colonial ethics and politics.

Given the failures of anti-racist posturing, I then return to the problem of anti-MENA racism and suggest that the complexity of our situation, which is only partly determined by the limits of white guilt, can be addressed by appealing to our own pre-colonial or indigenous relational practices. In other words, the critique I level here makes possible a more in-depth discussion of the indigenous reconciliatory practices that I believe MENA peoples, and dominated people more generally, can (and should) reclaim in an effort to build solidarity and combat racism. Chapter 2 can also be understood as setting a standard for *anti-colonial solidarity*, which is to reclaim social relations and interactions from the norms of domination through nonretributive dynamics. We must learn to hate the sin and not the sinner.

Chapter 3 marks the beginning of my affirmative account, which is a reconciliatory approach to decolonization. Here, I transition away from the negative critique of racial conflict in order to focus on the specific ways that naturalized objectified forms prevent MENA meaning-making and thus solidarity among MENA people. MENA actors are confronted with a dual problem of being targeted as part of a racialized collective and having the conditions that afford that domination catalyzed by in-fighting among MENA people who would otherwise share common interests. Hence, our ability to engage each other about our shared experiences and potentially form defensive, as well as affirmative, relationships—our meaning-making abilities—are often hindered by our micro-communal commitments that, for the MENA diaspora, were formulated in response to a different set of problems, from a different time, and often in a place that may or may not still exist. Internally, then, the racial hierarchy of coloniality takes on the specific form of nationalism among MENA peoples, thus transforming the primary contradiction into a racialized-nationalism. For the Orientalist-racist, however, all MENA peoples exist within the same racial collective, but the bounds of that collectivity are often conflated with recent national and continental distinctions, thus affording conceptual dissonance for MENA activists who are interested in formal recognition through a categorical MENA status.

The need to organize and work toward solidarity *is* a defensive move and the beginning of a potential self-determined future. And the act of forming communities is one of the oldest practices among the people who have only recently been categorized through imagined MENA boundaries and thus ought to be affirmatively maintained on its own terms as a continuation of our pre-colonial modalities. The insularity that prevents our collective action most often manifests as nationalism, which causes many problems beyond the permissive silence, or active participation in maintaining the coloniality of power, that is too often enacted by non-Black populations of color. Hence, in this chapter I also begin working toward an emphasis on the normative need to reclaim that pre-colonial ethos described above—and that I will define throughout the subsequent chapters as being driven by an anti-colonial principle.

First, however, I will extend this argument against insularity, specifically national insularity, amongst MENA peoples insofar as it is the primary blockage in the struggle for a new identity and modality that affords solidarity. That is, ethno-national chauvinism mediates the potential encounter between MENA peoples and too often prevents the encounter from unfolding before it has a chance to emerge. Therefore, I argue, in forming an anti-colonial identity, especially among MENA peoples, national identity must be softened, denaturalized, deproprietized, or, in some cases, rejected. Chapter 3 therefore reinforces the previously established standards—critiquing race in a global context and moving away from spiteful relation norms—and can also be read as a redefinition of *anti-colonial solidarity*, insofar as it is grounded in a challenge to the internalization of Orientalism, colonialism, and thus the mores of exclusion.

Chapter 4 marks a distinct shift from other decolonial or anti-colonial philosophies because the MENA world and the East/West divide emerge through unique historical-material circumstances, and therefore requires a custom strategically oriented response. Put differently, the question of cooperative-determination among MENA peoples is not just one of independence from Western power; rather, what is also needed is a reclamation of the historical modes that were either overwritten or appropriated by Western colonial forces. In this sense, the affirmative anti-colonial project among MENA people is also a project of taking back what is ours from the Western colonizers who have selectively whitewashed, proprietized, and thus claimed parts of our pre-colonial existence at the exclusion of others.

Specifically, the "West" has been determined through negation of the "East," such that the overemphasis on the known and barbaric *other* obfuscates its own ambiguity, instability, and contradictory character. Indeed, one often hears Europe or the United States spoken of with great certainty, not just as beacons of rationality, progress, and thus morality, but as fixed and eternal facts. It is assumed that the West is known, but it turns out that much is hidden by this knowing, which, when revealed, illuminates the myth for the teetering fabrication that it is. Dislodging reified historical claims that are grounded in natural hierarchies and dispositions—barbarian versus civilized, East versus West—requires an alternative critical historical framework and narrative that challenges the naturalization of our domination, as well as the Western frame (i.e., coloniality) more generally. And, as a historical critique, the alternative I describe in this chapter and the next also exemplifies possibilities that are foreclosed or obscured by the colonial story. Specifically, the Western mythos as mediating idea obscures the very thing that made it possible: relationality, exchange, diversity, and a world that is determined by people living from the ground-up, rather than a world that is imposed through the various forms of domination required for cartographic certainty.

I first illuminate this alternative historical frame and narrative through a more focused genealogical critique of the emergence of the Orient/Occident split—as it currently functions in the colonized mind along the Greco-Turkic or Europe/Asia border—that both describes and destabilizes that divide. The affirmative aspect of this genealogical critique also reveals that the colonial tourniquet that reifies current cartographic myths—instilling those myths as givens in the colonized mind and cementing an otherwise fluid world into a known oppositional thing—simultaneously obfuscates and rejects the indigenous reconciliatory practices that defined the broader MENA region prior to colonization, prior to MENAfication, and that are needed for a future that is liberated from colonial domination. Hence, I close Chapter 4 by "looking back" and recovering what I will call the ancient or pre-colonial principle, bringing it forward to the present as an anti-colonial principle. Chapter 4 can also be read as a reaffirmation of *anti-colonial solidarity*'s challenge to the Western imaginary and its fascist, exclusive, as well as fetishistic notions, but it is also a challenge to a-historicism or false historicisms. We must look back, honestly, while we move forward.

In Chapter 5, I respond to the problem of counter-historical method that lingers in the background of the previous chapter through a critical discussion of myth. I turn to myth because, as several theorists note, the heart of Euromodern, enlightenment, or colonial rationality is the simultaneous nominal rejection of myth and its tacit maintenance through a story about human nature and self-preservation.[35] Rather than abandon myth, I argue here that a new myth is needed to serve as an ideal that guides and transforms social-political relations in the face of the apocalyptic collapse that was and still is colonial domination. That myth is found in the story of Babel and brought to life through exemplary cases in the present.

I first discuss the tradition of the oppressed that drives much counter-historical work through José Medina's critique of epistemic resistance. Medina's work is invaluable, as he attempts to introduce a standard by which historical action might be judged through the concepts of guerrilla pluralism and solidarity, but, I argue, there is a risk that Medina's concepts might be mistakenly overdetermined by the misguided reader insofar as space remains for a reproduction of the sort of violent domination that defines *coloniality*. In other words, I argue that counter-historical narratives and anti-colonial movements need an explicit normative guiding ideal to prevent this misguided reproduction of coloniality. I turn to the myth of Babel to find that normative ideal and to defend the normativity that I began developing through the excavation of the anti-colonial principle in the previous chapter.

My goal is not to romanticize the nostalgic pre-colonial historical-material mythoscape. Like Walter Benjamin's Angel of History or the Sankofa Bird, I am interested in how people move forward while looking backward and create something that truly diverges from the violence of written (i.e., colonial) history.[36] I draw on the mythical pre-colonial in Ionia and Babel for this normative inspiration. Indeed, the normative force of history is especially powerful as it emerges in stories like the tower of babel—what once was could be again; the world as it is now is not how it always was; other worlds are possible—because such reflections help to clear the way for a grounded understanding of human interaction that, I think, will also help us to move forward from our present circumstances.

Chapter 5 can be understood as grounding the normative force of *Anti-Colonial Solidarity*, in that merely being oppositional not only is insufficient but also tends toward a replication of that which is being resisted. The capacity to act collectively, as a whole, requires an ideal of wholeness that replaces the divisive myths that allow colonial power to linger. It is not merely the case that race, nation, class, or gender, for example, are categories that have been fabricated to divide us against ourselves, but our collectivity is something that was taken and must be reclaimed.

In Chapter 6, I turn to the exemplar and specifically focus on the cases of Cyprus and Rojava. Both Cyprus and Rojava demonstrate the sort of reconciliatory meaning-making, normativity, and *anti-colonial solidarity* that I defend throughout the previous chapters. I begin by discussing the case of Cyprus as reflective of an ethics of reconciliation. I then turn to Rojava as an example of a politics of solidarity. Herein, I directly respond to Abdullah

Öcalan's uptake of the autonomist project and Rojava's uptake of Öcalan in order to lay the foundations for future works that follow similar social-political trajectories: namely, an unpacking of an ethics of reconciliation and a politics of solidarity. I specifically address the question of gender, or, as Khatibi put it, the margin of the margins, through my reflections on Cyprus and Rojava, and respond to Öcalan's demand to center women as both correct, necessary, and only possible when other objectified relational modes have already been softened to allow for the centering of women.[37] In this sense, I defend the general normative constraint that any *anti-colonial solidarity* must be a fundamentally feminist project insofar as it is a direct challenge to all forms of domination and thus an effort to reciprocally coordinate. Chapter 6 can be understood as a demonstration of what is perhaps the most important standard for *anti-colonial solidarity*: other worlds are both possible and emerging, so be ready.

I conclude this text by returning to the U.S. context and discussing possibility among MENA Americans. MENA Americans have much to learn from the exemplary cases of other MENA people coordinating and defending themselves from colonial violence, but the United States has its own unique set of complexities that must be attended to in the anti-colonial struggle. As I mention throughout the earlier chapters of the text, the MENA American situation is compounded by infighting that prevents cooperative-determination and by the specific colonial context of the United States that manifests through a Black-white binary. Hence, while MENA people work to establish a coherent and cohesive collectivity, we must also look beyond ourselves and toward the creation of solidarity with non-MENA peoples who are also dominated in and by the United States. Hence, *anti-colonial solidarity* has the potential to be fully realized in the United States because the space and its populations are marked by the plurality of colonial domination. Great power can be found in broader collectivization, and that solidarity can be realized without forgetting or fetishizing difference to the detriment of common histories and goals.

Chapter One

The "Unknown" Middle Easterner

Post-Racial Anxieties and Anti-MENA Racism throughout Colonized Space-Time

The title of this chapter is a reference to the performance of a predatory state actor who, in an effort to stoke fear and mobilize violence, described a group of refugees who were seeking security in the United States as criminals and "Unknown Middle Easterners."[1] This performance is revealing; it references much more than an isolated racist tweet, and that is why I have chosen to adopt it as the title. On the one hand, the response to the performance was not an inquiry into the "unknown" aspect of the claim because it turns out that Middle Easterners are known in many ways. For example, the *and* that connects the two descriptive terms—*criminals, unknown Middle Easterners*—suggests that they are synonymous or at least inseparable types of people: the predators would have us believe that criminals and Middle Easterners are one and the same—you cannot have one without the other. The equation of the type with criminality suggests that Middle Easterners disobey the law and are therefore potentially violent, nasty, brutish, and a threat to the United States as it currently exists. Also, *Middle Easterner* suggests foreigner, from a place that is known but also not known, and it is pluralized, which suggests a multitude of unknown quantity is coming.

This unknownness has a deep history—extending well beyond the U.S. border and the potential violation of its laws—that has been rigorously critiqued and conceptualized by Edward Said as *Orientalism*.[2] Said argues that the reification of Orientalism as discourse occurred in the nineteenth century, but as I suggest here, this emergence was not spontaneous and immaculate. For at least seven hundred years the unknown Middle Easterner, as an object of knowledge, has been a mythical collective that is simultaneously known and unknown—that is, the Western political imaginary as it relates to the fluctuating East is merely that, imagined, but that production acts as if it were something more, with shameless confidence, as an anti-epistemology.

And, for many, the Middle Eastern or Oriental object has long been fetishized because of this ambiguous status—as a monster, a vampire, a specter that haunts, a despotic world from which a princess or two might be saved, and thus always the appropriate target of violence.[3] Indeed, the predatory actor's utterance also included the call for a state of emergency, the suspension of law needed to mobilize the state's violent machinery to defend divisiveness. For all of these reasons, the performative "unknown Middle Easterner" is revealing, for it demonstrates the critique that Said was emphasizing, as well as my extension of that critique herein, that Orientalism informs coloniality and violence, at the very least by playing on and actually cultivating a fear that the Orientalists claim to be real: a frightening beast that might hurt "us" and that will certainly violate the sensible. Therefore, actual people who are designated as Middle Easterners are met with great violence—because, despite being unknown, the defenders of the order know what to look for in their efforts to defend or expand the boundaries.[4] On this point, Nadine Naber notes, "Arab American racial formations" in particular "have depended on shifting US imperialist agendas."[5] Simultaneously, the general practice of targeting the unknown-known—the criminal, illegal, or terrorist, the inferior but threatening races, the hordes at the walls—creates a great deal of vulnerability for those who are targeted and to a lesser extent, at least for now, those allies who resist what is happening.

In other words, persons of Middle Eastern descent are, to borrow Michael Omi and Howard Winant's terminology, racialized.[6] By *racialization* I mean an objectifying social and institutional relation that heavily relies on what Linda Alcoff calls "visible identities" that are used to target, denigrate, exploit, and ultimately divide to conquer.[7] As Mahmood Mamdani put it, we are defined and ruled.[8] Here, the claim that Middle Eastern persons are racialized is made in response to complexities that are definitive of our current post-racial situation—namely, that the language of race is seen as antiquated or misleading, and thus it fails to capture Middle Eastern American experiences for various reasons, such that some critics have called for different terminology (i.e., *xenophobia* or *Islamophobia*).[9] I maintain that it is crucial to hold on to the language of race, racism, and racialization for descriptive and normative purposes. We ought to call social-political violence that is committed against Middle Eastern people *racism* because to call it something else—Islamophobia or xenophobia, for example—is to ground the experience in an incomplete description that affords a lighter moral responsibility and that disconnects the experience from an ongoing historical conflict.[10]

The first part of this chapter elaborates the general problem of racial conflict in the post-racial United States and the specific problem of Middle Eastern racialization—namely, we are institutionally whitewashed despite being treated as non-white targets. I respond to this problem with a historical argument in the second section that emphasizes key genealogical markers in the co-emergence of Orientalism, colonialism, and racialization, which together act as the brass tacks—or, as Charles Mills frames it, the primary contradiction—of global conflict in the Euro-modern world.[11] In the third section, I address the conceptual problem by contrasting the idea of race with competing terms—*xenophobia* and *Islamophobia*—in order to emphasize why we ought to hold on to the concept for descriptive purposes. And, in the final section, I emphasize why the terminology ought to be maintained for normative or ethical purposes.

1.1. DESCRIBING THE PROBLEM: U.S. RACIAL CONFLICT IN A POST-RACIAL LANDSCAPE

The problem is twofold: (1) violence against people of color is constant, escalating, increasingly visible, permitted, and often carried out by the state; (2) but the language of race and racism, which carries with it a certain moral condemnation—we think of racists as morally flawed—has become increasingly fraught to the point of sometimes seeming meaningless. Regarding the second part of the problem—the anxious state of being without a coherent language to describe this objectified experience because that language is denied or taken away—there are various conflicting narratives that persist in popular discourse that dull our critical tools.

There is a popular sentiment that suggests that racist practice ended at some point. Referential events used to support the post-racial claim include rosy misrepresentations of the civil rights era and its perceived successes or, more recently, the election of Barack Obama.[12] This version of the post-racial position is problematic because of the self-evidence that the broader public can no longer be unaware of state and civilian violence against people of color, though this violence can be misinterpreted. Hence, much of the population continues to excuse racial violence through the deployment of objectifying terms that imply desert—*criminal*, *illegal*, and *terrorist*. Indeed, many support the mistreatment of people of color by demanding that more money be funneled into those various institutional forces (state and private) that perpetuate violence, while also defunding public services like education that might combat racism through nonviolent and reconciliatory means. Another marker for the post-racial claim is the collapse of racial science in the early twentieth century, which makes the use of racial language problematic because it no longer connects to the expert discourses it originally relied on for demarcation.[13]

At the same time that the world is supposedly post-race, the language of racism is still deployed in various, often absurd ways. Consider recent video propaganda that was released by the Sergeants Benevolent Association, a New York police union, titled "Blue Racism":[14]

> What do you see? Son, Daughter, Mother, Father? Aunt, Uncle or Cousin? Neighbor? Coach? Member of your church congregation? Community volunteer? The average person doesn't see those things that make me human. They don't even label me based on being African-American, Latino, Asian, Caucasian, and so on. They tend to see an even broader stereotype through an even more racist lens. When they look at me, they see blue. To be blue, I and over 700,000 brothers and sisters swore an oath to uphold the constitution of my country, my state, and my city, so help me god; yet, even in such numbers, I'm a minority as this strange form of racism continues to engulf the country.[15]

What the video is describing is obviously problematic. No person should be objectified or reduced to certain unchanging qualities such that those persons are not seen as having possibilities or potentials beyond those qualities. A table can be treated like a table, but a police officer is much more than just a cop. To be solely limited to the qualities of *cop* is to be understood like an object. And, insofar as objectification is the broader category under which racism is a subcategory, it is understandable—with great charity—that the terms would be conflated, especially when there is a political strategy to getting it twisted.[16] But the obvious difference between the objectification experienced by police officers and the racism experienced by people of color—a point that I will return to and expand on in the closing section of this chapter—is that the latter cannot escape their racialization, and their objectification co-functions with social-systemic oppression. This latter point was at least partly articulated by the controversial comedian Dave Chapelle in an infamous *SNL* monologue: "What, were you born a police? That is not a blue life, that is a blue suit. If you don't like it, take that suit off and find another job, because I'm going to tell you right now, if I could quit being black today, I'd be out of the game."[17]

Despite the conceptual error that makes claims about blue racism absurd and disconnected from the experience of oppression, the concepts of race and racism are overdeployed in part because they carry a moral and political force in the present post-racial discursive landscape, a power that is eroded as the terms are misused. We are supposed to feel like bad people if we admit that objectifying the police is the same as being racist, because being racist is wrong. But objectifying the police and being racist are not equivalent, and to admit as much is to obfuscate racialized experience.

Chapelle's critique gets to the heart of contemporary racism, as he cannot quit being Black, which means that even if biological racism is an artifact, like witchcraft, or what Barbara and Karen Fields call "racecraft," there is something about one's body and habits that leads to racialization or the experience of being treated as being of another, hierarchically situated, race, and thus the appropriate target of violent domination.[18] *Racecraft*, which "originates not in nature but in human action and imagination," helps capture the source of dissonance that characterizes race and racism: "Witchcraft and racecraft are imagined, acted upon, and re-imagined, the action and imagining inextricably intertwined."[19] In this case, the original imaginary of hierarchically distinct natural kinds that was made real through its enactment, despite being imagined from the beginning, is formally abandoned but then reimagined and thus reconstituted, leaving a path of chaos in its various transformations. Again, what is being described is an anti-epistemology.

The conceptual chaos surrounding race and racism is further complicated for Middle Eastern peoples, and especially Middle Eastern Americans, who are legally politically categorized as white, yet judged and mistreated in the social world as a racialized population. One might say that if I call the experience of violence against Middle Eastern people "racism," then I am making more or less the same move as the police and misapplying a dead terminology. My response to this concern is both historical and conceptual.

1.2. THE CO-EMERGENCE OF ORIENTALISM AND RACISM IN GLOBAL CONFLICT

The experience of racism and racialization is rooted in an Orientalist imaginary that drove colonialism and continues to drive neo-colonialism. If I were only concerned with distinction, then I would argue that the more appropriate term for *racism*, especially as it is deployed against those presumed to be Middle Eastern, is Orientalist-racism. There are countless historical markers that support this position, especially once one treats Orientalist-racism as a hermeneutic lens through which history can be read. For example, la Reconquista, which afforded what is now Spain, wherein social-political status—the formal expression of which we now call citizenship—was attributed to blood and birth (*limpieza de sangre*) beyond the royal family, is often cited as a key moment in the emergence of racial thought.[20]

Similarly, as Western forces colonized the Americas, a debate over the status of the indigenous peoples or first nations of the Americas occurred within the Catholic Church. Bartolomé de las Casas famously defended the Indians on the grounds that they were the type of barbarians who could be converted and saved, but the grounds for his defense and how that defense was taken up are worth noting precisely because they demonstrate what the West thought of the East, wherever it was assumed to be encountered. Enrique Dussel emphasizes that this discursive moment, wherein las Casas tries to persuade the crown and the church to have mercy on the Americans because they too could be Catholic, is definitive in the early stages of Euro-modernity because the response to las Casas defined who could be included in the modern project and who would be "excluded" while also being exploited.[21] If the Indians were not really barbarians, then who were the barbarians that las Casas believed did deserve such violence? Las Casas speaks for himself:

> The Turks and the Arabs are a people said to be well versed in political affairs. But how can they be honored with this reputation for uprightness when they are an effeminate and luxury-loving people, given to every sort of sexual immorality? The Turks, in particular, do not consider impure and horrible vices worthy of punishment. Furthermore, neither the Greeks nor the Romans nor the Turks nor the Moors should be said to be exercising justice, since neither prudence nor justice can be found in a people that does not recognize Christ, as Augustine proves. When, therefore, those who are devoid of Christian truth have sunk into vices and crime and have strayed from reason in many ways, no matter how well versed they may be in the skills of government, and certainly all those who do not worship Christ, either because they have not heard his words even by hearsay or because, once they have heard them reject them, *all these are true barbarians*.[22]

Though the formal outcome of las Casas's plea is unclear, the colonizers clearly disregarded it in their practice, meaning that the Americans were seen as equally barbaric as the Arabs, Greeks, Romans, and Turks.[23] Although religion still functioned to justify colonization, it is clear here and in the colonial response to las Casas's plea, that the barbarian was seen as a natural kind, even if that kind was not yet described as a race. Falguni Sheth's work emphasizes the importance of the rejection of las Casas's plea by pointing out that a central component of racialization as an ongoing process is the representation of the objectified as an "unruly" collective—that is, we remain the wrong type of barbarians.[24]

In other words, what Said describes as an Orientalist attitude precedes racial thought and racism—as well as Orientalism as a formal discourse—and thus racism, as it operates in the United States, is partly determined by these discourse-shifting historical events, even if most people do not recognize the historical influence. And, as colonization intensified, a more robust discourse emerged about the natural inferiority of the colonized that shifted objectification to a racial categorization that continues to justify colonial practice.[25] Further, given that the primary opposition in the United States is racial, which is to say race is the standard through which conflict is reduced, oversimplified, and thus misunderstood—especially when elections are about to occur—it is important to situate the color line in a global context because these experiences do not occur in a vacuum.

Indeed, like colonial Spain, the United States has largely defined itself through rigid policies of inclusion and exclusion, and the primary framework through which race is understood in the United States, even now, is a Black-white binary.[26] Socially, this binary informs how racialized actors are understood and relegated, such that one's racial status is more or less determined by how the racist gaze perceives one's proximity to Blackness, but the bounds of that proximity fluctuate over time, space, and class, which is why certain groups that may have once been racially perceived (e.g., Irish Catholics) are now considered white in most places.[27] Hence, the obfuscation of the Orientalist origins of racist praxis in the United States is rooted in both a lack of historical memory—or a highly selective and provincial memory—and the way that conflict in the United States is defined through practices of inclusion and exclusion according to a Black-white binary.

For example, the 1792 naturalization act restricted citizenship to "any alien, being a free white person of good character." The Fourteenth Amendment expanded this to anyone born in the United States except for those first nations who were chased and restricted to Indian territory/reservations. And the 1870 naturalization act allowed anyone of African nativity and persons of African descent to also become citizens. These various shifts in citizenship law matter because they set the stage for the legal debates that would occur in the early twentieth century over who counts as white and would be granted state protections, as well as rights as a citizen. Like the Reconquista, inclusion and protection were at stake.

Whiteness becomes the debated concept because, as Ian Haney López points out, migrants did not typically apply for citizenship as African descendants, a guaranteed second-class status, and because whiteness in the United States was not practically defined to account for persons beyond Western Europe prior to the late nineteenth and early twentieth centuries.[28] Except for first nations, the U.S. legal-political apparatus was gradually forced to address the fact that the world is not Black and white, and its response to the fact of peoples who do not fit the binary ham-fistedly afforded our current problematic.

There are three important cases that defined the U.S. stance on race/racism and specifically the racialization of Middle Eastern peoples. What I take to be the most important case involves Costa George Najour, an Eastern Christian who sought refuge from the crumbling Ottoman empire and its genocidal policies.²⁹ He applied to naturalize, and his application was denied on racial grounds, but the appeal case that granted Najour whiteness ultimately destabilized the courts. In Sarah M. A. Gualtieri's invaluable analysis of the Najour case, as well as the other early legal events that ultimately shaped the current MENA American racial bind, she emphasizes

> Najour . . . seemed to understand his whiteness only in relation to a racialized Other, to a group he described as "yellow." He did not so much affirm his status as a "white" person as *negate* that he was something else.³⁰

Gualtieri goes on to point out that part of the ambivalence in Najour's positioning stems from the fact that post-Ottoman refugees' "premigratory conceptions of difference were rooted primarily in religion."³¹ Religion was the primary marker of difference in the Ottoman and post-Ottoman world in part because phenotype was not a reliable marker; hence the idea of whiteness was in many ways foreign to the early MENA American migrants, and just as the idea was being taken up, it was soon to be officially abandoned by state actors.

The Najour case marks the beginnings of a shift away from scientific racism to the use of "common knowledge" for deciding race. Throughout the early twentieth century, the courts were largely inconsistent and split concerning the deployment of racial category. As Haney López notes:

> In contrast to the early racial prerequisite cases, the prerequisite decisions from 1909 to 1923 are riven by contradictory results and rationales. . . . Judges continued to rule that people with mixed or Asian antecedents did not qualify as White. . . . A court in 1909 ruled that Armenians were White, even though their origins east of the Bosporus Strait . . . made them at least geographically Asian. More perplexing still, judges qualified Syrians as "white persons" in 1909, 1910, and 1915, but not in 1913 or 1914; and Asian Indians were "white persons" in 1910, 1913, 1919, and 1920, but not in 1909 or 1917, or after 1923. Significantly, these contradictory results correlated with the rise of a marked antagonism between scientific evidence and common knowledge as racial meters.³²

With Najour, the judge hearing his case appealed to a racist text to grant him whiteness. The judge notes:

> Although the term "free white person" is used in the statutes, this expression, I think, refers to race, rather than to color, and fair or dark complexion should not be allowed to control, provided the person seeking naturalization comes within the classification of the white or Caucasian race, and I consider the Syrians as belonging to what we now recognize, and what the world recognizes, as the white race. . . . Quite a recent work, which I have before me now, "The World's

People," by Dr. A. H. Keane, classifies . . . Syrians as part of the Caucasian or white race.[33]

The judge's appeal to the Keane text is historically crucial because it demonstrates that although the United States postures as if it were exceptional and functioning independently from world history, its norms and beliefs are still directly informed by broader discursive norms. Any history of race in the United States that presents itself as only focusing on Anglo-America, in isolation from broader racial discourse and practice, is therefore an incomplete history precisely because it treats the concept and practice as if occurring in a vacuum when in fact racial thought has always been a global project. Nevertheless, many were furious that the judge in the Najour case made a distinction between race and skin color, and that the term *Caucasian* was equated with whiteness. Indeed, some judges continued to appeal to phenotype despite the Najour precedent, and as Gualtieri points out, "in cases where personal qualifications were in doubt, and the applicant was deemed unworthy of citizenship, color continued to serve as an additional marker of ineligibility."[34]

With the lower courts conflicted, the Supreme Court intervened through the cases of *Ozawa* and *Thind*. Takao Ozawa was a Japanese man who attempted to naturalize as a white person.[35] One of Ozawa's key arguments appealed to the precedent set in the Najour case, namely that he was white because his skin was white. The justices upheld this element of the Najour case, noting that skin color is not the defining attribute of one's race—one could have dark skin and be racially white, and one could have light skin and be racially non-white; but Ozawa was ultimately denied recognition because he was understood as being part of the Mongolian race. This move upheld certain aspects of racial science but also destabilized skin color as a reliable designator.

The second case, *United States v. Bhagat Singh Thind*, involved a Sikh man who petitioned for citizenship on the basis of his belonging to the Caucasian race.[36] The Keane text used in the Najour cases held that the Caucasian race expanded across most of the Eurasian continent, which included populations that did not align with the common belief about whiteness. And, in denying Thind's plea, the court also rejected the Caucasian-white equivalence, while delegitimizing racial science as such through an appeal to that same text.[37] Haney López suggests that Keane's writings here became not evidence that the term *white person* should be broadly interpreted, but proof that science could not be trusted to define whiteness.[38] Gualtieri adds to this point: "These two Supreme Court rulings suggest that when science failed to reinforce popular beliefs about racial difference it was discarded but that when it confirmed them it was conveniently embraced."[39]

Racism was still very much alive, as it is today, but the foundation for that racism formally shifted through these cases to common knowledge, which is harder to analyze, as it makes social myths authoritative while also erasing the fact that those myths were produced by experts before being abandoned in expert discourse.[40] The *Ozawa* and *Thind* decisions undermined the claims of *Najour*—especially the equation of Caucasianness with whiteness—yet the *Najour* decision stands such that Middle Eastern people remain white, despite being socially treated as non-white targets (i.e., MENA Americans have been whitewashed). To add to this problem, the rise of political correctness in the post–civil rights era has led to the increasing use of coded racism such that previous terminology is replaced by talk of criminality, illegality, and terrorism, which continues the work of racist designation by justifying the erosion of basic protections that accompany citizenship, cosmopolitan hospitality, or human rights.[41] We remain unruly barbarians.

1.3. XENOPHOBIA, ISLAMOPHOBIA, AND RACISM

I now shift from the historical problematization of Middle Eastern American racial experience to the conceptual problem. I make this shift because one proposed analytic response to the contradiction of ambiguously situated non-white and non-Black minorities in the U.S. context has been to use different language to address the problem. The rationale here is that since racial science is dead and racists no longer publicly admit to their racism—though this is shifting in recent political time—resistance requires that descriptive and normative claims be updated to reflect current complexities.[42] The alternatives I discuss here, xenophobia and Islamophobia, are necessary for parsing out the complexity of objectified experience, but are neither descriptively nor normatively sufficient replacements for the language of racism.

Xenophobia—fear or hatred of foreigners—seems to function as a permissible objectified relation when treated as analytically, and thus historically, distinct. Most communities have some concern with and aversion toward outsiders, just by virtue of self-defense, and I say this not as a justification but merely as a recognition of the position. Further, following Ron Sundstrom and David Kim, I maintain that xenophobia informs the way Middle Eastern peoples are treated—as well as other racialized people who fall outside of the Black-white binary—but it is not exhaustive of the experience in part because it is too general and fails to account for the ongoing experience of foreignness that a second- or third-generation German simply does not experience in the same way as those of the second or third generation who fall outside of the Black-white binary.[43] Many U.S. citizens with white great-grandparents from

Western Europe describe a migratory experience that included prejudice and physical violence. What is also common is that the next generation, assuming they did not marry or reproduce with folks from outside of their ethno-national community, was able to blend in to whiteness without question or concern, because they were no longer foreign *and* they were white.

At the same time, people of color who have a similar background are unlikely to enjoy this whitening effect. We remain X American, X being wherever your family came from that gives you a phenotypic quality that evokes questions like "Where are you from?" or "What are you really?"[44] Neda Maghbouleh emphasizes this point in her critique of the early twentieth-century court cases, noting that "one feature that has not been analyzed in these types of racial prerequisite cases are the roles played on- and offstage by liminal claimants' American-born or raised children."[45] In other words, the experience of racism that is masked as xenophobia has a transgenerational quality that includes, at the very least, a constant awareness that our security is conditional.[46] Thus, I stand by Sundstrom and Kim's claim that the experience of being permanently foreign is central to being a nonbinary person of color, but xenophobia is neither descriptively nor normatively sufficient to fully describe what's going on.

The second position, Islamophobia, is more popular in mainstream discourses about the experiences of Middle Eastern peoples and rightly highlights the image that anti–Middle Eastern sentiment conjures: namely, an Arab-Muslim terrorist, and even more specifically Osama Bin Laden or a figure in a black *niqab*. And, at the institutional level, much of the rhetoric or propaganda that is used to justify endless war in the Middle East is based in anxiety about groups who have debased Islam by deploying its name for violent ends. The fear and hostility that Islamophobic propaganda reproduces in the social world is visceral and imprecise. The average American knows little of the Middle East, its peoples, and especially not Islam or Muslims; yet the false image and narrative about the Middle East are entrenched. The Orientalist image is projected into the world through an unknowing and fearful population, influencing and harming a broader population than the term *Islamophobia* suggests.[47]

Many who are assaulted because of anti-Muslim sentiment are neither Arab nor Muslim, such that even if the driving force behind their mistreatment is Islamophobia, the way that it functions is more like racism precisely because it consumes anyone who looks like the false image at the epicenter of white fear. Indeed, returning to the title of this chapter, "The 'Unknown' Middle Easterner," fully captures the fluidity of racialization in our post-racial landscape such that the Arab-Muslim epicenter is also eroding as racist sentiment intensifies. Here, whiteness is also defined against Middle Easternness, while security is associated with whiteness such that Middle Eastern people are encouraged to assimilate and become "Good Muslims" (i.e., white).[48] Many colonial apologists make an argument from the "good Muslim" position, suggesting that the objectification of Middle Eastern peoples is only a problem for those who are "bad Muslims."

Even the conforming "good" Muslim is vulnerable, however, because racists use bird shot when they unleash the racial gaze, and they hit anything that looks like a target. Even if the popular image of the racialized Middle Eastern person is an Arab Muslim, the range of people who that impacts is much broader than just that category. The people being targeted are both Muslims and non-Muslims, because the targeting is not really about Islam and is instead about strategic control, power, and the ongoing assault against a population because of where they are at or where they are perceived to be from, biologically, historically, and politically. And the type stands out in relation to other populations regardless of religious practice.

So racism in this context encompasses all of those institutional forces that produce a story and image of a people, toward the production of a people, and then the ways that that production is used to subjugate the general target populations. The racist does not have to be accurate. The racist sees markers, and sometimes those markers are more or less obvious. Alia Al-Saji describes this in terms of cultural racism, suggesting that certain practices (e.g., wearing a hijab) accent or highlight racial markers that afford a specific sort of objectification and violence.[49] Expanding on Al-Saji's claim, I have argued that even if one is an Arab Muslim who does not practice in an obvious way, one's body is still a possible object of racialization, though one may move into different spheres of racial expectation. Indeed, because Middle Eastern Americans embody a wide range of phenotypic expressions and ethnic habits, they are often misinterpreted as of another racial background and, especially when the mistaken identity is white, these identities are sometimes taken up for defensive purposes.[50]

The fluidity of racialized experience is not typically voluntary, however, nor is it one-directional, as we witnessed in the aftermath of the San Bernardino shooting. When the shooting first occurred, nobody knew what was happening, and media helicopters were deployed to monitor the scene to see if it was or was not a terrorist attack. The media was looking for signs on the bodies of the shooters, and when it was revealed that the shooters were Middle Eastern and Muslim, the event was also determined to be a terrorist attack, because *terrorist* is the politically correct racial code word for Middle Eastern.[51] I mention this event because the story goes on to include the neighbor of the shooters, Enrique Marquez, who was charged with supporting the shooters and also described as a terrorist.[52] The fluidity of the post-racial categorization illuminated in this example is important because it demonstrates that any racialized body can be deemed a terrorist, if they have proximity to other bodies that are racialized as such and are also racialized bodies. If a white gun-store clerk had sold the weapons to the San Bernardino shooters, they would not have been racially categorized as terrorists despite their instrumental role, just as the folks who supply weapons to Al Qaeda and ISIS, American companies run by white people, are also not designated as terrorists despite their active role in perpetuating global terror.

So, Islamophobia and xenophobia inform the objectification and mistreatment of Middle Eastern peoples—as do gendered and class expectations—but neither alone is satisfying as a description of the objectification experienced by Middle Eastern peoples; and, more importantly, racism carries a greater moral weight. Indeed, xenophobia seems to be broadly acceptable by many people if it is equal in its discrimination—the conservative will claim that we ought to be careful when any and all strangers enter our home—and Islamophobia seems to be overly narrow insofar as it is focused on fear and hatred of Muslims, while overlooking the mistreatment of all Middle Eastern peoples—the "unknown Middle Easterners"—and anyone who seems Middle Eastern. Further, many non-Muslim Middle Eastern people are wary of Islam and may even be Islamophobic, while simultaneously being relegated to the racial category of Middle Eastern and thus mistreated.[53] On this point, Islamophobia has a pernicious tactical effect insofar as it is encouraged within non-Muslim Middle Eastern populations as a way of separating out, delineating the "good Muslims" from the "bad Muslims," which undermines our potential to function as a collective.

1.4. IT'S THEM THEY KNOW, NOT ME: A NORMATIVE RESPONSE

Who we are must be open to possibility. There are many ways to be Middle Eastern. For critical descriptive purposes, this experience includes having been subject to or producer of Islamophobia and xenophobia—as well as sexism, classism, ableism, and so on. These various experiences are necessary for understanding the complexities of Middle Eastern American experiences, yet the colonial conflict is not sufficiently captured by these categories. I have argued that racism is the appropriate framework for describing our current conflict because the history of colonial subjugation is a history of the refinement of tactics of division that ossified as racist thought and practice. The divisions imposed and reproduced through racial hierarchy were never reconciled and thus remain the lingering fact of our conflict. Normatively, the appropriate negative frame for condemning contemporary objectification is to call said behavior and institutional arrangement *racist* because that language carries with it greater moral weight, despite attempts to undermine that moral force, and it is multidirectional.

I have made two central claims that demonstrate and defend the moral and multidirectional force of anti-racist critique in relation to Middle Eastern experiences of violent domination: First, as I demonstrate in my appeal to the tweet from which the title of this chapter draws, the claims of las Casas, and the San Bernardino example, a much wider range of persons are potentially objectified and dominated as Middle Eastern peoples than just Muslims. This includes a wide range of non-Muslim Middle Eastern peoples, but also includes those who are assumed to be as equally "barbaric" as Middle Eastern peoples because of a perceived and projected proximity to the imagined racial epicenter.[54] In this sense, there is fluidity in racialized experience such that persons who have nothing to do with the MENA region can and often are mistreated as if they were Middle Eastern.[55]

Second, Middle Eastern peoples can be racialized and mistreated accordingly while also being Islamophobic. Hence, parsing out the modalities—racism, Islamophobia—is important for holding our own communities accountable for the ways that they reproduce division while also recognizing that racist mistreatment is real. This second critique is crucial because part of the way that the Middle East and its extended peoples are portrayed through the Orientalist imaginary is as a naturally warlike and thus fragmented collective. In reality, our divisions were produced or catalyzed by colonial actors, and we have maintained those divisions through ethno-nationalist boundaries, narratives, and erasures that include contempt for the enemy *other* who is deemed naturally inferior based on their religious-national lineage. Being able to point out the extent to which we are mistreated and that certain beliefs or habits contribute to our subjugation is crucial to any liberatory future. We need to be able to call racism by its name at the same time that we condemn Islamophobia or xenophobia.

Finally, the normative force of calling something or someone's actions racist is obviously important; otherwise, other groups would not be trying to co-opt the language in order to make a moral point. Hence, the question remains: What about blue racism? Well, we ought to be able to emphasize the absurdity of calling the objectification of police officers racism while simultaneously condemning the objectification of police as morally questionable. But condemning the objectification of police is less morally forceful because the language lacks the historically situated weight that is found in the language of racism, and because the police are effectively the domestic militant force that maintains colonial power relations. Yes, objectification is often morally reprehensible, especially when that objectification affords exploitation, but, following Martin Buber, we often have to objectify in order to function.[56] I do not treat my mechanic the same as my best friend because our relation is pragmatic. The police operate like mechanics, or like firefighters and postal workers, making their relation to the world when they are doing their jobs pragmatic. Unlike my mail person, however, the cop has a great deal of explicit power over me that does not invite reciprocity. I am intimidated by the police—they have guns and can kill me—and so my pragmatic relation to such actors is also one of survival. Meanwhile, my mail person delivers books I ordered, checks, and tinder for my stove—they are like Santa Claus and probably deserve better pay.

At the same time, because of the sorts of practices I pursue outside of academia, I have known several police officers personally—off-duty, unarmed, and in civilian clothes—and in those circumstances I felt less concerned for my safety, especially when I did not know they were cops in our initial getting to know each other. I even think of myself as being friends with some of the folks I have known under these circumstances. As James Baldwin puts it: "A cop is a cop. He may be a very nice man. I don't have time to figure that out. All I know is that he has a uniform and a gun."[57] Unlike the police, people of color do not have the luxury of taking off the markers of their objectification. A phenotypically Middle Eastern cop is both a cop and Middle Eastern, but when not wearing a uniform, the cop remains Middle Eastern. Of course, the phenomenology of racialized experience will vary when the uniform comes off, and anti-MENA racism is distinct from anti-Black racism for various reasons, some of which I have noted above.[58] Similarly, I still might objectify someone in civilian clothes who is an off-duty cop and tells me they are a cop—independent of their racial status—but the meaning of that objectification is more easily changed because I can engage and learn about the person through our encounter if they are willing to engage with me. However, being racialized often prevents this sort of reconciliatory encounter because the racist remains hesitant to engage and transform their objectified expectations, and people of color might also hesitate to be more vulnerable—especially when the gaze of the other is clearly hostile.

In this sense, racialization and racism are far more morally repugnant precisely because they shut down the conditions of the possibility of their own transformation (i.e., reconciliation as interpersonal knowing through a direct encounter), while the objectification of the police only prevents the transformation of that objectification while the police are known as police. If the police were only ever seen as police and they were unable to escape their "policification," then we might say that their experience is similar to racism and maybe similarly morally problematic. But even if morally equivalent, the historically emergent processes that define the police as police and racialized persons as raced are distinct and should be described as such.[59] Nevertheless, we ought to strive for more direct and open encounters with all persons, within the reasonable limits of our safety, and any real anti-racist future will have to find a way to enact this contact work.

Chapter Two

Changing Lenses

Anti-Racist Posturing versus Praxis, an Enactivist Critique

The tragedy of this experience, and indeed of so many post-colonial experiences, derives from the limitations of the attempts to deal with relationships that are polarized, radically uneven, remembered differently. The spheres, the sites of intensity, the agendas, and the constituencies in the metropolitan and ex-colonized worlds appear to overlap only partially. The small area that is perceived as common does not, at this point, provide for more than what might be called a rhetoric of blame.

—Edward Said[1]

In Chapter 1, I argued that the language of race, racism, and racialization ought to be maintained for normative, as well as descriptive, purposes. I emphasized that the normative force of calling racism by its name is crucial because such accusations or critiques carry greater moral weight than other objectifying categories. Nevertheless, a problem remains concerning the practical force of naming race/racism/racialization.

I understand this problem in two ways: First, generally speaking, when racism is named in interaction, the common response is defensive—to deny, deflect, or double down. But second, and more specifically, those who are seen as Middle Eastern by racists, or more precisely Middle Eastern and North African (MENA), and subsequently mistreated, generally lack the legitimacy to even declare the racist action as racist—after all, in many contexts MENA people are, in the absence of institutional recognition, categorized as white, or the experience of racialization is explained away through other terms that are less morally forceful (i.e., *Islamophobia*). Hence, I argue that anti-racist praxis must diverge from the colonial norms of condemnation—what I will describe as posturing and which is epitomized by certain forms of "calling-out" that maintain institutional power and social division (i.e., racism)—and move toward social meaning-making labor (i.e., reconciliation) that emerges through face-to-face encounters.

The specifics of a face-to-face encounter will vary based on what mediating forces are already present or must be intentionally produced, but the foundational characteristic of the encounter is the direct material being together with others. As I mention in the introduction, for proto-agential beings (e.g., young children), material conditions must be produced and sometimes carefully stewarded in such a way as to afford cooperative meaning-making encounters. An ideal classroom might act as the moderated or structured place wherein social relations are refined in interactions. At the same time, for relatively peaceful agents—those who have presumably been well-socialized in the basics of meaning-making—the social encounter presupposes the capacity and will to make sense together. Indeed, under the best conditions, people maintain a thin sense of trust that others will coordinate and satisfy basic expectations for the sake of mundane meaning-making.[2] In the absence of this thin trust, basic social activities—such as safely walking through a world that includes other people—become impossible.

As people cultivate relations, a more robust connection emerges that is often described as friendship or through the convoluted languages of love. In this sense, the ideal meaning-making encounter is a meeting of friends that transcends the constraints of time and warps certain social norms because defenses have been lowered, allowing the other "in" and simultaneously being let "in." Of course, for conflicted social relations the ability to have a face-to-face encounter is undermined beforehand by presuppositions, mistrust, or maliciousness, such that human relationality defensively mutates to account for (i.e., defend against) a world of predatory actors.[3] It is under these sorts of anti-social conditions that racism functions and that relationality is blocked before a possible encounter—a point that I will expand on below but which is especially true in a world mediated by social media platforms.

In the first section, I expand on the general problem of condemning racism, which I suggest is rooted in atomistic notions of agency and sociality that are integral to the coloniality of power, and thus taken as given. I develop this critique in section 2, through a distinction between anti-racist posturing, which positions the judging actor beyond the interactional situation and is most recently witnessed in the rise of call-out culture, and praxis that takes the encounter and exchange between persons as the starting point of all meaning and value—indeed, of personhood as such.

In section 3, I suggest that there is a feedback loop between systemic posturing, as witnessed in the response of major political and thus corporate actors to claims of racism, and the social world that unfortunately follows this lead. In section 4, I argue that social responses to racism must diverge from the institutional lead, which is mere posturing, but that call-out responses are nevertheless invaluable when directed from sociality toward the untouchable institutional experts who stand beyond the world of encounter. In section 5, I return to the question of MENA social-institutional subjectivity and rearticulate the complexity of condemning anti-MENA racism with this more general problem of accountability in mind. My normative call for encounter and social labor remains, but the capacity for anti-racist praxis among MENA people is complicated by the additional vector of racialized nationalisms, which I critique in Chapter 3.

2.1. THE GENERAL PROBLEM OF CONDEMNING RACISM

Francisco Varela makes a helpful distinction between ethical know-how and ethical know-what that further elucidates this problem of condemning racism: "As a first approximation," Varela says,

> let me say that a wise (or virtuous) person is one who knows what is good and spontaneously does it. It is this immediacy of perception and action which we want to examine critically. This approach stands in stark contrast to the usual ways of investigating ethical behavior, which begins by analyzing the intentional content of an act and ends by evaluating the rationality of particular moral judgments.[4]

The distinction between ethical modes being captured here is one of rational deliberation or know-what—that is, we decide beforehand, outside of interaction, what is right or wrong—versus ethics as an emergent and spontaneous activity, know-how. The active know-how, wherein our choices and reactive attitudes may be more or less informed by various and often-competing rational frameworks, as well as the environment within which the event occurs, occurs in the moment and often without immediate rational deliberation on the myriad operative conditions of said moment. I think a great deal of conflict over the rightness or wrongness of one's actions rests on how much we have cultivated our ethical know-how, yet our actions are often judged according to a rigid conception of ethical know-what. Indeed, at least some well-intended people do not think of themselves as racists—which is to say they know that racism is rationally wrong—but they still act in racist ways, in the spontaneous moment, because, at the very least, rational deliberation is not all that is required for ethical action: Combating racism and the coloniality of power requires social labor, not just rational reflection and judgment. Given that liberal-colonial systems fail to adequately address issues of racial conflict in the social world—despite causing and maintaining those divisions—some activists and academics have taken to cultivating or policing ordinary social interactions.[5]

I think this move to the social is correct—especially if the goal is to establish a legitimate institutional form. The concern that drives this chapter, however, is the normative force of calling something or someone racist—that is, the "policing" of interaction demands critique. The full implications of naming racism will vary based on the positionality of the person whose actions are being condemned, yet recent forms of condemning racism—what I will call anti-racist posturing—have failed to appreciate the nuances of power and the importance of social work, such that a blanket approach to moral failure has been taken that produces greater division among folks who ought to otherwise stand in solidarity. The mode of condemnation I am alluding to has been recently witnessed and critiqued as call-out and cancel culture.

The first part of my critique is therefore focused on examples that fit these specific forms of moral failure and responsive outrage, though the claims I make here can also be extended to include other moral failures and call-out responses. I argue that calling-out racism too often reinforces racism, yet I also defend the call-out as an appropriate reaction to actors whose power positions them beyond sociality. My critique of call-out culture rests on a distinction between anti-racist posturing and praxis—modes with different paradigmatic starting points and different ends—so I begin by elaborating that split and defending a certain notion of praxis in order to create a clearing for an anti-colonial ethics and politics. Given the failures of anti-racist posturing, I then return to the problem of anti-MENA racism and suggest that the complexity of our situation, which is only partly determined by the limits of white guilt, can be addressed by appealing to our own indigenous relational practices. In other words, the critique I level here clears an opening for a more in-depth discussion of the indigenous reconciliatory practices that I believe MENA peoples, and people of color more generally, can (and should) reclaim in an effort to build solidarity and combat racism.

2.2. ANTI-RACIST POSTURING VERSUS PRAXIS: A PLEA FOR NUANCE

Racial conflict in the United States has morphed in certain key ways since I began writing this book, and especially since the public murder of George Floyd, which demands a more careful analysis of racist tactics. I maintain that social and institutional racism persist through denial from the right or from an emphasis placed on reform through a rebranded political correctness from moderate liberals. (Explicit racist forms still emerge in public spheres.) On the one hand, right-leaning politicians and their followers not only deny the reality of racism or the ongoing genocide that accompanies that sort of denial, but also often argue that discussing race/racism is itself racist. The right believes, or instrumentally deploys language that suggests, that the United States is post-race.[6] Even if the right only relates to the language of race/racism instrumentally, enough people maintain this position—presumably at least half of the U.S. voting population—that it is worth taking seriously.

On the other hand, moderate right and thus liberal politicians, as well as their followers, have been forced to admit that racism persists, but, as is standard to the liberal problem-solving method, the response has been one of, at best, incremental reform and individualistic blaming that fails to address the roots of the problem. Most of my argument in this chapter is directed toward the liberal audience, though I think it is crucial to name the right and its strategies/tactics too.

The eventual racist derogatory that demands liberal concern and the performative responses it elicits also reveal a second key feature of the Orientalist-racist colonial project as it presently operates. Namely, social and institutional practice takes on what I will describe as an anti-racist posture—condemning, shaming, and ultimately isolating the exposed actor—that is rooted in an individualistic, objectifying, and ultimately carceral ethos. Extending the claims of Aníbal Quijano, Sylvia Wynter, and Martin Buber, it is not merely the case that the coloniality of power relies on hierarchical racial categorization (i.e., Orientalist-racism) and a knowing that emerges through a problematic subject-object relation, but value as such is also overdetermined and thus limited by this same objectifying modality.[7] Hence, despite the intentions or critical awareness of the condemning actor, the anti-racist posture and the shaming call-out can have devastating consequences for sociality—that is, more often call-outs reinforce racism. The anti-racist posture therefore seems to be just that, a positioning, a presentation, a superficiality that relies on and reinforces racism, thus maintaining the status quo while making the poseur seem morally superior. Part of the reason for focusing on the moderate liberal anti-racist poser is because that bad-faith performative mode has been taken up by actors who might otherwise really believe that racism, as well as social division more generally, ought to be combatted and not just rebranded to maintain the status quo of coloniality.

By contrast, the anti-racist praxis that I am defending throughout assumes a reconciliatory relation to the world as possibility and attempts to create meaning with others that undermines reification and affords possibility. Anti-racist posturing and praxis both rely on different paradigmatic notions of personhood and value, and thus different notions of what it means to be "good" or in this case anti-racist. Hence, the exigence and complexity of what Howard Zehr describes as *Changing Lenses* is more fully captured by Quijano as "epistemological decolonization," which, "as decoloniality, is needed to clear the way for new intercultural communication, for an interchange of experiences and meanings, as the basis of another rationality which may legitimately pretend to some universality."[8]

The distinction between anti-racist posturing and praxis is complicated, however, by the positionality of the actors condemning or being condemned. For example, the discussion over call-out culture has become so active that even former president Barack Obama has chimed in, recently saying:

> "This idea of purity and you're never compromised and you're always politically 'woke' and all that stuff," Mr. Obama said. "You should get over that quickly." "The world is messy; there are ambiguities," he continued. "People who do really good stuff have flaws. People who you are fighting may love their kids, and share certain things with you."

And:

> "I do get a sense sometimes now among certain young people, and this is accelerated by social media, there is this sense sometimes of: 'The way of me making change is to be as judgmental as possible about other people,'" he said, "and that's enough." "Like, if I tweet or hashtag about how you didn't do something right or used the wrong verb," he said, "then I can sit back and feel pretty good about myself, cause, 'Man, you see how woke I was, I called you out. . . . That's not activism. That's not bringing about change," he said. "If all you're doing is casting stones, you're probably not going to get that far. That's easy to do."[9]

Obama's call-out of call-out culture was subsequently lauded by conservatives and democrats. And Obama's claims contain a great deal of truth. The problem, however, is that Obama stands outside of society such that his performance is patronizing, though given the leviathan-like power of hashtag activism in contemporary politics, these calls by experts to be more compassionate come across as an attempt to pacify or control a new and uncertain power. In other words, moral condemnation and the tactic of naming or calling-out moral failure, especially racism, is a tool that has consequences, and the specificity of power needs to be accounted for in judging these movements.

2.3. SYSTEMIC POSTURING AND LIBERAL NICETIES

I begin with examples of systemic posturing, as these are the most well-known and inform social norms in problematic ways. Mainstream discursive forces, especially the televised news media, and persons with institutional power respond to explicitly racist performances through a set of predictable scripts—the content of which will vary with ideological position. Typically, liberal actors posture as beacons of moral purity, such that they will cannibalize their own if moral failures are brought to light, while unabashedly right-leaning actors relate more strategically such that racism, and moral failure more generally, are regarded or disregarded as the response augments power. For the strategic right, racism is a tool that can be weaponized. For the more ideologically committed right, race is a reality that must be defended. Michael J. Monahan and Grant Silva describe this latter position as self-love, which cashes out as a preservationist mentality in relation to some imaginary ancestral collective and its honor.[10] The critique I level here is aimed primarily at those liberals who posture as anti-racist, because despite potential good intentions, anti-racist posturing, especially of this scripted variety, ultimately reproduces or reinforces racial conflict.

Before moving into my critique of the liberal position, however, I want to clarify my critique of the right. Returning to the initial example from the previous chapter, the condemnation of "criminals and unknown Middle Easterners" appeals to both elements of the above described right mentality. For the conservative realist, what matters in the performative is that the border must be secured such that none shall pass, but within the utterance there is also an appeal to the white nationalist mythos because it is not just criminals who are challenging sovereignty; it is a non-white collective—which includes the original mythological threat to whiteness, an Eastern Nosferatu-like monstrosity—who will presumably further taint the nation. The right is clear, almost certain, and as El Hajj Malik el-Shabazz repeatedly asserts, it acts as the wolf showing its teeth:

> When he opens his mouth and shows you his teeth you think he is smiling and when you look at a fox you think a fox is smiling, but actually the objective of the fox and the wolf is the same. They want to exploit you, they want to take advantage of you. Both are canine, both are dogs—there is no difference. Their methods might differ, but their objective is the same.[11]

The liberal position, the above-noted political fox, is far more pernicious and tactical insofar as it avoids accountability by presenting itself as well-intended, thus displacing agency and responsibility. Among foxes, consider the more recent example of Shane Gillis, a comedian who briefly worked for NBC before a video surfaced of him making racist and homophobic claims in 2018.[12] Gillis positioned his claims as humor, such that his public response to the event felt, he said, "ridiculous." Gillis's response to his own claims, and NBC's response to the public realization of those claims, both represent elements of anti-racist posturing and how that posturing avoids responsibility. For Gillis, the status of comedian is assumed to absolve him of responsibility, such that it is ridiculous for him to ever perform a serious utterance—he can't be racist because he is merely a chuckling nihilist. NBC assumes an equally innocent posture in the hiring and firing of Gillis, because they did not know what Gillis said, and when they found out, they did the right thing, they assume, by firing him.

The anti-racist posture taken by NBC reveals a common institutional failure to adequately address racism by avoiding it at all costs and quickly sanitizing when it is on their hands. Nevertheless, Gillis's position is also important because it reflects the individualistic paradigm that weakens the anti-racist posture, such that it is only a posture and not successful action. Luvell Anderson's distinction between merely racial, racist, and racially insensitive humor helps clarify why Gillis's claims were morally problematic:

> An instance of racial stereotype humor is *merely racial* just in case (i) the speaker has an aim to subvert the stereotype associated with the target group and (ii) the audience can reasonably be expected to recognize this aim. A racial joke is *racially insensitive* if the speaker (i) lacks an aim to subvert the associated stereotype or (ii) has a subverting aim but cannot reasonably expect audience uptake of that aim. And finally, racial humor is *racist* if either (i) it wrongly harms the target in virtue of that person's membership in a particular racial group or (ii) the speaker is motivated by a malevolent attitude or one of disregard.[13]

Anderson's description of merely racial humor suggests that it could even be morally valuable insofar as its clear aim is to undermine and ideally transform problematic social norms that stem from various institutional forms of domination. Gillis was clearly not engaging in merely racial humor, which means he was at least being racially insensitive, though the content of his performance seems to be simply racist. Whether he was being racially insensitive or racist, what makes Gillis's claims morally wrong is his distinct disregard for or even violent animosity toward potential others. Gillis was only thinking of himself and people like him—in fact, the video of the podcast shows him conversing with his near doppelganger. The objects of humor in his worldview remain just that, objects with which he has no meaningful relation.

The atomistic modality that underpins Gillis's moral failure is also found in NBC's response to fire him. Andrew Yang emphasized this point in his criticism of NBC's response, saying that Gillis should not have lost his job: "I think that our standards have become unfair, and we've become unduly vindictive and punitive. . . . We move on, but that person [Gillis] still doesn't have a job or that person's life has still been changed irrevocably."[14] Yang ultimately offered to meet with Gillis, presumably to talk and potentially build a relationship. My goal here is not to defend Gillis—he was clearly being racist—or Yang, who has a problematic relationship with appealing to stereotypes to, presumably, be seen as a viable presidential candidate among white voters.[15] Rather, Yang's response to the failed attempt at accountability for moral or legal failures—which includes NBC's anti-racist posture, as well as Gillis's claims to innocence—in many ways mirrors critiques made of punitive methods more generally.

Consider, for example, Angela Davis's argument in *Are Prisons Obsolete?*[16] In her critique of the prison-industrial complex (PIC), Davis emphasizes that carceral norms and racism are codependent, such that anti-racist praxis requires the abolition of the prison system as it is currently known. What can be easily missed in Davis's materialist critique—especially among eager activists longing for action and justice—is that the carceral state depends on a collective ethos that responds to crime, conflict, and difference through violent retribution. The retributivist modality, as common knowledge and not the worked-out ideal theory of a philosopher, relies on an atomistic notion of personhood and responsibility. When someone steals a loaf of bread and they have their hand cut off, the circumstances that afforded the conditions wherein theft is a necessary or viable option are not considered. Indeed, the social-environmental circumstances that afford conflict are seen as unfortunate excuses from the retributive perspective, because at the end of the day, a choice to commit a crime was made knowing that there would be potential consequences. Unlike Hammurabian retributivism, however, the neo-colonial state is far more vicious in its spiteful retaliation. Rather than simply remove a hand, the PIC disempowers and enslaves those who are caught up in its machinery, and as Davis rightly argues, those typically on the receiving end of punishment are racialized.

But the PIC is not racist just because it systematically targets racialized bodies. The deeper point that I think undergirds Davis's claim is that the spite of the punitive ethos is also racist insofar as it forecloses the possibility of transforming social relations in a way that would combat racism by removing racialized actors from meaningful interaction, while keeping white populations "safe" in differently gated communities. This is why Davis closes her critique by referencing alternative ways of dealing with conflict that draw on a communal sense of justice—reconciliatory modes. Condemned to the periphery, or once formally marked as criminal—what Orlando Patterson describes as social death—the relationship between social worlds in the liberal-colonial landscape remains divided against itself because the moment conflict occurs, the punitive reaction exacerbates rather than mends or repairs the micro and macro fissures.[17] Rather than having to know those who cause harm and deal with conflict ourselves, external agents simply cut off the offending actor; the symptom of the problem is mistaken for the source—what is known of others is only narrated by expert actors, and our festering open wounds continue to poison the social world. Biblically speaking, the sinner is taken for the sin, condemned and removed from meaningful relations. A mythical objectified narrative is all we are given by the overarching propaganda machine, and it is through that false narrative that the other is produced as a known "thing." How could we possibly solve our own problems under such divided conditions?

Further, the PIC and the carceral ethos that reproduces racial conflict in the United States is the emergent result of both liberal and conservative politics. Indeed, as Naomi Murakawa argues: "Partisan racial criminalization is precisely the kind of practice that legitimates racist realities in a systemic fashion. Liberal racial pity mirrored conservative racial contempt, and, as mirror images, 'competing' partisan frames locked blackness to criminality."[18] Left pity is a key element of the anti-racist posture because it is a condescending relation to racialized people that positions the subject beyond the circumstances of the racialized object, such that the liberal is compelled by their own presumed goodness to intervene and help—not because their actions and positionality directly produce the problem. In other words, racism is a problem that liberals have to deal with, because self-righteousness demands, but it is not a problem that liberals think of themselves as producing. In terms of policy, Murakawa notes, this plays out through a law-and-order mentality that ultimately "constrained the ideological terrain for addressing racial violence."[19] Consider Murakawa's critique of democratic policy decisions during the Clinton administration:

> The 1992 national democratic party platform referred to geographically discrete inner cities as "crime-ravaged communities" where "crime is not only a symptom but also a major cause of the worsening poverty and demoralization that afflicts inner city communities." Even as New Democrats punished the "Willie Hortons," they also positioned themselves as protectors of respectable, middle-class people of color, a distinction achieved by Clinton's personal rhetorical savvy and, more significant, the internal economic stratification of African Americans.[20]

In her 2016 election campaign, Hillary Clinton was called-out concerning claims she made when these policies were being forced on the social world by her husband, so that, Michelle Alexander rightly emphasizes,

> she used racially coded rhetoric to cast black children as animals, echoing anxieties around the "Willie Hortons" who were out to get "good" people: "They are often the kinds of kids that are called 'super-predators.' . . . No conscience,

no empathy, we can talk about why they ended up that way, but first we have to bring them to heel."[21]

Hillary Clinton's being called-out on what is clearly a racialized description of people of color fully captures the hypocrisy of liberal nicety-politics. Like Gillis, Clinton attempts to distance herself from the force of her past claims, though through the lens of regret rather than nihilistic dismissal: "Looking back, I shouldn't have used those words, and I wouldn't use them today."[22] Fair enough, maybe she would not use those words today, but not because she has transformed her racist beliefs and habits through intentional social work; rather, the rules of liberal politics have changed such that what counted as coded language in the 1990s no longer works in the present. Clinton would avoid calling racialized youth "super-predators" now because that language would expose her as a racist, which would presumably hinder or force her to pivot in her ongoing pursuit of power through domination. Of course, not much came of Clinton's claims—after all, she won the popular vote but not the electoral college vote—but other less powerful popular actors are not so "lucky," and their racism can lead to similar tough-on-crime reactions.

In other words, the sort of punitive relation to racism that is captured in the case of Shane Gillis is reproduced more locally and more problematically. Those who work in the academy often witness this sort of punitive call-out happening between students. In the best cases, the anti-racist call-out is understandably righteous, the speaking actor feels a moral responsibility to call it when they see it, ideally creating a moment wherein the racist is expected to reflect on their racism and change. After all, "See something, say something!"[23] The assumption underlying the best form of call-out culture reflects a misunderstood version of what John Braithwaite coined as "reintegrative shaming," which he describes as follows: "Reintegrative shaming communicates disapproval within a continuum of respect for the offender; the offender is treated as a good person who has done a bad deed."[24] The emphasis on shaming behavior is key, however, because most call-out events fail to separate the "sin" from the "sinner," and thus the shamed actor is, following Braithewaite's critique, stigmatized. Stigmatization has a tendency to reinforce or increase shameful behavior; as Braithewaite puts it,

> Stigmatization is disintegrative shaming in which no effort is made to reconcile the offender with the community. The offender is outcast, her deviance is allowed to become a master status, degradation ceremonies are not followed by ceremonies to decertify deviance.[25]

Of course, it is understandable why one might struggle to separate racism from the racist, especially when the prevailing assumption about human agency is that individuals are fixed over time—we have something of a soul, but with the death of god, we secularize the notion as a "mind," which serves the same purpose of cutting us off from ourselves—and also deliberate from a position of radical freedom. Indeed, for many it seems ridiculous to even suggest that someone could say or do something racist and still be, over the course of their existence, a good person. The goals of anti-racist praxis, however, demand that it at least be theoretically possible for a racist to become a good person and ultimately become anti-racist themselves.

Unfortunately, the Western world, and especially the United States, relies on and thus idealizes a punitive mode that permanently stigmatizes while simultaneously obfuscating other possible modes. Hence, along with unpacking the arguments made above, I also turn in the subsequent chapters to examples from the MENA region to help work out what is required to enact social work that affords meaningful anti-racist communities—that is, I clarify what the MENA world can offer to correct for the ongoing failure of Western social-political arrangements.

2.4. THE DIVIDES THAT BIND: "SOCIAL" POSTURING AND PRAXIS

I imagine most left-leaning persons have at some point felt the desire to call-out racism, and I am certain many of us have, and the results are clear: calling-out in the everyday encounter and the attempt to shame not only fail to combat racism but also often cause the racist actor to either dismiss the critique or double down on their position, especially if the accused is an active racist, thus further polarizing an already divided sociality. Loretta Ross emphasizes this same tension in her critique of call-out culture:

> Call-outs are justified to challenge provocateurs who deliberately hurt others, or for powerful people beyond our reach. Effectively criticizing such people is an important tactic for achieving justice. But most public shaming is horizontal and done by those who believe they have greater integrity or more sophisticated analyses. They become the self-appointed guardians of political purity. Call-outs make people fearful of being targeted. People avoid meaningful conversations when hypervigilant perfectionists point out apparent mistakes, feeding the cannibalistic maw of the cancel culture. Shaming people for when they "woke up" presupposes rigid political standards for acceptable discourse and enlists others to pile on. Sometimes it's just ruthless hazing.[26]

Note the difference between Ross's critique and Obama's: Ross emphasizes the value of the call-out in relation to those beyond our reach, especially as it helps to humble presidential candidates with a racist past. Calling-out Hillary Clinton is, it seems, the only way to engage her or hold her accountable. We have no other real means of engagement, especially with powerful elites like the Clintons, who have an armed security team and mobile fencing, to keep us from engaging them. Speaking truth directly to power, as in confronting those who hold power, is necessary in our current colonial arrangement because we have no other recourse, no space where power can be confronted. Indeed, a key difference between democratic societies of the pre-colonial MENA world and the liberal-colonial polis is, Michel Foucault argues, the distinct lack of the conditions of the possibility of parrhesiastic speech-acts. On this point, Foucault specifically notes:

> Parrhesia may be organized, developed, and stabilized in what could be called a parrhesiastic game. . . . The people, the Prince, and the individual must accept the game of parrhesia; they must play it themselves and recognize that they have to listen to the person who takes the risk of telling them the truth. Thus the true game of parrhesia will be established on the basis of this kind of pact which means that if the parrhesiast demonstrates his courage by telling the truth despite and regardless of everything, the person to whom this parrhesia is addressed will have to demonstrate his greatness of soul by accepting being told the truth. This kind of pact, between the person who takes the risk of telling the truth and the person who agrees to listen to it, is at the heart of what could be called the parrhesiastic game.[27]

Foucault leaves us wondering what might be required to play such a game. Who would listen to the harsh truth of another and be willing to really hear it? For the truth to stick, in the parrhesiastic game, both parties must commit in a sort of dual vulnerability where one's status in relation to power is suspended and the confrontation occurs between fellow humans. The vulnerability and power shift required for the successful call-out of a high-level politician is, under our current colonial arrangement, not possible.

Ross's focus on the cannibalistic and arrogant quality of the anti-racist posture as it is performed through a call-out between similarly situated actors is also crucial, because as an anti-racist posture, the call-out is a hierarchically situated position; it condemns from above when it judges—even if those judging are not differently empowered—aiming to make an example of the morally flawed by hurting them, sacrificing them in public. And the sacrifice is seen as just because the failure is heinous. But, the call-out also objectifies, inverting the colonial power dynamic. It is not just that the condemned individual failed, but they are a failure, a racist, and thus must be punished, made an example of, stigmatized, and exiled. Hence, for the ordinary person, those who are not beyond social encounter, the call-out has consequences that differently reinforce racism because of a difference in positionality.

Those working in small liberal arts colleges witness this entrenchment regularly. A student says and does something that is not politically correct, and another student calls them on it, accusing them of various things. The accused is shamed, the accuser is righteous, and the interaction, especially if it occurs outside of a classroom—or within a misregulated classroom—often ends with this asymmetry. Social divisions are solidified in this act, friends pick sides, and rather than actually solving a problem, the students have made the problem worse. Little concern is given to where the students are coming from, what they have or have not experienced, whether or not they would be willing and able to learn with others.[28] Friendships can abruptly end where the parrhesiastic game is not able to be successfully enacted. And the possibility of other modes of life, wherein these now-oppositional students could have collaborated in order to collectively cultivate a different sensitivity, awareness, and thus engagement with the world, all of this is lost with the erecting of yet another border.

It is easy to confuse positionality, however, when much interaction now occurs through the dual medium of objectified knowledge and the anti-social technologies of the internet. In other words, the megaphone of the internet affords what seems like a platform for all and thus makes everyone seem like an expert because of their distance from the world of encounter. And, because information is mistaken for wisdom, just as rationality is mistaken for virtue, it is also assumed that everyone should already know, like an expert, because the information is all available. Further, the knownness of the other that is already enforced through overlapping discursive mechanisms is verified in comment sections that are selectively interpreted. To be clear, the other can only be an object through digital relations, because they are only our own unchecked interpretation, a Cartesian wax that we shape and manipulate with our minds—what I call *digital onanism*.

Coupled with this digital onanism, the call-out polarizes and further divides, as any attack will. The call-out has the opposite impact of what one thinks ought to accompany anti-racist action. Part of the reason that stigmatized shaming fails as an anti-racist method is that it assumes racists will feel shame when engaged in this way, and more importantly, our social situations lack the necessary structures to simultaneously reintegrate those who are shamed. Consider, for example, when a student of color calls out a white student in a classroom setting that is not effectively mediated by the professor or TA. The unfolding is fairly consistent: There may be a hostile exchange, and both parties will walk away offended. Where do these students "return" to? The white student is likely to retreat into whiteness, peers and family who will understand and reinforce a reactionary sense of victimization—the experience will be framed as an angry person of color attacking an innocent white person—and the shame will be recalled as a slight against an already-frail white ego.[29] The student of color will continue to experience racism and may become increasingly frustrated, or hopeless, if not already, at how unwilling or unable white people are to confront their role in the perpetuation of white supremacy. The result of this sort of experience is that already-reified groups are reinforced because there is no structure in place to follow through on the shaming such that both parties fall back into the same problematic patterns. The sinner is mistaken for the sin, and the shamed are left with a limited range of possible responses—in this case, retreating to whiteness and thus denial as the typical response—while the judges who rallied against the condemned are at least satisfied for not simply sitting back and allowing the racist to do their thing.

More important to the goals of this text is the way POC and subjugated classes more generally fight each other, engaging in what some have described as an "oppression Olympics," where the experience of violent domination receives hierarchical and comparative treatment. Here, all racial violence is understood through a limited hermeneutic framework—in the U.S. context, a Black-white binary—that conflates descriptive facts about how racism operates with also being normatively arranged. Subsequently, anti-racism is reduced to a politics of purity, forcing all racialized actors to pick sides, reduce their experience to the experience of others, and since this is an impossible demand—or a demand that leads to bad faith—the end result is too often infighting among racialized groups that ought to otherwise be working together. And the white anti-racist can be the most egregious in their picking of sides and may maintain a politics of purity, often then reproducing racism against non-Black people of color by treating them as white adjacent.

One thing that guarantees that realization of the truth of the parrhesiast, like all speech-acts, is that the other actors in the total situation validate or support the performance. Where the other members of a performative world do not take up the parrhesiastic utterance, then it is less likely to stick. Hence, retreating to whiteness when called-out is in many ways a practice of protecting white subjectivity, as well as reinforcing its perceived dominance. Similarly, despite being in self-defense, the call-out as it occurs in an ill-equipped total situation ends up being nothing more than retribution—despite the best intentions. As my friend Hannah Baer recently noted through her meme account, *malefragility*: "It's interesting how much you love calling out other people's racism when your framework around wrongdoing and punishment seems kind of carceral."[30]

Hence, the claim now being leveled by those experts who want to regulate the call-out is that we need more compassion and forgiveness, which is also problematic because such calls tend to ignore or oversimplify the failures of anti-racist posturing and because they are working to pacify moral outrage with an overdetermined and imposed sense of moral repair. The consequences of a public call for forgiveness have been witnessed in South Africa, wherein Desmond Tutu's power afforded a national confessional for past harms that left many involved feeling far worse than they did prior to calling-out and then forgiving their many perpetrators.[31] And, of equal importance, much of what needed repair and decolonization in South Africa was left to continue festering.

To be unnecessarily charitable to those experts calling for compassion, I could understand the call to be a plea for an attempt at meaningful engagement with the other, to try and understand where they are coming from, what was intended, and to work to convey why the failed action was problematic such that it might be recognized and future behavior might be corrected; but, that encounter might not itself be forgiving or compassionate in the typical sense of those terms. Indeed, when persons are willing to actually work out their problems, together, those engagements can be full of righteous rage.[32] That anger might be necessary before anything else is possible. And people can coexist and create new meaning together without ever engaging in confessional-forgiveness activities when the total situation of their meaning-making is such that they do not immediately retreat to embattled enclaves that reinforce divisiveness by virtue of their existence.[33]

Nevertheless, what seems to be the fundamental element of anti-racist praxis, and the reconciliatory activity more generally, is that people are willing and able to engage each other, face to face, in a meaningful way. Loretta Ross's normative pronouncement to "call-in," rather than "call-out," reflects the need for real encounters as the starting point of cooperative meaning-making that moves us beyond the positional warfare of liberal-colonial politics and thus acts as the conditions of the possibility of solidarity. In other words, we might be motivated to reconcile for all sorts of reasons, but the collapse of colonial institutional existence forces our hand, in many ways, such that we have only two real options: death through perpetual war—which ultimately fulfills the colonial expectation—or choosing to become something else with other dispossessed people of the world. In this sense, solidarity is our only hope.

2.5. COMBATTING ANTI-MENA RACISM: STRIVING TOWARD SOLIDARITY FROM THE LIMITS OF RACIST GUILT

The problem of naming and condemning racism is further complicated for Middle Eastern peoples, and especially those presumed MENA in the United

States, because those from spaces like the former Ottoman and Persian worlds are legally and politically categorized as white, despite being mistreated as a non-white population, and racial conflict is constantly oversimplified according to the mores of a Black-white binary. Indeed, part of the desire for formal institutional recognition is that said status would simultaneously legitimate claims of racism insofar as there is an apparatus that reinforces the possibility that MENA people could be mistreated on racial grounds. Presently, if someone is mistreated for being presumed MENA in the United States, the condemnation of that violence risks being met with dismissal if made on racial grounds because MENA people are miscategorized as white.[34] And the dismissing racist will say as much. Hence, an appeal to religious discrimination ends up being useful for those who can and are willing to make that sort of claim—and this ends up being a problematic way of categorizing the racial mistreatment of MENA peoples, as discussed in the previous chapter.

But even if systemic recognition were granted and people were pressured to admit that the violence that bolsters their existence impacts even larger portions of the world's peoples than previously conceded—a concession that is rarely made for those groups already formally recognized—it is not clear that this sort of recognition would actually do anything beyond shifting the way that racism categorizes those who do and do not count. Racists are amazing at pivoting around anti-racist norms. The shift in racialized language in the post-racial era reflects this pivoting, insofar as racists can still enact racism—domestically and abroad—without using explicitly racist language, by instead appealing to politically correct terms of condemnation. And, concerning foreign policy specifically, the United States is unlikely to change, even if recognition of domestic domination is granted, because it maintains a relation of violent domination toward other subjugated peoples who are already recognized in various ways—that is, the United States justifies its ongoing intervention and domination of the global south, as well as the peoples perceived to be from the south, on other grounds (e.g., combatting communism and now terrorism) and because racism is often misunderstood or reduced to a purely subjective act-based phenomenon rooted in a worked-out or intentional positionality.[35] Hence, the call-out of anti-MENA racism not only fails insofar as it potentially reinforces conflict lines, further entrenching us against ourselves, but also fails because MENA peoples are not recognized by the overarching discursive apparatus such that anti-racist condemnations are nominally legitimated by the law and expert utterance. Nevertheless, as John Harfouch emphasizes, the failure is still a success.[36]

As I argue in the previous chapter, this lack or muddled systemic recognition is central to how Middle Eastern peoples have been categorized and treated throughout colonial history. And, while some Middle Eastern people have attempted to assimilate and adhere to their whitewashed status, with more or less success depending on their location and how they relate to the features that contribute to their Middle Easternness, many have responded with ethno-national insularity. Maintaining closed communities within the broader social-political system seems to afford short-term security, but it is ultimately a failed strategic position. Hence, systemic recognition is only one side of the social-political coin, and in the absence of social recognition, safety, security, and equality will not be guaranteed. Of course, anti-racist efforts should be made to educate and transform popular sentiment and representations within the social world. But of equal importance is transforming relations between the various fragmented Middle Eastern populations who see themselves as enemies because of internalized Orientalist tactics that pit all against all.

In other words, adding yet another layer to this complex identity is the uptake of naturalized national identities among MENA people that reinforces objectification and the condemnation of other MENA peoples. Insofar as systemic recognition fails, the focal problem for the remainder of this text are those conditions that prevent MENA solidarity and the conditions that are needed to overcome those obstructions. In this case, the overlapping forces of racism, nationalism, and sexism that are reified by and thus bolster the coloniality of power, keep us divided. The goal of noting these internalized divisive forces is to combat them, and as I have argued throughout this chapter, that struggle begins with social encounters.

In other words, we must find a response to violent domination that does not rely on or reinforce the coloniality of power in all of its insidious forms—while also challenging the liberal-colonial system. The claim being built in this chapter is that we begin this liberatory work by actually engaging with other people, especially other MENA people, to build real community coalitions wherein people are known in all of their complexity—not just as boxes to be carefully navigated in an effort to remain righteous and condescending. The first, and perhaps most important, condition of the possibility of a reconciliatory process that affords political solidarity and thus liberation is the face-to-face encounter.

Enrique Dussel, drawing on Emmanuel Levinas, emphasizes this starting point throughout his work: "When I am face-to-face before another *in a (practical) relationship*, in the presence of praxis, that person is *someone* for me and I am *someone* for him or her. The being face-to-face of two or more is *being* a person."[37] And Dussel extends this position in his description of why las Casas moved to defend the first nations:

> Las Casas would not have been able to formulate and articulate his critique of the Spanish conquest of the Americas if he had not lived in the periphery and

heard the cries and witnessed the tortures to which indigenous people were being submitted. It is that Other who is the actual origin of this counterdiscourse that took root in Europe.[38]

Dussel's reading also clarifies why las Casas was less friendly toward the Eastern barbarians by which he contrasted the indigenous Americans in an effort to save them, for he did not exist in the periphery of the near-East and was thus unable to have his objectified knowledge destabilized by the facticity of life. The near-East was unknown, to las Casas—or at least to his contemporaries—or was only known as an object of fear, a thing to be conquered. What is striking about this emphasis on the face-to-face is that it was the norm for those people from the broader MENA world prior to colonization. Prior to nationalism and the fetishism of a colonial-carceral state, MENA peoples coexisted in various ways that afforded encounters.

Hence, MENA peoples are particularly primed to do this sort of face-to-face coalition-building because we have an extensive pre-colonial or indigenous history of community-building to draw on, which I will discuss in the following chapters through an analysis of myth and exemplarity. Beforehand, however, I will say more about the nationalism that negatively mediates MENA social labor and thus obfuscates *anti-colonial solidarity*.

Chapter Three

Calling in MENA Nationalists

Why Recent Geopolitical Boundaries Fail to Account for MENA Subjectivity

Racism is a practice of abstraction, a deathdealing displacement of difference into hierarchies that organize relations within and between the planet's sovereign political territories. Racism functions as a limiting force that pushes disproportionate costs of participating in an increasingly monetized and profit-driven world onto those who, due to the frictions of political distance, cannot reach the variable levers of power that might relieve them of those costs. Indeed, the process of abstraction that signifies racism produces effects at the most intimately "sovereign" scale, insofar as particular kinds of bodies, one by one, are materially (if not always visibly) configured by racism into a hierarchy of human and inhuman persons that in some form the category "human being."

—Ruth Wilson Gilmore[1]

The ability to successfully challenge and transform anti-MENA racism, specifically through a face-to-face encounter, is obstructed because of institutional misrecognition and violence that is coupled with the social failures of anti-racist action. The failures of anti-racist action are further complicated in relation to MENA subjectivity because neither the racist actor nor the anti-racist poseur are coerced or taught to recognize MENA difference.[2] Thus, even a retributive call-out of racism against MENA peoples seems impossible, and often fails, because the necessary conditions for the successful illumination or condemnation of anti-MENA racism are not in place.

Subsequently, scholars and activists are increasingly calling for systemic recognition of MENA racial identity so that anti-MENA racism might be better challenged. The success of recognition is unclear and certainly unsatisfying, but for MENA people the challenge of recognition is further complicated by internal conflicts over who counts as a part of the group.

My focus in this chapter is on this tension among MENA peoples over who counts, but before jumping into that debate, it is important to clarify what is at stake, which is the goal of section 1. Here, I argue that the primary blockage to community between MENA peoples is an insular and often genocidal ethno-nationalism.

My broader goal in this chapter is to begin the transitional work away from purely negative critique toward an emphasis on normative ideals that are rooted in pre-colonial modes—modes that have been obscured by nationalist projects. Hence, in section 2, I extend my argument against national insularity among MENA peoples by discussing the ways that race and nation are too often conflated when discussing MENA people. That is, national chauvinism and its imagined boundaries are also naturalized in a way that mediates the potential encounter between MENA peoples, thus preventing the unfolding of face-to-face relationality and also undermining greater defensive possibility. My critique of the race-nation conflation is an extension of my critique of xenophobia in Chapter 1, though with a specific emphasis on the uptake of national identity both among racialized MENA peoples and by those who would support formal recognition.

In section 3 I argue that enacting *anti-colonial solidarity*, especially among MENA peoples, requires that national identity be softened or completely rejected and ultimately replaced by an affirmative identity that is grounded in more immediate experience. In the U.S. context, this immediate experience is of being MENA in such a way that clumps us together with little regard for the national differences over which we foolishly infight.

3.1. COMPLEXITIES OF MENA DEFENSIVE RESPONSES TO COLONIAL DOMINATION

In the absence of formal racial recognition, MENA subjects have limited options for making sense of and thus protecting themselves from violent domination. Some MENA American actors will continue to attempt to assimilate. Others will identify through alternative categories that are already overdetermined by the Orientalist-racist colonial arrangement and thus legible, especially when the objectified being is not easily categorized according to Blackness. In other words, some will attempt whiteness, while others will emphasize religious and national identity, or a combination of both, even when it is common knowledge that all of these categories fail to capture or protect from violent domination. Thus, the MENA actor operates along the border of the Black-white binary, distanced from whiteness in daily interactions and general self/other understanding, but simultaneously relegated to whiteness in discourse and institutional practice.

Here, consider Neda Maghbouleh's revealing analysis of the popular television series, *Shahs of Sunset*, a reality TV show that focuses on Iranian-Americans living in Los Angeles:

> Iranian-Americans talk about white people in surprising ways. Reza Farahan, the show's gay, mustachioed breakout star, is also its racial id. Whether hollering at "yummy white hos," asserting "a white guy [can't] make a Persian man jealous" or assessing a rack of gingham-checked bikinis as "the white section . . . Persians wouldn't be caught dead in that," Reza says things about race no Iranian has ever said before—on TV, that is. The paradox is that Iranians and other Middle Easterners have been (often happily) categorized as "white" in the United States since their earliest arrival in the 19th century. Recent efforts among these groups to gain federal recognition as "Middle Eastern" are reflective of internal and external cultural shifts.³

Maghbouleh's analysis echoes my own experience and the experience of other folks I have known from the broader MENA region who grew up in the U.S. context. We know we are not white, we critique and thus distance ourselves from whiteness all of the time, but, as Maghbouleh emphasizes, we tend to do this within our own ethno-national communities or, when we extend beyond those communities, sometimes hesitantly, with other people of color. Like most institutional arrangements under the coloniality of power, television is produced for comforting or reaffirming coloniality even when an occasional attempt is made from within that system to challenge that power. And the hesitation among MENA people to voice their racialized sight-beyond-sight on television reflects a more common social norm of silencing critiques of whiteness, as well as racialized experience. On the one hand, defenders of whiteness do not want to hear it—they believe they can do no wrong. On the other hand, white "allies" too often fail to see beyond their own binary positionality—that is, they maintain a more rigid racialized worldview that is solely Black or white. The white ally ultimately reinforces the binary opposition by dismissing nonbinary racialized forms, thus forcing people of color into one side or the other.

The response to MENA critiques of whiteness from the right can be met with the standard post-racial dismissal of racial critique—racism is over and discussing it is racist—but those critiques can also be met with the above-noted relegation, especially from so-called "anti-racist" allies who only understand conflict according to the Black-white binary: "What are you talking about? You are white too." Hence, the second part of Maghbouleh's claim, that MENA peoples have often happily occupied whiteness, is at least partly rooted in this dismissive rejection, or purely instrumental relation (i.e., policing), that whiteness levels against any racialized bodies who are non-Black. (Of course, as noted above, white supremacists and their complacent supporters differently dismiss claims against racism that are made by subjects who are perceived to be Black.)

In light of this ongoing gaslighting—committing violence and then denying the reality of that violence, which is a foundational move in the colonial playbook—many subjugated peoples from the broader MENA world reinforce their ethno-national communities to defend from and also form positive meaning in spite of the coloniality of power. The retreat into ethno-national enclaves occurs in many ways, including by those who are attempting to assimilate and those who are appealing to religion to make sense and find a place that seems secure.

Further, despite recent efforts to organize and build a broader community among MENA peoples—an effort to which this book will hopefully contribute—many MENA subjects are resistant to organizing or speaking out against the problem of the color line with other MENA people. Resistance to critique is both defensive—"don't rock the boat"—and a cultural replicant for reasons that are baked into the national identities through which we allegedly are defending ourselves—"My enemies' enemy is my friend," says the nationalist whose interests are backed by colonial force. Hence, our ability to engage each other about our shared experiences and potentially form defensive, as well as affirmative, relationships is often hindered by our micro-communal commitments that were formulated in response to a different enemy threat, from a different time, in a faraway place, and by a false belief in the willingness and ability of the "new world" to make good on the promises of liberty and justice for those who play by the rules.

It is in light of these complex circumstances that the need to organize and work toward solidarity is a defensive move and the beginning of a potential cooperatively-determined future—not just a plea for recognition. The act of forming new communities is a longstanding practice among the people who have only recently been categorized and incarcerated through imagined MENA boundaries. And, as I will argue in the following chapters, the practice of cooperative-determination or community formation ought to be affirmatively maintained on its own terms as a reclamation our pre-colonial existence and is in fact being mobilized among some MENA populations (see Chapter 6). Presently, however, nationalist insularity prevents collective action, which causes many problems—beyond the permissive silence, or active participation, that is too often enacted by non-Black populations of color—some of which I address in the next section.

3.2. MENA WHO? A CRITIQUE OF THE RACE-NATION CONFLATION (OR, WHY NATIONAL BOUNDARIES FAIL TO DEMARCATE RACIAL GROUPINGS AND EXPECTATIONS)

The internalization and championing of the categories through which we have been dominated is specifically problematic for MENA subjects, as well as the larger project of solidarity toward which identity politics is supposed to be oriented, because those categories keep us pitted against ourselves even when they are masked as working toward coalition. In other words, obstructing the relational history and practice that defined the broader MENA region prior to colonial imposition is the internalized Orientalist-racist narrative that manifests itself among MENA peoples as ethno-national identity.

Informed by the Orientalist-racist attitude, nationalist narratives operate throughout the social world and rely on selectively closed histories that disregard the presence and importance of those who are objectified as beyond the nation. The internalization of these Orientalist-racist scripts plays out in present calls for recognition of MENA peoples as a racialized collectivity insofar as they include, and in fact rely on, a colonial account of who is or is not MENA. Not only does this sort of plea reinforce Orientalist-racist realism, but it also masks that realism through the fetishization of nationalism.[4]

The failure of understanding MENA people through colonial geospatial markers is that it conflates two ambiguous identity categories, race and nation, while simultaneously maintaining that both categories are real. In this way, the national realist also acts as a racial realist. Nevertheless, I believe that historical-cultural commonalities can be maintained and political geography can be critically understood such that a meaningful discussion of and with MENA peoples can occur without also holding on to the imported Orientalist-racism and thus nationalism that is too often unreflectively relied on to delimit MENA subjectivity.

Born from the West, ethno-national identity is taken up, throughout the colonized world, partly because the violent means of building solidarity around the imagined community of the timeless nation and the end of that national effort—self-determination through a nation-state—are legible to Western powers.[5] (The fact that Việt Nam's declaration of independence opens with an almost identical phrasing as that which was deployed in the formation of the United States is a testament to this intentional effort to be legible to the oppressor.[6]) Unfortunately, attempts to liberate or decolonize that rely on nationalist techniques and strategies ultimately fail because, as Audre Lorde notes, "the master's tools will never dismantle the master's house."[7] Rather than liberate, the nationalisms of the early decolonial effort led to further violent domination and thus division (a repetition). And, despite the various problems with nationalism (including its colonial origins), nationalist imaginaries continue to inform how the peoples of the broader MENA region are categorized and represented in discourse.

Here I use the language of nationalism, or ethno-nationalism, rather than ethnicity, for several reasons that I will expand on throughout Chapters 3 and 4, but should be clarified upfront. First, the idea of a uniform and affirmative ethnicity that binds any people, Latin American or MENA, is suspect, and those attempts to categorize based on cultural or linguistic histories are marked by compounding exceptions—dialects, divergent historical records, change over time, and so on. For example, as Abdelkebir Khatibi carefully emphasizes, "the name "Arab" designates a war of naming and ideologies, which bring to light the active plurality of the Arab world."[8] Khatibi goes on:

> This unity is, for us, for the past, to be analyzed in its imaginary insistence. And besides, this alleged unity that is claimed so vehemently includes not only its specific margins (Berber, Coptic, Kurdish . . . and the margins of margins: the feminine), but also covers the division of the Arab world into countries, peoples, sects, and classes—and the divisions of divisions, up until the suffering of the individual, deserted by the hope of his god, forever invisible.[9]

Here, Khatibi critiques the MENA ethnic category, Arab, by pointing out the various ways that the term's meaning shifts as its marginal forms are considered. Ideally the Arab unity would respond affirmatively to the question: Where do the Coptic, Kurdish, Armenian, Greek, or Turkish people fit within the Arab ethno-imaginary?

Unfortunately, however, that affirmation is uncommon, which leads to a second problem with ethnicity among MENA peoples; namely, the recent history of the MENA region has been marked by genocide, exclusion, or coercive assimilatory practices with the goal of creating a homogenous identity from a hyperplural collectivity. The Asad family's Arabization tactics in Syria are at least partly to blame for the instability that led to the present civil war. Turkey's ongoing efforts at Turkification create similar instabilities because any effort to force a plurality of people into a singular form will produce resistance and animosity.

Third, it is precisely this sort of ethnic chauvinism that afforded the partitioning of the post-Ottoman world with the support of Western colonial powers in the nineteenth and twentieth centuries. The post-Ottoman state formation is a "homeland" for an imaginary ethno-national population that is presumed to be real in a historical and biological sense, but that imaginary homogeneity fails because MENA peoples carry with them at least a thousand years of historical existence that traverses empires, languages, and cultural forms. So when I am talking about nationalism among MENA peoples in this chapter, I am specifically talking about those who hold on to a rigid notion of the MENA world that is based in an imaginary or highly selective, as well as naturalized, historical memory and thus grounded in the exclusion of other MENA peoples. And this nationalism matters because, independent of what nationalists from the MENA world think, all MENA people are lumped together in the colonial mind with their imaginary enemies as being the same sort of people (i.e., an inferior race that can be manipulated for Western purposes).[10] My critique is of how these nationalist forms misdirect MENA peoples in ways that afford greater vulnerability, even if the immediate insularity of national cloistering appears to be secure. (One final point is that the nationalist claims an ethnicity or culture but simultaneously denies the very thing that makes those forms vibrant and real—namely, difference, exchange, and appreciation among free people. I would love to see culture liberated from the colonial and national tomb, to revive the processes that afford great civilizations.)

The uptake of nationalism in the broader MENA region and its ongoing reproduction in discourse does not simply fail because it reproduces conflict among people who have coexisted in pluralistic communities throughout history—most recently in the former Ottoman empire, as well as the Qajar and Pahlavi arrangements that afforded modern Iran; rather, the depth of the failure is that the imported nationalism catalyzes the conditions needed for the territories to be reorganized by Orientalist-colonizers into what is now myopically understood as the Middle East.[11] In our attempts to liberate, we divide against ourselves and have been subsequently conquered. By holding onto national identities, we remain divided against ourselves and estranged from our siblings.

Consider, for example, John Tehranian's pivotal work, *whitewashed*, wherein he argues for formal recognition of a MENA racial category by appealing to the current understanding of the MENA geopolitical world to demarcate who counts.[12] Here, Tehranian raises several cases of Persians and Arabs who conceal their national origin, sometimes claiming to be Jewish, Greek, or Indian, presumably as an attempt to defend themselves from racial violence, which demonstrates the need for racial recognition and a protected status. Tehranian says, "With the simple change of a revealing first or last name, many Middle Easterners can become Italian, French, Greek, Romanian, Indian, Mexican, Puerto Rican, or Argentine."[13] The national masking Tehranian describes could be likened to a Japanese American attempting to change their identity during internment to something like Korean or Chinese in order to avoid persecution and prosecution; that is, it is not a deracialization, but rather an attempt to not be seen as the national enemy through which the perceived race is currently being relegated. The actor who stands out as potentially Japanese, Arab, or Persian, stands out on racial grounds and is therefore racialized in interactions.

The legal and geopolitical claims made by those who appeal to recent divisions fail to explain the racialization of Middle Eastern–perceived persons—regardless of whether their national or ethnic identity is Italian or Iranian—because in reality all Middle Eastern populations are legally categorized as white, but are nonetheless interpellated and mistreated in relation to a Middle Eastern racial epicenter. If one has a Persian background but covers this identity when confronted (e.g., by claiming to be Italian or Jewish, as if one cannot be simultaneously Persian and Jewish or Italian), one is not avoiding racialization—though one may avoid immediate assault—because racialization is what made the confrontation occur. Indeed, depending on who is asking and how they are asking, the questioning of one's origin that is initiated by awareness of phenotypic difference is not just insulting but is also a threat. MENA people may actively attempt to live the bad faith of whiteness through a self-induced historical amnesia, but if one is picked out as raced and confronted on said grounds, then pivoting to other national identities, at best, merely moves the racialized target into a realm of more non-white expectations and thus white violence.

Even if the racialized actor were waving a national flag that was not affiliated with the presumptive enemy group, they would remain suspect to the racist, and we witness this fact, all too often, as the many migrant-refugee populations of the United States continue to be persecuted despite concerted efforts to assimilate and even bleed for the U.S. flag.

Tehranian extends the race-nation conflation in the following claim: "We unquestionably define any individual of Irish, Italian, Slavic, or Greek descent as white."[14] Here, Tehranian's view of populations who identify with a national space that is now geopolitically understood as "European" not only reveals the race-nation conflation but also contradicts the more general plea for recognition of other Middle Eastern Americans who are also categorized as white despite their race-based mistreatment. After all, the grounds on which people are or are not unquestionably defined as white are debatable, but if we are going strictly by institutional recognition, then all of the people Tehranian is attempting to categorize as MENA would also be white. But, as Tehranian and I both know, the grounds of inclusion are not simply determined by institutional recognition. Rather, social forces—and specifically the white supremacists who have a clear sense of whiteness that does not include most of the people Tehranian mentions, including Irish Catholics—play a major role in determining one's racial status and, more importantly, one's safety.

Tehranian's appeal to national groups who stand outside of the geo-conceptual bounds that currently demarcate the MENA region, and his use of these groups in defining MENA people through contrast, is problematic for more insidious reasons than simple contradiction. After all, we can and often do live with contradiction. The uptake, or the failed uptake, of national boundary as the grounds of inclusion or exclusion ultimately reproduces and reinforces an Orientalist-racist understanding of the world that is rigid and ahistorical, as if the current geographic palimpsest has been fixed through history and its delineations accurately reflect racial grouping. Hence, it is not merely the case that the race-nation conflation fails to accurately describe racial interpellation, but appealing to and relying on the terms set out by the coloniality of power to demarcate a category of recognition in fact reproduces colonial power discursively as well as practically, insofar as the maintenance of such boundaries actively undermines solidarity.

The race-nation conflation, which treats national identities as a natural demarcation and also as the grounds for a collective notion of, in this case, MENA racial identity, is problematic and not helpful for the same reasons that colonial partitions of hyperplural life-worlds are problematic: namely, both operate as a top-down roundup of a collectivity with complete disregard for the complexity and nuance that defines the life being partitioned. The MENA identity category that uses the Orientalist-racist concept of MENA people and place is particularly problematic because the geo-territorial lines it relies on are only recently imposed and are still highly volatile. I will focus here, and in the next chapters, on two specific lines that have recently been deployed in the post-Ottoman landscape to create the East/West distinction: the continuously fracturing lines of the Greco-Turkic boundaries and those that have come to define the Levant and broader Syria.

But, before deconstructing the East/West boundary at its present seams, I think the point can be made from a less ambiguous locality. For example, Tehranian uses a range of identity categories that a MENA-perceived person might mask through in order to, presumably, deracialize—these include Italian, Greek, Jewish, Indian, Mexican, and Puerto Rican! I will use Italian, since many scholars maintain that Italians enact whiteness in various ways. So what happens if and when a Middle Eastern–looking person responds to the unreflective white supremacist by identifying with an Italian national origin—a highly plausible scenario for some southern Italians who are, historically speaking, directly linked to the imagined communities of the presently produced MENA region (e.g., Arab, Persian, Turkic, Greek, Jewish, etc.)?[15] Does the white supremacist make the unprecedented concession that they were wrong? "Ah, my mistake, I thought you were Arab!" Of course not. The white supremacist would never admit to being wrong—that would be a recognition of their non-supremacy, which would lead to all sorts of meta-problems for their teetering whiteness. Rather, in the best-case scenario, the interpellated subject will be reinterpreted through a different range of stereotypical traits.

Popular options for the racialized Italian are a subrational, animalistic, and hypersexual character such as those presented in television shows like the Jersey Shore, or the explanatory media rhetoric of events like the European economic crisis, which is narrated as being caused by the lazy and dishonest southerners (P.I.G.S.) who just want to drink and party.[16] Another option is the dangerous gangster who will "whack" those who disagree with his ill-logic—consider the award-winning six-season HBO program *The Sopranos*.[17] A third option is the antiquated type, wherein the raced subject is framed as having at one point had great and important ancestors who collapsed (or degenerated) into backwardness because of their proximity to, and thus mixing with, Africa and the East, which caused Geist to move north and west, leaving its previous forms eternally behind.[18]

Racialized bodies with Italian national relations, or racialized bodies who either hide or are misrecognized as Italian, are not alone in being selectively framed; the point is that "covering" oneself, trying to claim another identity that is close to but not quite Arab, does not deracialize one's experience when one has been racialized, as these other groups are also relegated to subrational race-based expectations when they are racialized, and thus they are already under attack. The ability to claim a different religious, geopolitical, or national origin within the same racialized whole is not a deracialization: it is a survival tactic that has a long history as a practice, especially among MENA peoples who, as moving targets, have been fighting for their lives for centuries.[19]

Similarly, by relying on imposed lines, many who would otherwise be perceived as MENA, and who maintain a familial historical relation to the broader MENA region, are unjustly excluded. I will say more about the current East/West boundary in the next chapter, but for the purposes of calling in my MENA siblings who maintain the race-nation conflation and, hopefully, bring a bit more nuance to the conversation, consider the case of the famous Thesalonian/Salonician Mustafa Kemal Pasha or Kemal Atatürk.

Most widely known as the father of modern Turkey, few who do not study the former Ottoman empire know that Atatürk was born and raised in what is now the Greek state. You can visit Atatürk's former home in Thessaloniki, though technically it is a Turkish territory and consulate within Greece. Here is the address: Apostolou Pavlou 17, Thessaloniki 546 34.

Like many of the populations who comprised the former Ottoman empire in its final days, Atatürk's identity would shift quite dramatically from the time that he was born to the time that he helped reorganize what is now Turkey. Prior to the rise of Turkey and Greece, and the nationalisms that accompanied those emergences, the primary identity of persons from the region was religious. Atatürk's family would have identified as Muslim, not Turkish, and the other subjects of the region who would become Greeks, Turks, Armenians, Assyrians, and a wide range of other national identity groups, would have similarly self-identified primarily according to their religions. The emphasis on religious identification is crucial because there are few other reliable ways to delineate the Ottoman populations—phenotype is especially unreliable. Indeed, it is possible that Atatürk had Christian or Jewish relatives, for example, who at some point converted to Islam. Conversion, whether voluntary or forced, was not atypical in the Ottoman world—especially as adherence to Islam afforded social-political benefits under the millet system of taxation and representation.[20]

Linguistically, Atatürk's home language would have been some version of the dialect that became modern Turkish, but he also would have been well versed in the local Christian languages, namely the Hellenic that is associated with the orthodox community in Thessaloniki, as well as the other languages that were needed to engage with the plural community that made up his hometown. Had Atatürk been a Christian, instead of a Muslim, then he would have likely become differently nationalized—for example, he could have become Greek, North Macedonian (FYRoM), or Bulgarian, had his familial trajectory been slightly different one generation earlier, or if he had converted to Orthodoxy. And, if someone with a similar background as Atatürk had moved to the United States from Thessaloniki, then they might have been categorized as having a non-Turkic national origin.

Of course, all of these possible national affiliations do not change the way that the interstitial subjectivity of a character like Atatürk would be seen when racialized. That is, it is impossible to distinguish the peoples of this region according to phenotype because the population shares in a common cultural, environmental, and genetic history. A hyper-emphasis is clearly placed on religious or linguistic difference to demarcate national affinity precisely because phenotype is not a useful internal marker (and because we all quietly admit to being siblings when the nationalist attitude is allowed to soften).

So how would someone like Tehranian make sense of a figure like Atatürk in the U.S. context if a MENA identity category relied on recent national boundaries to categorize? Do we just exclude him? Politically, he would have been classified as white, the same way that all people from the region were misidentified in the early twentieth century, but socially, Atatürk would have stood out as an obviously non-white body. Atatürk's interstitial experience is not exceptional, as most of the former Ottoman populations can tell a similar story about themselves and their families—despite the genocidal efforts of nationalists to deny and thus erase those overlapping narratives—such that being from the region is to be between spaces, Afro-Eurasian, and thus according to one-drop rules, rules of degeneration, and the common knowledge of white supremacists who determine social-institutional norms in the West, not white.

For a final example, consider what it takes to be a U.S. national. Here, there are at least two general ways of understanding U.S. national identity. On the one hand, there is the ideal civic-national identity that is realized by participating in and defending the norms, ideals, and laws of the nation to which one claims membership. On this ideal view, one can become a member of the nation through civic engagement because the nation is not a racialized construct but is a set of values that one does or does not uphold. This is ideal, of course, because the reality of national membership is largely not defined by whether or not one upholds the right values—in fact, most of the strongest advocates for U.S. ideals, especially liberty and equality, have been people of color who were murdered, by the state and white nationalists, largely because of their unwavering advocacy for the ideals on which the nation is supposed to stand. Hence, on the other hand, nationalism is understood and enacted as a racial-ethnic project, such that, in the United States, one can be a citizen, descendent from several generations of patriotic citizens, and still not belong to the nation because of one's non-whiteness. The tension between civic-nationalism and ethno-racial nationalism is not unique to the United States. There are plenty of people who have lived in Western Europe for multiple generations who will not be recognized by the ethno-nationalists as belonging precisely because those who determine inclusivity imagine the nation as being sanguineous and not dependent on values or linguistic norms.

Here, the civic-nationalist might argue that we should not base our understanding of the nation on that of the ethno-nationalist. Though I concur with the normative sentiment that social-organizations ought to be co-determined through collective meanings and meaning-making processes, the failure of those processes is too often caused by violent resistance from those who fetishize genetic nationalist supremacy. Those most comfortable with violence that is aimed at destabilizing heterogeneous collectivities are the nationalists who believe in their own manifest superiority. So, descriptively, it only makes sense to use the violent threat as the baseline for understanding possibility within the current arrangement, not just because we must defend ourselves and thus recognize real threats, but because that potential violence lingers in the background of social life, determining who is or is not a potential target and thus who does or does not belong.

Being honest about the presence and possibility of violence is not an endorsement of violence. A society can be perfectly organized on paper, ideal, but where that organization meets reality, praxis, and in this case enforcement reveals the truth of those ideals. The same can be said for resistance. The ideal of peace ought to guide thought and action, but the moments between intentional reflections, what William James referred to as our flights, are marked by a vulnerability and reflexivity that cannot be simply denied in the name of ideals—that is, the act of self-defense can be an immediate movement, nonreflective, or reptilian.[21]

3.3. AFFIRMING IDENTITY

The claims of those who conflate race and nation nevertheless reveal an important question: On what grounds should we define ourselves? The claim that I have made and will continue to develop throughout this book is that we, insofar as there is a future wherein *We* are collectively self-determined and thus enact solidarity, *We* cannot define ourselves according to the palimpsest that is colonial geopolitical boundaries. We are not our national origin. At the same time, the need for collective-determination and solidarity that is grounded in a meaningful identity is motivated by a defensive reflex because the well-known threat that bolsters the coloniality of power is white supremacist violence. But if identity is defined according to the negation of others—which is how nationalists have traditionally identified themselves—then it has not avoided the trappings of coloniality or the sort of organizing that fractured the broader MENA peoples throughout the twentieth century.

Of course, recognizing the complexity of the original "melting pot" societies is antithetical to the coloniality of power. Several volumes would be necessary to capture all of the nuanced distinctions by which the various populations of the broader MENA region have distinguished themselves throughout time, and even this sort of ethnographic work would fail insofar as human life is fluid, transitional, and thus defies category. If, however, MENA spaces are considered according not to their present illusory form but in terms of war, with specific attention to how these spaces have expanded and contracted over time, then it becomes clear that those who could qualify as MENA, those targeted and victimized by the Western war machine as it forced the MENA region into its present form, come from places well beyond the Orientalist bounds presently ascribed as MENA. A broad historical view of the "Middle East" includes persons from Portugal, Spain, Italy, Northern Africa, much of what is now Southeastern "Europe," the Aegean, north into the Caucasus, and eastward into India. Indeed, if the spread of Orientalist-racism to the Americas is taken as a continuation of the same war tactics, a historical connection between Latin American and Middle Eastern experience becomes obvious, as I emphasized in Chapter 1. Yet selective and reified Orientalist political narratives that ignore the long history of white supremacy would have us believe these spaces are not connected by a common history of strategic Orientalist-racist war tactics. Still, Istanbul was once Constantinople, while Ceuta remains claimed by Spain and the EU.

The sort of nationalism that blocks recognition of the broad impact of coloniality and its racial violence has a much deeper root, however, than surface-level identity politics and thus requires a deeper critique. Indeed, the objectifying Orientalist-racist mentality that drives nationalism is definitive of thought in the colonized world, as I continue to argue in the next chapters, such that overcoming its rigid bounds requires a total transformation of our relations through anti-racist praxis or reconciliation. In other words, the coloniality of power has embedded itself like a parasite into our identities, such that overcoming its endless desire for blood requires the cultivation of an identity that is not merely resistant and thus negative, but that causes an allergic reaction to that parasite when it attempts to embed itself once more because of its overwhelming affirmative power.

The new identity is not a posture but a distinct and habitual modality that destabilizes the coloniality of power with every performance. Or, as Abdullah Öcalan frames it, "It is our foremost duty to bring about the birth of a new ideological identity in our minds and souls, an identity coherent and holistic, original and robust, an identity that will prevail."[22] The terms of this enactive movement will vary by location. What is needed by MENA people in the U.S. context is distinct from what MENA people need in Kurdistan, yet what is clear is that a common foundation links these struggles and simultaneously allows for divergence such that our connections remain visible but not overdetermined and thus carceral. Of course, this linkage is not unique to MENA populations, but emphasizing it as a possibility is necessary given the intensity of nationalist fracturing and the limited ways of existing that are scripted by those fractured forms. The exact terms of this identity cannot be decided beforehand, either, as they must emerge organically if they are to be properly anti-colonial. And, though an organic emergence is necessary, the heart of anti-colonial identity forms is an embrace of multiplicity that is antagonistic to domination. In other words, rather than offer a blueprint, I have discussed and will continue to discuss, for the remainder of this text, strategy, tactic, and thus the conditions of the possibility of a new modality that celebrates multiplicity, as well as non-domination.

For example, when accosted with "where are you from" or "what are you really," the attack also leaves a tactical opening—in this moment, coloniality can be reaffirmed and the pressure to do so is great, or the destabilizing work needed to enact something new can be initiated. There are a range of possible responses beyond the expected racial-national resignation, from playful to deadly serious. Depending on who the questioning actor is and how they intentionally position themselves as social-political representatives, the encounter may or may not proceed. The proper colonizers, with their unjustifiable confidence, will fight so hard to find the category, their category, wherein you can be safely objectified, and to get you to say it: I am x, just as you knew I was.

Resisting this resignation involves telling a more complicated story, trapping the colonizer in the moment through an extended counter-education. Or, depending on your mood and willingness to educate, simply have fun with the moment by playing their expectations against them—for example, I am a level 50 mage in a popular role-playing game. We are endless possibility, colonial categories are weak, and power can be inverted, even if just momentarily, under the right circumstances and with the right defiant attitude: Why do you want to know? What makes you curious? Do you ask everyone these sorts of questions?

The colonizing mind despises ambiguity; it wants to know, with certainty, which is why it pushes to objectify whenever and wherever it can. Hence, counter conduct of the above described form, micro-resistance, is necessary to destabilize, but of course it is not sufficient.

The emergence of an affirmative identity is not merely a tactical pursuit, however, and requires an openness to possibility and difference that can take a great deal of time to relearn—perhaps generations. Indeed, as I have argued in this chapter, coordinating identity and thus expectations between MENA subjects takes on an added layer of complexity due to the uptake of selective historical forms—national identity—such that certain responsive modes can immediately shut down the potential exchange or afford violence. The naturalization of hostile antagonism between the different possible MENA identities is common knowledge among MENA people more generally, such that the wrong national response to the identity inquiry can afford immediate conflict. I have witnessed these failed encounters many times. Somewhat recently, I became acquainted with an Armenian national and an Azerbaijani national, both of whom initially interpellated the other as a friend and compatriot purely because the phenotypic norms of MENA-perceived peoples are not reliable markers of difference—though, as this case exemplifies, phenotype can be a reliable marker for commonality. In this case, the figures looked like brothers. Nevertheless, as soon as the identity dance began and both parties became aware of their inherited and naturalized oppositions, the encounter did not merely collapse but led to open hostilities. People who are otherwise strangers hate each other because of national affiliation and a history of violence that is baked into those national identities. Of course, that violence is real, so the problem becomes one of mediating that tension before the encounter collapses.

The ability to transform and realize new identities that are guided by an ideal of solidarity requires encounter; but, though necessary, encounter alone is not always sufficient to afford a liberatory future. Indeed, the predatory actor who is glorified within the colonial context is skilled at taking advantage of interpersonal relations, and thus the encounter is not a singular moment—ultimately this is how we were divided against ourselves in the first place, by opportunistic colonial forces who manipulated already-existing tensions into war.

Consider, as an example, the rise of "pick-up" culture and sexual predation more generally. Here, the predatory actor intentionally encounters the other, typically female, and manipulates the situation in disingenuous ways for their own personal conquest. The sort of encounter I am advocating is an ongoing reconciliatory activity wherein persons cultivate relationships that are grounded in shared meaning and understanding that ultimately afford trust or respect—relations based in reciprocity, not the surreptitious domination seen in the pick-up. Moving from a starting point of indifference or an acquaintance-level relation to trust and respect is sometimes easier than moving from open hostility, but not always. Either way, what is required to build relationships is a contextually distinct criterion that can be thought of as a mediating condition.

Mediating conditions, like mediating actors, can be seen as neutral, which is to say their operation may obstruct collectivity or it may afford it, depending on how the mediating force is interpreted. A mediator can be an individual, an idea, a physical event, or an object—that is, many forces mediate our encounters such that they can potentially emerge in various and unpredictable ways. The distinction, however, between a mediating force that might cause conflict and the mediating force that affords relationality rests on abstraction and presence. As Ludwig Feuerbach puts it, "Something is true only when it is no longer mediated; that is when it is immediate."[23] In the case of negotiating and enacting meaning with others, the immediate or the moment that is unbounded, wherein relationality can unfold in unpredictable and often intense ways, is sometimes made possible by a mediator, but the immediate transcends abstraction and returns persons to a preobjectified mode, a mode of action and wonder that is most often witnessed in young children.

The role of mediator or mediating force in social interaction is massive and multifarious. As more parties are involved, so too will variability and unpredictability increase. Moving from a mediated divorce to larger-scale processes like truth and reconciliation commissions is no easy task. The complexity that defines interactions between two persons is difficult to understand, but a third actor can dramatically shift the gravity of the situation in positive or negative ways. And what mediating forces demand attention, or what sort of mediating forces are needed to transform conflicted situations—so that persons can engage others in an immediate sense, momentarily free from the chains of abstract objectification that keep us vigilant—will vary across space-time.

Of course, the primary mediating force for all global conflict—at this historical moment—is the role of colonizer in the history of local conflicts and thus finding a way to undo or transform the damage done by that force. Many truth and reconciliation commissions fall short because they fail to address the role of coloniality and often the formal mediator, as peace worker, is either a direct or indirect advocate for Western colonial norms (e.g., universalists of the liberal-capitalist variety).[24] In other words, the formal mediator attempts to establish immediacy such that conflicted parties might establish new relations, but the mediator's relation to colonial power ultimately prevents the full realization of something new among the conflicted—especially when the direction of the encounter inevitably veers into the realm of anti-colonial and anti-capitalist solidarity.

It is not possible to account for all mediating forces in interaction, which is why it is generally good practice to interpret others carefully, but also in charitable ways—which is not to say that suspicion should be totally abandoned; rather, each interpretive mode has its place in interaction. While some mediating forces are unpredictable and perhaps impossible to know, in the moment, other forces are clear—especially when actors intentionally take up certain positions, such as the nationalist uptake of hate toward the enemy other through which the nation is defined.

Hence, as I have argued in this chapter, a central mediating force that obstructs MENA solidarity is the nationalist modality and its naturalization of us/them relations. This mediating force once functioned to build a certain form of solidarity, the nation, but it has since become an obstruction. Historian of Arab nationalism George Antonius emphasizes this claim through a fact that is well-known among post-Ottoman peoples—though it may not always be publicly admitted—namely, that Arab nationalism, and non-Turkic post-Ottoman nationalism more generally, as a liberatory form of solidarity, emerged as a direct response to Turkish domination: "Although its immediate causes were not everywhere identical, its outward manifestations tended to one end—liberation from Turkish rule—and gave it the deceptive appearance of a concerted insurgence."[25] The oppositional tendency that drove the nationalist struggles of the nineteenth and twentieth centuries has persisted, however, and it is a clear case of a mediating force that vacillated from solidarity to exclusion.

This is not to say that the Arab identity is not still meaningful or worth holding onto, or that the history of Ottoman domination that it was formulated to resist was not real and worth memorializing—roughly four hundred years of domination is real. The claim is that the national identity tends to overdetermine sociality and prevent the realization of other liberated futures, especially once it has done the work for which it was originally formulated—liberation from Ottoman domination. It is time to move beyond the tool of nationalism, as it no longer usefully rallies us to a meaningful immediacy, which might mean changing the terms of collective identity.

The post-Ottoman national identity, in this case "Arab," does not cease to exist in this shift; instead, the identity becomes a past form, a historical movement that is meaningful for who we are but not central to present identity forms—just as other past forms are also meaningful to identity even if they are no longer centered as a primary modality. To emphasize this point, I turn in Chapter 4 to another example of post-Ottoman nationalism that has gone awry and thus formalized a division that has dire consequences for MENA peoples, as well as the possibility of thought more generally. Within this critique, however, I also expand on the previous claims about the transformative character of identity by recovering Hellenism as a past form that many MENA peoples ought to be able to claim as central to their historical being.

Chapter Four

Decolonizing the Ancients
Or, The Known West and the Anti-Colonial Principle

Thus, the tendency in anthropology, history, and cultural studies in Europe and the United States is to treat the whole of world history as viewable by a kind of Western super-subject, whose historicizing and disciplinary rigor either takes away or, in the post-colonial period, restores history to people and cultures "without" history.

—Edward Said[1]

It looks as if the term continent, *as applied to Europe despite the land continuum of Eurasia, embodies only some European fantasies, and no more: the fantasy of a Europe that wants to imagine itself different, that wants to separate itself from Asia; the fantasy, moreover, of a Europe that wants to think itself as a geographical, natural, and factual unity. But then again, where does Europe end? On the Adriatic? In Yugoslavia? Turkey? Or perhaps even Russia.*

—Roberto M. Dianotto[2]

As I suggested in Chapter 3, a fundamental aspect of the colonial obstruction that prevents solidarity among POC and MENA peoples in particular are rigid identarian frameworks that depend on an oppositional relation to an enemy other, coupled with a problem-solving mode rooted in violent domination (e.g., a carceral or philopolemical ethos). The Black-white binary cannot be overcome so long as whiteness is defined and enacted in opposition to Blackness, and vice versa, and racial violence cannot be overcome so long as POC in general are pitted against each other in similar oppositional ways.

Of course, the reality of racialized experience is not binary—despite the racist or colonial gaze that reduces all life to simple objectified forms, dots and lines on a map—and it is precisely the multidimensional quality of life, its complexity, that requires attention in our overcoming divisiveness. In other words, what might be called *intersectionality* can be understood as both a critique of legal thought—as it was originally articulated by Pauli Murray and Kimberlé Crenshaw, and recently critiqued by Tommy Curry—but also in a broader sense as a normative demand to transcend objectified colonial thinking.[3] Concerning this latter form of intersectional, complexity analysis, or more simply the ability to transcend colonial thought, this type of critique requires a radically different epistemic and habitual framework.

Various figures have emphasized this need to move away from objectified thinking and an ethos of domination—what might also be called "philopolemia," and which manifests at the domestic level in the United States as a carceral ethos. Martin Buber calls for an *I-you* relationship, Enrique Dussel demands that we hear the voice of the poor and act, Sylvia Wynter calls for a new human, and Gloria Anzaldúa pushes this all forward with great clarity as she challenges us to consider the interstitial nature of all things. Here, I hope to add to this collective critique by focusing on a division—which has been central to the emergence of Western philosophical thought as the defining characteristic of philosophy and thus the West—that permeates the colonial modality and that reproduces itself throughout contemporary thought as if it is given. This division that I will discuss, the "naturalized" split between East and West, affords, and is afforded by, the imagined MENA world and a false image of the people defined through that palimpsest. The Orientalist-racist framework depends on this divide, which obscures possibility, and is a fundamental mediating force for MENA people that demands further critique.

Specifically, the "West" has been determined through negation, such that the overemphasis on the known and barbaric other obfuscates its own ambiguity, instability, and contradictory character. Indeed, one often hears Europe or the United States spoken of with great certainty, not just as beacons of rationality, progress, and thus morality, but as fixed and eternal facts. It is assumed that the West is known, but it turns out that much is hidden by this knowing that, when revealed, illuminates the myth for the teetering fabrication that it is. Dislodging reified historical claims that are grounded in natural hierarchies and dispositions—barbarian versus civilized, East versus West—requires an alternative critical historical framework and narrative that challenges the naturalization of our domination, as well as the Western frame more generally. And, as a historical critique, the alternative I describe in this chapter and the next also exemplifies possibilities that are foreclosed or obscured by the colonial story. Specifically, the Western mythos as mediating idea obscures the very thing that made it possible: relationality, exchange, diversity, and a world that is determined by people living from the ground-up, rather than a world that is imposed through the various forms of domination required for cartographic certainty.

I illuminate this alternative historical frame and narrative in the two sections titled "Greece, the (Other) Crown Jewel of Colonialism" and "Reciprocal Hellenism in Discourse" through a more focused genealogical critique of the emergence of the Orient/Occident split as it currently functions in the colonized mind along the Greco-Turkic border, which both describes and destabilizes that divide. These sections also unfold as a critique of Said's notion of Orientalism, since one of my aims, throughout my work, is to extend Said's works. The affirmative aspect of this critique also reveals that the colonial tourniquet which reifies current cartographic myths, by instilling those myths as givens and reifying an otherwise-fluid world into a known oppositional thing, simultaneously obfuscates and rejects the indigenous reconciliatory practices that defined the broader MENA region prior to colonization (i.e., prior to MENAfication). Reclaiming these obfuscated practices is exigent, as they are needed for a future that is free from colonial domination. Hence, in the last section of the chapter, I "look back" and begin to recover what I will call the ancient or pre-colonial principle, bringing it forward to the present as an anti-colonial principle.

4.1. GREECE, THE (OTHER) CROWN JEWEL OF COLONIALISM: FETISH, EAST/WEST FORMATION, AND RELATIONAL POSSIBILITY

In his "Anti-Cartesian Meditations," Enrique Dussel explains that the age of Western European power emerged through the dual deployment of (1) three cooperating discursive tools that were reified via (2) war and other colonial tactics: "The Enlightenment" Dussel tells us, "constructed three categories that concealed European 'exteriority': Orientalism (described by Edward Said), Eurocentric Occidentalism (fabricated by Hegel among others), and the existence of a 'South of Europe.'"[4] And, although Dussel recognizes the significance of Said, as well as Martin Bernal's *Black Athena*, his emphasis on these figures is underdeveloped in ways that are consistent throughout the decolonial tradition.[5] Concerning this silence within decolonial thought, John Harfouch offers the following pointed critique:

> These patterns of silence are generated by institutional commitments structuring the rules of discourse around who power is willing to recognize as "marginal," "decolonial," or "other." The university's margins must be constituted and validated to ease consumption. Its margins, be they "critical," "decolonial," or what have you, will be constructed for the purposes of domination and control. This is the basic lesson of Orientalism, and to the extent philosophers either forgot that lesson or never knew it to start, it continues unabated.[6]

Harfouch rightly recognizes neo-Orientalist patterns that require a rigorous critique. Even if Said's *Orientalism* is well known among some critical decolonial thinkers, especially Dussel, the work of the processes of Orientalism and colonial powers more generally persists in key ways that require vigilance. Orientalism is not a thing of the past. Europe, Asia, Africa, and the Americas are discussed as real, distinct, and eternal social-spatial life-worlds, the boundaries of which also seem to demarcate reified racial conceptions, but only because of a historical process that simultaneously forced those objects into being through war while also overwriting the reality of their non-homogenous and fluid existence through nationalist narratives. At the very least, then, decolonial thought must treat Said's work with greater care and take the problem of Orientalism as ongoing.

Here, I focus on an aspect of this historical movement that is particularly problematic for various discursive and practical fields, including decolonial thought: the reification of the East/West split as it currently stands, dividing the Eurasian continent at the Greco-Turkic boundary, and the fact or knownness of this distinction such that our students remain uncertain of how many continents can presently be found on this planet.

The Greco-Turkic divide acts as the general conditions under which Euromodern chauvinists discuss civilization, rationality, Europe and European history, and the standards of exclusion or inclusion.[7] If, as Dussel argues, the early modern period can be demarcated by the colonization of the Americas and the degradation of its peoples as subhuman barbarians, while mid-modernity is attributed to the Cartesian movement of the seventeenth century, then late modernity can be demarcated by the completion of the Reconquista that I describe below through the reification of the East/West boundary.[8] As Dussel emphasizes, "Modernity originates . . . in a 'place' and in a 'time.' The geopolitical 'displacement' of this 'place' and this 'time' will mean equally a 'philosophic,' thematic, and paradigmatic displacement."[9] It is not coincidental, then, that the displacement of the reified East/West situation is one of the stages on which contemporary debates and critiques of Edward Said's *Orientalism* unfold.

For example, recent work on the role of the East/West boundary in the colonial project has focused on select passages in Said's 1994 "Afterword" response to Bernard Lewis's review of *Orientalism*, wherein Lewis compares Hellenic studies or classics to Orientalism in order to claim that both are unrelated to the colonial project.[10] In his response, Said argues that Orientalism and Hellenism are

> radically incomparable. The former is an attempt to describe a whole region of the world as an accompaniment to that region's colonial conquest, the latter is not at all about the direct colonial conquest of Greece in the nineteenth and

twentieth centuries; in addition, Orientalism expresses antipathy to Islam, Hellenism sympathy for classical Greece.[11]

Critics of Said's response who are otherwise sympathetic to his work seem to agree that he is simply wrong to claim that Hellenism and Orientalism are incomparable.[12] Yet much more than a pedantic debate rides on interpreting Said's response to Lewis. For Said's positive project, recognizing and recovering the reciprocity that defined pre-colonial central Eurasia is what guides his response to Lewis and is the ideal conceptual framework that must be exemplified in the struggle of Middle Eastern peoples to reconcile toward solidarity.

Here, I agree with critics of Said, insofar as I maintain that a certain form of Hellenism is Orientalist, and yet I am struck by Said's comments and believe they deserve further consideration. In other words, I also maintain that Said was correct, Hellenism *as such* is not an Orientalism, but because his comments were underdeveloped and potentially reactionary, Said did not explain that there are multiple Hellenisms, and certain forms are Orientalist and thus integral to the European colonial project.

In this chapter I focus on two forms of Hellenism. First, there is the Hellenism of Hegel and the Western European Orientalists, an instrumental fabrication, what Stathis Gourgouris calls a *Dream Nation*, which was ultimately brought to life through violent domination.[13] In other words, the Greek national ideal—which is the Orientalist form of Hellenism—was imported into the tumultuous Ottoman empire and eventually taken up by Ottoman Christians in the name of national liberation, but the success of this project was due to foreign interventions and, like all liberal movements, the purpose was at best nominally liberatory for most people.

Second, there is the Hellenism defended by Said that reflects a pre-colonial reciprocal modality that resists the very structures and habits of coloniality. Thus, I will unpack both forms of Hellenism, with a specific focus on reclaiming the classical modality defended by Said and the relational ethics it represents, which operated throughout the pre-colonial world that has been cut off from itself through various boundaries. Further, I set this ethos up as an ideal that persists in the present through Cyprus and Rojava, which I discuss in Chapter 6.

4.1.1. Orientalist Hellenism and Its Colonial Impact: Why Said Was (Partially) Wrong

A central part of the story I am critiquing suggests that Europe, rationality, and thus philosophy began in Greece and moved West, and all other cultures and civilizations that are outside of Europe are/were merely immature and backward states of society.[14] The popular Euro-nationalist story sets both Greece and Europe up as historical constants, and as superior to all other social worlds. This Euro-nationalist history began emerging in the fourteenth and fifteenth centuries as it was accompanied by colonial conquest, but solidified in its exclusivity in the eighteenth century.[15] For example, prior to the late eighteenth century, Peter Park argues, "historians of philosophy were in agreement that philosophy began in the Orient," but the late-modern thinkers fully reject the non-European world and claim philosophy, among other things, as European.[16] This exclusive European nationalist history displaces, overwrites, and denies alternative narratives and experiences, while at the same time appropriating and claiming exclusive ownership over a history, a place, a peoples, and resources. This appropriative practice is typical of colonialism, and I focus on Greece because of its interstitial geopolitical status, its discursive deification, or its centrality to the European colonial myth, and because Greece is not typically given appropriate critical treatment as having a colonial past.[17]

Regarding the Orientalist Hellenic past in particular, Western experts have, as Maria Koundoura rightly suggests, projected "onto the past a Greece of their imagination."[18] It is this process of producing a history external to the indigenous peoples and place that ultimately makes the myth of the Greeks an Orientalist practice. As Anna Carastathis adds, "The representational activities of displacement, appropriation, erasure, renaming and derealisation are significant, as they mark the exteriority of Hellenism to Greece, which, as Said tells us, is a crucial structural feature of Orientalism."[19]

The Orientalist production of the Greek ideal can be connected back to various movements in the pre-Enlightenment and Enlightenment periods of Western European history. For example, David Constantine's *In the Footsteps of the Gods* analyzes the shift from infatuation with the Roman to an obsession with the Hellenic world.[20] The fetishization of the ancient world was also a longing for a romanticized and seemingly better time, when the Western *reich* ruled the East. Constantine's text specifically follows the work of "travelers, scholars, and poets who, in their various ways, discovered, described, and celebrated Greece and took the land and the idea and ideal of it into their own lives."[21] In his introduction, Constantine clarifies exactly what is being discussed in his text, a moment worth quoting and analyzing at length:

> The chief components of the experience of Greece—then and still—are severance (or discrepancy) and continuity. What continues? The language, for one thing. The landscape and real places in it, for another. Homer and Ritsos share a language, they are far closer to one another in their speech, though much further apart in time, than are the author of Beowulf and his translator Heaney. And

no one steeped in the poetry, myth, and histories of Ancient Greece ever quite gets over the fact that Delphi, Olympus, Thebes, Sparta, the Eurotas, Parnassus and countless other such celebrated places are there on a modern map and can be visited. You can better understand the battles of Marathon and Thermopylae by going where they were fought. The physical structure of Greece—the sea, the archipelago, the mountains, the severe hinterland, the flowery well-watered valleys—this is all still very apparent. Early travellers and the poets dwelled on that vast survival.[22]

This first section of Constantine's introduction reveals what was at stake in the exploration of the Ottoman world. The colonial scouts were interested in finding evidence of a history they were simultaneously creating.[23] The emphasis on ruins is an obvious anchor point for any historical narrative, and it did not take long for these various "disregarded" and unkempt artifacts, fetishized rocks, to be exported back to the Western world, where they could be traded, sold, and displayed as evidence of Europe's great cultural past.[24]

Along with the idolization and hoarding of ruins, there is also an emphasis on linguistic continuity, which has been internalized by the colonized subjects on both sides of the East/West boundary. The Hellenic language is sacred to the nationalist, especially among the diaspora communities, because it is supposed to be proof of the unbroken connection between the past and the present. Of course, the language is not and cannot be the same idiom of the ancient world, both because our understanding of the ancient tongue is speculative and because languages are fluid and emergent aspects of the broader relational process that defines human life.[25] Further, modern Hellenic dialects have various commonalities with other languages, specifically Arabic and Turkish. Cappadocian Greek, for example, is an explicitly blended Hellenic-Arabic-Turkic idiom that was denied and shamed by nationalists who were trying to revive and impose the ancient form, which would supposedly be pure from external influence.[26] Along with having various dialects, most Ottoman Christians were also able to speak the languages of their neighbors. Indeed, in Cyprus, where the East/West divide was only recently imposed and which is now undergoing an important transformation, there are persons still living on both sides of the border who can speak the language of the other and remember living together before the war, not primarily as Greek and Turk, but as Cypriots who were Muslims or Christians.

Alas, as Constantine demonstrates in the next passage, the Orientalist explorers were at best instrumentally interested in the people living in the territory of their fantasies; most were not interested in the people in themselves and for themselves, at all:

> Some [explorers and poets] included the people too—still there, in that place, after so many centuries. But just as strong, or in the more elegiacally minded

even stronger, was the sense of loss, severance, discrepancy. The people were not the same, they had been under Turkish rule for three hundred years, they were Christian, not heathen, they were mixed, they were ignorant of the arts and sciences of their own illustrious ancestors. The remnants of the great cities and cult places, where they could be discovered, were in ruins—against which (this was especially the case in Athens) most modern building looked like slums and shanties. Discrepancy between what had been and what was, stared the travellers, and the poets reading them, in the face. Some then took all the consolation they could in the continuing earth and sky, the mountains, the islands and the sea. The place survived, the locus of a once and—some hoped—a future humane civilization.[27]

The erasure of, disregard for, and condescending relation to those Ottoman subjects who would become the modern Greeks, Turks, Armenians, and Assyrians—to name a few of the many people whose lives were upended by the extended reconquista—is symptomatic of, as Koundoura argues, one of the central organizing principles of Orientalist Hellenism.[28] What mattered in the formation of the myth of the Greeks was the realization of the imaginary ideal and the future humane civilization—that is, a hegemonic Europe—regardless of the cost. The mythologizing Hellenization project had nothing more than an instrumental interest in the real-life descendants of the people they were mythologizing. Rather, the "ignorant mixed people" who spoke some version of the Hellenic language were useful to securing the museum space that proved the West's exclusionist history and also its potential failure. The need to transform the backward inhabitants of the idolized territory was paramount for the Euro-nationalists, and the drive for that transformation was bloody. And, after five hundred years as second-class citizens under the Ottoman millet system, the Christians were primed for such a narrative, a story that evoked self-respect, victimization, and a justified need for liberation. Of course, countless lives have been lost, and yet the promise of liberation remains unfulfilled.

The Ottoman Christians had to be taught who they were or, more precisely, who they once were—white, European, and rational. The Germans were, and still are, particularly obsessed with reviving or producing the Greece of their fantasies.[29] It took some time for the Germans to enter the scene, however, and before their intervention, the powers now referenced as Russia, Britain, and France were the main external paternal forces engaged in arming, disuniting, robbing, and murdering the Ottoman subjects.[30] As David Fromkin describes it, Western powers were engaged in a "great game" to dissolve and gain control over the Ottoman world.[31]

4.1.2. The Bloody Transition from Theory to Practice: 1821 and 1923

The pseudo- and overtly Orientalist moves of the Renaissance, which centered on what Said calls an "imaginative geography," created the conditions for the possibility of a narrative that would spread like wildfire when coupled with the nationalist mentality.[32] And Western nationalist vanguards—spearheaded by diaspora groups like Filiki Eteria, or the society of friends—engaged the Ottoman world to spread the nationalist message and begin stirring revolutionary embers throughout the pluralist Ottoman world. At the same time, Ottoman merchants were enjoying increasing trade as the Western war machine was slowly claiming territories and transferring the East to the West. For example, the 1718 treaty of Passarowitz formally ended the "great Turkish war" and transferred power over much of what is now Serbia to the Habsburg Monarchy of Austria, affording a much wider access to the Aegean market. Among those Ottoman Christians who would become the Greeks, this nationalist narrative was packaged alongside the experience of being subjected under the Ottoman millet system—which was equivalent to a second-class status in the Ottoman world. In other words, the Big Idea (e.g., the nationalist idea) initially took real material problems and co-opted those under the banner of national consciousness and advocated violent self-defense against the Ottoman enemy.

There are two key events in the history of the Greek state that are worth emphasizing, wherein this exterior discourse was realized in practice, such that a certain past was cut off and certain possible futures were made unthinkable: the revolution of 1821, which is when the Greek nationalist forces claimed independence from Ottoman rule and the Greek state began to emerge; and the exchange of Christian and Muslim populations in 1923 that solidified the Greek and Turkish states in their homogenizing trajectories. In other words, in exploring the material circumstances from which the fetishization of an ancient and strictly European starting point emerged, I am also exploring to what end that fetishization has functioned; that is, the discourses surrounding the ancients were transformed with the emergence of the Orientalist tradition in order to justify and excuse the goals of conquest.

Through this recent European fetishization of the ancient world, the Greeks became a material possibility in 1821, and the solidification of the Greek ideal, housed in the museum-vacationland of the Greek state, really congealed in 1923. This is not to suggest that 1923 was a stabilizing moment, but it is during this time that one could really begin to speak of Greece and Turkey as distinct worlds, with independent histories and peoples, with some sort of certainty and authority—outsiders could foresee eventually visiting Greece and witnessing the reality of the place, which is really a projection of someone else's making. Of course, the certainty of Greece and Europe has repeatedly come into question since 1923, most recently with the Greeks preparing to reject Europe, leaving Europeans, specifically Germans, scrambling to make sense of their unraveling identity and economy. To be clear, I am not suggesting that the Greeks were not discussed before 1821; rather, before 1821 the Greeks were nominal and exclusive to certain discourses, while the inhabitants of the near-East understood themselves primarily through religious identities and saw the Hellenic world as part of their shared human past.

These two dates, 1821 and 1923, are crucial moments in the history of the fall of the Ottoman empire that bracket the creation of the Greco-Turkic or Orient/Occident divide that is now treated as given. The year 1821 is celebrated as the successful initiation of the Greek war of independence or condemned as a part of a broader Christian uprising, and 1923 is the year that the treaty of Lausanne was enacted. I say that 1821 represents the successful initiation of the revolution because there were previous attempts, driven by Prussia's Katherine the Great, to undermine Ottoman power by stoking and arming Ottoman Christians in the name of national liberation. The Orlov revolt, for example, was a failed attempt by the Russians to use the pre-Greek Ottoman Christians to destabilize and claim Ottoman territory, and after the revolt failed, the Christians returned to coexisting with other Ottoman subjects, with their identities anchored in Christianity not Greekness, and as if the revolt had never happened.[33]

After one hundred years of war, the signing of the Treaty of Lausanne in 1923 formally solidified the Greek and Turkish states and thus the current East/West divide by way of population exchange or the forced removal of those populations whose very existence undermined the overarching Orientalist Euro-nationalist story—that is, those remaining populations who did not buy into the Greco-Turkic/Orient-Occident split and were part of a pluralist community.[34] Crucial to both of these events and the space-time between them is the overt redaction and erasure of alternative historical records, specifically the stories of those people who were opposed to the nationalist project and Westernization. Much like the invention of the Greeks in discourse, the manifestation of that imaginary is intended to be hermetic and absolute. The initiation of the Greek revolution, which I am arguing is the moment wherein the Greeks began, marks the start of an ongoing effort to forget or deny a relational history marked by coexistence, a general peace, and blending, while the population exchanges of 1923 represent the destruction of many of the last remaining relational communities that resisted the Western-made divisions and its volatile universalism until it was no longer possible.

All of this is to say that before 1821, the people who would become Greek were not Greek any more than their neighbors who would become Turks,

Arabs, or Armenians; and, had things been otherwise in and around 1923, our understanding of the Greco-Turkic peoples, or the Ottoman peoples more broadly, might be quite different. But, in 1821, along with various other revolutionary movements throughout the Ottoman world, the Greek state declared its independence and the nationalist uprising was in full force. Here, in this declaration, the Greek people began to transform from a Western imaginary to a real material collective.

Of course, Western powers funded and backed this revolution, and when the first war of independence was complete, the Greek state had its first king: Otto Friedrich Ludwig of Bavaria. After Otto, who was of the family Wittelsbach, every king of Greece until 1973 was German (with royal ties to Denmark and the rest of the Western royal family). However, 1967–1974 marks a shift in indirect colonial rule. In 1967, the military dictator Giorgos Papadopoulos, backed by the CIA, seized power only to be ousted by his colleague, Dimitrios Ioannidis, whose failed coup attempt gave way to the emergence of nominally democratic politics. Greece then joined the EU in 1981, formally rebinding itself to Germany and maintaining a relation of indirect rule.

Prior to joining the European Union, countless Greeks were disappeared and murdered for being enemies of the state. Large chunks of history, such as the Greek civil war period (1946–1949), are underdiscussed in part because of the horrors that were committed in order to preserve and justify the Greek nation that the Western world wanted. Neni Panourgiá's critical work *Dangerous Citizens* illuminates part of this genocide that specifically targeted anyone who was suspected of having left political leanings.[35] Turkey continues to pursue such anti-leftist policies and practices, as Banu Bargu demonstrates in her crucial work *Starve and Immolate*.[36] And, of course, during the revolutionary periods prior to the civil war and the left purges, many Ottoman Christians were killed by their own, as well as their supposed enemy, for similar reasons.

To be clear, the fear of the left and its violent suppression was not driven solely by Cold War ideology. Left-leaning citizens of the newly emergent Greek state, and left-leaning Middle Eastern folks as a whole, generally oppose nationalism, tend toward building solidarity across communities, and reject rigid divisions such as national borders. Middle Eastern leftists defend a politics of reciprocity, fluidity, and appreciation. Hence, the existence of the left destabilized what had been achieved in establishing the Greek state and thus threatened Western identity.

Upon entering the EU, the contemporary Greek state finds itself in a similar Orientalist and colonial condition, which Carastathis elegantly spells out:

> If Hellenism refuses Greece its actual history, cultural heterogeneity, linguistic hybridity, and political complexity, by fetishising a retrojected, imagined past,

constituting a "colonisation of an idea," as Gourgouris would have it, the neocolonial politics of debt and austerity refuse Greece (as one among many nation-states relegated to the peripheries of the global economy) its future.[37]

The rise of Greek nationalism, despite its liberatory call, was an example of colonial tactics—namely, divide, conquer, and as Mahmood Mamdani suggests, indirect rule.[38] And, the goal of rule over Greece remains the reification, opening, and appropriation of the non-European world, through the simultaneous maintenance of the East/West divide, and the ongoing domination of Middle Eastern/Mediterranean subjects. Alongside the political and military tactics that keep central Eurasia in a perpetual state of conflict are discourses that justify that conflict. Indeed, certain discourses surrounding the Greeks, and especially mainstream philosophical history, are guilty of maintaining an Orientalist ideal that justifies death and domination in the near-East. It is under these conditions that Hellenism is Orientalist, but beneath the palimpsest that has gradually covered over the pre-revolutionary Ottoman world, there is another Hellenism that must be recovered.

4.2. RECIPROCAL HELLENISM IN DISCOURSE: BANTU-GRECO-ARABIC OR WHY SAID WAS (PARTLY) CORRECT

The relational modality that sustained ancient philosophy and the pre-colonial world more generally is held captive by the Euro-modern colonial project. In my more cynical moments, I would go so far as to say that philosophy died or became decadent in the solidification of the Greek state, but I maintain that the pre-colonial relational modality can be recovered despite being transformed by the events between then and now. This section is dedicated to continuing the recovery of that relational modality and hopefully resuscitating that which made philosophy possible before it was appropriated and dominated into its present rigid form.

Prior to 1821, the Ottoman territories of interest to the West were home to various groups that had coexisted and intermixed for countless generations. Prior to the revolutionary nineteenth century, various types of Christians, Muslims, and Jews, along with many other groups, comprised the communities of the Ottoman world. In the better days of the empire—especially prior to the Young Turks' genocidal actions—these communities were relatively peaceful, cooperative, and a stark contrast to the West's universalizing motives. The Ottoman millet system did not demand assimilation or attempt to implement a strict cosmopolitan order, although it did have serious and inexcusable problems that created the unstable conditions that afforded the uprisings that led to its downfall—especially in the later parts of its existence when genocide was committed against the Christian populations (as well as those populations that were not the right type of Muslim). Prior to the nationalist and liberal-colonial shift of the nineteenth and twentieth centuries, however, the Ottoman world maintained the pluralism that was definitive of the pre-colonial world, as did nearly every civilization prior to colonial Europe's modernity.[39] Indeed, the schism of the eleventh century was not merely a difference of opinion; rather, it was akin to an embargo and worked to seal the Eastern world from the West, separating out a communal political system from a universalist system, and ultimately setting the stage for Europe's medieval crisis and eventual Orientalist renaissance.[40]

It was from the shambles of medieval Europe that the Orientalist ideals were formed and eventually deployed through the colonial war project, elevating and enlightening Western Europe after ten centuries of darkness. In other words, the "enlightenment" and the empowering of Western territories, such that we speak of their recent history as *Modern* or their past as a nonhegemonic force as a "dark age," was not some arbitrary phenomenon wherein Westerners spontaneously learned to think and organize; rather, the Dark Ages ended because the colonization of the Americas and Africa afforded resources and thus military power, which were used to embark on yet another crusade to claim and open the East to Western power. As Said, Dussel, and many others argue, the creation and the colonization of the South of Europe and the rise of the Modern West to global power are the same movement. Europe has defined itself through colonial acquisition, and taking the Peloponnese, Aegean, Attic, Anatolian, or the broader Levant territories—much of which it has failed to fully claim—has been crucial to that process.

Just as the communities of the pre-colonial world were grounded in relational reciprocity—based on exchange, the honoring of treatises, and cooperative problem-solving—so too were discourses surrounding the ancient world relational. Various discourses about the ancient world existed long before the rise of Modern European power and its Orientalist apologetics. The ancients included and were inspired by various peoples from various regions, and subsequently inspired many other groups long before those discourses were Orientalized and deployed as tactics of war.[41] Al-Kindi, Al-Razi, Al-Farabi, and Al-Ghazali are only a few of the countless "Arabic philosophers"—or simply nonideologically Western philosophers—who engaged with and in some way claimed the ancients, making their work discursively continuous and thus part of the non-Orientalist tradition.[42] It is well known that if it were not for Arabic philosophers, many of the central texts of the ancient period would be lost. Similarly, Hellenism clearly emerged through the thinkers and indigenous populations of, for example, Kemet, Sumer, and the Indus valley.[43] Hellenism has a history in the near-East and the South, and the Western appropriation of the tradition is not simply bad history, but it also operates to close off and refuse other worlds their own past. Yet, as I suggest in the previous section, there is a specifically Orientalized form of ancient studies (i.e., philosophy) that has been selectively whitewashed and weaponized. Thus, critical scholars have a minimal obligation to resist and condemn those who harbor the Orientalist perspective of the ancient world and propagate the myth of the European Greeks, and a much larger obligation to excavate and defend the longstanding tradition of relational coexistence that afforded the Hellenism defended by Said.

In order to defend Said's impulse to distinguish Hellenism from Orientalism, and also to condemn those who defend the myth of the Greeks, I will focus on the worry that despite the nationalist uptake of a whitewashed Greek ideal, there were still Hellenic-speaking peoples in the past that we can appropriately discuss and even relate to without being Orientalist. Maintaining that the ancient Athenians, Spartans, Cretans, and so on were all a part of the same indigenous European collective that we have come to call the Greeks is ultimately a commitment to the Orientalist form of Hellenism. The Aryanized position maintains that the Greeks were somehow independent and only later corrupted by the surrounding African and Asian civilizations. Europe and the contemporary Greeks are a direct byproduct of this once-glorious and now-resurrected civilization. But following the supremacists' Aryan perspective is problematic, not merely because it is a justification for violent domination, but also because it is a baseless position with various glaring gaps that reveal its dubiousness.

First, it is clear from various historical records that the societies now haphazardly clumped together and labeled "Greek" did not understand themselves as a unified whole, even if a common language allowed for intergroup engagement. Indeed, the so-called Greeks of the ancient world spent a significant amount of their time at war with other so-called Greeks. Thucydides's *History of the Peloponnesian War* is a record of the long-standing animosity that separated some communities that are now mythologized as a whole.[44] If we are going to speak of the Spartans and the Athenians as one people, then we ought to also speak of the inhabitants of ancient Cairo and the Chaldeans as a part of the same prenationalist collective because the only thing really binding them as a singular people is that they existed in a similar region, around the same time, and successfully came into contact on more than one occasion and had fruitful encounters. Of course, the contact between these groups was crucial to their existence and form, but it is not grounds for a nation, nor is it grounds for a linear historical narrative.

Secondly, since language is an idol of nationalism, it is not clear that the mythical Greeks shared a common tongue. What is clear is that the scribes of the ancient world were able to write in a shared idiom, but this tells us little about the common languages of these historical collectives, and it does not give us the grounds to speak of a Greek nation. The more likely situation is that the ancient elites spoke multiple languages or had translators who helped maintain cross-societal contact. Even if the ancients did speak a common language, this does not mean they understood themselves as one people—the Athenians made a sharp divide between the citizenry and the slaves, which is just one example, but an important one because Athens holds a special place in the imagination of the Western chauvinist.

When we reject absurd nationalist history, however, we are confronted by a new set of problems. Namely, the backward application of Orientalist thinking on the ancient world has made it difficult to discuss the past without appealing to Orientalist language, specifically terms that separate Europe from Asia and Africa. Indeed, this problem is akin to the more general problem of trying to reclaim pre-colonial experience from our hybrid and overdetermined present. Thus, the less exclusive histories that work to resist the Euronationalist model still maintain nationalist notions, and this is a potentially unavoidable problem. Various thinkers suggest that the ancient Greeks were indebted to Asian and African cultures. The latter reading is more likely—the ancient civilizations cross-pollinated, and anything that we might take from the ancient world must have roots beyond the bounds of modern Europe. But even this reading maintains an Orientalist influence insofar as it treats recently produced groups (i.e., "Asian" and "African") and national identities (i.e., Greeks) as transhistorical forms. It is not just that the legacy was stolen, as George G. M. James argues, but that it was objectified and proprietized in a way that erased the relational and connected character that made it possible, hence making it a thing that could be stolen.[45] Prior to Western colonization, the land, the people, and the history of the ancient world were common and thus communal, not a singular thing over which one people laid claim.

A third option extends this second historical reading by demanding that we abandon the Orientalist and white supremacist distinctions between Europe, Asia, and Africa, because they did not function in the past, at least not as we are using them now, and maintaining them in our critical histories unintentionally pays tribute to white supremacist tactics. If we say that Socrates was a Greek and that Greek civilization was influenced by African and Asian cultures, then we are still maintaining the false distinction between Europe, Africa, and Asia. What we ought to say is that Socrates might have been an Athenian, and Athens existed in a pre-Orientalist space that included the spaces that we now call Cairo, Damascus, Baghdad, Tehran, Dehli, and so on, and these spaces and their peoples mingled, mixed, and shared in various ways. Even this is a stretch, for it still relies on selected histories that have been canonized over others. Socrates, or more specifically Plato, was one figure among many in the pre-Orientalist world, but various classical figures have been deified, omitted, or misread for the purposes of creating and maintaining a continuous story about Europe and its power. The problem with this third interpretive approach is that it is ignoring the need to counteract or rebalance the tilted situation that has been produced by the Orientalist colonial movement.

Regardless, on the second and third interpretive approach, Hellenism can maintain its focus on certain figures and texts, but not at the exclusion of others because both hermeneutic stances are in resistance to the Orientalist and nationalist tendency to create boundaries that make an outsider an outsider and their influence foreign. The broader and ethical form of Hellenism, which is the older and healthier tradition, is concerned with a civilization that has come and gone, not because it seeks to revive the dead, but because the people of a past time dealt with real and persistent problems and had valuable insights into how problems may or may not be solved. More importantly, other past civilizations were informed by and also informed the ancients, such that we can trace a history of problem-solving and liberatory practice across multiple times and places. Orientalist Hellenism, on the other hand, is necromancy and obfuscates the liberatory quality of historical thinking.

Whether or not Said had this broad form of Hellenism in mind in his response to Lewis requires only a bit of hermeneutic charity. Indeed, given the spirit of Said's thought, his personal identity, and various key moments in his work, it is not difficult to believe that he had a similar distinction in mind and simply did not want to participate in the fetishization of select parts of the ancient world.

Regarding key moments in his work, Said was well aware of the Aryanization of European history and how eighteenth-century actors violently fabricated a continuous narrative that begins with ancient Greece. The following passage from *Culture and Imperialism* stunningly demonstrates Said's awareness of the relational modality intrinsic to Hellenic thought:

> Consider, for a more complex example, the well-known issues of the image of classical Greek antiquity or of tradition as a determinant of national identity. Studies such as Martin Bernal's *Black Athena* and Eric Hobsbawm and Terence Ranger's *The Invention of Tradition* have accentuated the extraordinary influence today's anxieties and agendas on the pure (even purged) images we construct of a privileged, genealogically useful past, a past in which we exclude unwanted elements, vestiges, narratives. Thus, according to Bernal, whereas Greek civilization was known originally to have roots in Egyptian, Semitic, and various other southern and Eastern cultures, it was redesigned as "Aryan" during the course of the nineteenth century, its Semitic and African roots either actively purged or hidden from view. Since Greek writers themselves openly

acknowledge their culture's hybrid past, European philologists acquired the ideological habit of passing over these embarrassing passages without comment, in the interests of Attic purity.[46]

More importantly, Said was himself descended from Ottoman Christians and was therefore well aware of what was at stake in keeping some form of Hellenism safe from appropriation; namely, proper Hellenism is the glorification of a tradition of pluralism, exchange, and creativity—what might be called appreciation, as opposed to appropriation—that was rooted in all of the communities of what has become the Middle East/Mediterranean and beyond. In the worst possible situation, Said did not know the history of modern Greece and was mistaken, but even in this scenario, he was not actively participating in the Orientalist production, and given that there are many experts who shamelessly do take part in reproducing a false historical ideology that justifies violent domination, it is best, I think, to grant Said the friendly reading I am suggesting: the pre-colonial world of central Eurasia maintained an appreciative relation to Hellenism that modified and extended the tradition—just as Hellenism modified and extended, for example, Bantu thought—and that relational continuity ought to be seen as central to the indigenous practices of the region, as well as its people.

4.3. THE ANCIENT PRINCIPLE AS ANTI-COLONIAL PRINCIPLE: ISONOMIA, APPRECIATION, AND THE LOST HEART OF PHILOSOPHY

Thus far I have critiqued the East/West as it is currently reified along the Greco-Turkic boundary in order to undermine the confidence with which Europe, and thus Euro-modern thought, is discussed as a historically distinct constant—such that even the continuous Eurasian landmass is described as geologically distinct, separated by nature and not politics or war. The critique of the East/West also makes space for a reclamation of that which was lost as the divide was forced into existence, namely, a relational modality grounded in experiences wherein boundaries are permeable or nonexistent and human relationships emerge through intentional coordination and appreciation. Reclaiming what was lost should be understood not as a duplication, but as distillation of the metanormative conditions that made reciprocal relational practices possible. I encapsulate this distilled modality in terms of an ancient or anti-colonial principle—that is, the normative demand to live the ambiguity of our primordial tension without reducing that tension to atomism or holism, such that we are simultaneously rooted with our ancestors but also free to diverge and reconstitute the meaning of history.

It is from this anti-colonial principle that I will, in the subsequent chapters, defend the overarching normative call for *anti-colonial solidarity*. The distillation of the ancient modalities into an anti-colonial principle is also pragmatic, as those metanormative conditions are what is needed to build solidarity and ultimately other worlds that resist domination, which is to resist the sort of universalism that makes colonialism malignant; thus, these practices act as the open-ended framework through which something new can emerge in the present: an ethics of reconciliation and an *anti-colonial solidarity*.[47] This critical historical work also raises the question of how to bring pre-colonial or indigenous practices into the colonized present in a way that is not overly romantic and does not reproduce the violent domination said practices are being brought forward to overcome, which I clarify in the next chapter through a discussion of myth and exemplarity.

As Said notes, there are various historical interactions that are intentionally overlooked or obfuscated in the production of the West, which, when recovered, can act as evidence of the reciprocal-relationality that continues to define the MENA region.

> Thus, the tendency in anthropology, history, and cultural studies in Europe and the United States is to treat the whole of world history as viewable by a kind of Western super-subject, whose historicizing and disciplinary rigor either takes away or, in the post-colonial period, restores history to people and cultures "without" history.[48]

Rather than restore history, the point of this normative reclamation is to excavate the conditions that made certain worlds emerge, over and against others, such that a different future modality might be collectively determined from the present. Consider, for example, Kojin Karatani's groundbreaking *Isonomia and the Origins of Philosophy*, which emphasizes the reciprocal-relationality that defined the Ionian, now Anatolian, territory in the ancient world, as well as the contemporary case studies that I discuss in subsequent chapters, Cyprus and Rojava, illuminate the continuity of this obfuscated ethos.[49]

The relational modality introduced here is grounded in experiences wherein boundaries are permeable or nonexistent and human relationships emerge through intentional coordination and appreciation. I allude to Karatani's work on isonomia because he describes the Ionian worldview as being reciprocal in a similar sense. Isonomia is, according to Karatani, nonrule that cashes out in politics as absolute equality: "Without economic equality, the political equality of isonomia remains a lifeless ideal. And this equality can only be realized by the confiscation and redistribution of land."[50] And, for Karatani, isonomia is a material relation that he explains as operating in relation to four other modes of exchange: mode A, reciprocity through the gift as described by Marcel Mauss; mode B, which is grounded in "ruling and protection"; mode C, elaborated by Marx as commodity exchange; and mode D, which returns to while also transforming mode A from the failure of positions of B and C.[51] Mode of exchange D, isonomia, is distinct from A insofar as the material actors are not bound by tribal affiliation, which is to say isonomia is marked by one's ability to choose one's community.[52]

Extending Karatani's analysis, it is not simply the case that mode A dissipates in its transcendence to D; rather, reciprocal exchange can still operate at the local level through the "gift" and its appreciative reception, but the transmission of the gift is not limited by tribal laws or affiliations. The higher-order mode of exchange is a reciprocity that allows for appreciative emergence to be opened in radically unforeseen ways. In other words, isonomia is the realization of a hyperplurality of other possible modalities and thus other possible worlds. This appreciative modality is not possible when exchange is grounded in debt, obligation, and thus the servitude that affords capitalist profit. Under the capitalist mode of exchange, relations are largely limited to appropriation even when persons do their best to avoid said mode. Karatani discusses several historical groups that embody the isonomiac mode, with his emphasis on the Ionians, though he also attributes this modality to the Babylonians, which is significant for the exemplary cases I critique in the next chapter.[53]

Isonomia also has a problematic affiliation with colonization in the general sense of the term, which is to say the occupation and claiming of territory that often accompanies human migration. For freedom and space or territory go hand-in-hand, such that when a person or group desired a new community, they simply moved to another location and reestablished themselves. Sometimes this involved engaging with other, already-existing communities, and other times it did not. Speculative history suggests that the Americas were originally colonized in the general sense by persons crossing the Beringia strait. The general sense of colonization stands in contrast to the notion of European colonialism as coloniality that I have thus far been deploying, which is defined by the overt erasure of other modalities and the imposition of a system of domination that simultaneously traps and subjugates the colonized.[54] In the absence of constraint, the people of a colonized land who are not able to coexist might also find refuge elsewhere, but with the militarization of boundary—national, but also in terms of property and thus identity— that accompanies European coloniality, the peoples are treated as slaves to the colonizers. There is no exit built into the Euro-colonial system—unless one understands resignation or death as real options—which is why we must become a *We* that can build a new way.

The inability to fully escape the colonial world-system through its own machinations is further complicated by the dual pressure of not wanting to repeat the colonial project—to simply recolonize, as we see happening in Israel/Palestine, for example, is not an escape from the trappings of Euro-modernity but is a "replicant."[55] The reclamation of the isonomiac mode is therefore complicated, perhaps impossible, given the pitfalls of our colonized present. Nevertheless, the reciprocal and appreciative elements of the Ionian and Babylonian way can be drawn on in the formulation of a new ethical principle that might guide social-political praxis. For example, Karatani attributes the origin of philosophy to this isonomiac mode, but Karatani's modest position can be made explicit by arguing that the reciprocity and openness that defined the indigenous ways of the Ionian peoples represents the heart of philosophical thought that was lost in the Euro-colonial appropriative process.

The central contradiction of Euro-modern thought then is that it is grounded in rigidity and objectification—through national boundaries, what Lewis Gordon calls disciplinary decadence, and also temporally insofar as it understands itself as the "end" of history—but appeals to a system that was only able to successfully function through openness, reciprocal exchange, and constant transition.[56] As Césaire admits, "It is a good thing to place different civilizations in contact with each other; that it is an excellent thing to blend different worlds; that whatever its own particular genius may be, a civilization that withdraws into itself atrophies."[57] And, of course, Césaire rightly concludes, from this powerful description of the appreciative and reciprocal exchange of life-worlds, that the coloniality of power works against civilization, pitting people against rather than bringing together. In other words, coloniality is opposed to "civilization" and solidarity, thus raising the question: How do we realize an alternative possible future where we are a *We* that coexists in relative peace and thus in cooperatively-determined communities? The ancient world succeeded, to some extent, in realizing this sort of self-determined coexistence, but that world was not poisoned to the same extent as the present by ideological overdetermination—the world was not so completely objectified and thus known—and though the pre-colonial can be used to inspire the anti-colonial in various ways, the anti-colonial principle must also stand on its own so that it cannot be dismissed as history belonging to the other. Chapter 5 takes up this problem of inspiration through a discussion of mytho-historical appeal and exemplarity.

Chapter Five

Flip the Script

Myth and Example from the Shores of Shinar

For more than two centuries whole populations have had to assert their identity in opposition to the processes of identification or annihilation triggered by these invaders. Whereas the Western nation is first of all an "opposite," for colonized peoples identity will be primarily "opposed to"—that is, a limitation from the beginning. Decolonization will have done its real work when it goes beyond this limit.

—Édouard Glissant[1]

Decolonization, therefore, implies the urgent need to thoroughly challenge the colonial situation. Its definition can, if we want to describe it accurately, be summed up in the well-known words: "The last shall be first." Decolonization is verification of this. At a descriptive level, therefore, any decolonization is a success.

—Frantz Fanon[2]

Thus far, I have discussed contemporary conflict through a dual framework wherein bodies are strategically demarcated (Orientalist-racism) and targeted (coloniality). In Chapter 4, I developed a genealogical critique of the East/West division that reveals alternative possible relational modalities (i.e., isonomia and the general practice of appreciation) that are obscured or erased through reified naturalized narratives. The counter-historical narrative through which I am developing an anti-colonial principle raises two problems: a problem of legitimacy and one of possibility.

First, the problem of legitimacy is that hindsight makes judgment simple, but living conflict is complicated by the absence of an evaluative standard. What seems correct "now" might turn out to be quite wrong depending on how things unfold, which raises a question: What is the standard by which we can evaluate present social-political claims or actions? Second, the problem of possibility is that coloniality has reified divisiveness in the contemporary mind and thus effectively erased alternative experiential modes. The colonial mind is rigidly, as well as unreflectively, determined—"That's just the way it is" or "What is the alternative?"—and the problem of possibility challenges whether alternatives that draw on or destabilize mytho-history can be realized in the present.

The problem of possibility is connected to the problem of legitimacy, for even if a standard of judgment is established, it remains unclear how to relate to those who stand on the wrong side of history—after all, the oppressor thinks they are oppressed, thus problematizing a victim-centric notion of liberation. The ability to reconcile or make meaning with the objectified other requires that persons be willing to realize themselves differently, and the rightness of that co-determining or its failure must be judged in an effort to avoid cyclical violence.

Here, I respond to these problems by focusing on myth and exemplarity. I turn to myth because, as several theorists note, the heart of Euro-modern, enlightenment, or colonial rationality is the simultaneous nominal rejection of myth and its tacit maintenance through a fetishization of self-preservation.[3] Rather than abandon myth, I argue here that a new myth is needed to serve as an ideal that guides and transforms social-political relations in the face of apocalyptic collapse. That myth is found in the story of Babel, and it is enacted through the exemplary cases of Rojava and Cyprus. A new myth is needed because previous forms have either failed, exhausted their usefulness, or are not sufficiently anti-colonial. The myth that I am developing and appealing to here might be compared to other historical figures and movements, specifically the Arab awakening discussed by Fayez A. Sayegh, or the historical critiques of Kurdish identity found throughout the works of Abdullah Öcalan.[4] I understand this work as complimenting Sayegh and Öcalan, but with a specific eye toward the conditions of the possibility of *anti-colonial solidarity* and thus accounting for the difference of space-time, as well as historical transformations, that have made national or linguistic ideals less helpful, especially for the MENA diaspora community.[5]

In the first section, I discuss the tradition of the oppressed that drives much counter-historical work through José Medina's critique of Foucault and his call for an epistemology of resistance. Medina's work is useful, as he emphasizes a method by which historical action might be judged through the concepts of guerrilla pluralism and solidarity, but I worry Medina's concepts leave space for the reproduction of the violent domination that defines our present. In the section titled "Myth/Fiction and Exemplarity," I turn to the myth of Babel to claim that the legitimacy of alternative modes found in insurgent subjugated knowledges rests in the openness of those modes toward difference and possibility, through material relationships, and *not* their oppositional quality. Here, the problem of possibility is also partly answered insofar as exemplars are appealing to—as well as rejecting, in certain ways—mytho-history through practice. Hence, I suggest that the standard by which social-political and historical claims ought to be judged is rooted in that same openness, as social-material practice—a face-to-face labor—and critical-philosophical reflection ought to orient toward clarifying the characteristics that are central to this openness and opening.

5.1. LEGITIMATING SUBJUGATED KNOWLEDGES

The critique of the East/West conflict developed in Chapter 4 reflects a more general process, excavation, and analysis of what Michel Foucault classifies as "subjugated knowledges," or those persistent, reemergent subjectivities, experiences, and modalities that the colonial-liberal palimpsest attempts to obscure, hide, erase, and deems naïve or nonrational.[6] Yet these subjugated modes linger and call for attention from those who live them, as well as those who are willing, able, or cannot do otherwise—the palimpsest always fails to cover what came before. Given that these sorts of subjugated modes are integral to counter-historical narratives, revolutionary organizing, and other movements seeking to transform the world, their reoccurring emergence raises methodological and ethical questions.

It seems subjugated knowledges operate as a historical force that Foucault would treat in his genealogical descriptions as ever-present and potentially neutral—that is, he does not maintain an explicitly normative judgment about said discourses.[7] Subsequently, an insurrection against prevailing discourse and practice could be waged from various epistemic positions, including wildly conservative and philopolemical positions, as have been witnessed in the various national liberation struggles that failed the decolonial spirit, as well as more recent so-called alt-right or neo-fascist movements. Similarly, what was once a useful insurrectionary epistemic mode with liberatory aims can easily transform into a reified and authoritarian mode, as is witnessed in the various nationalist projects that have defined the broader MENA region, as well as the history of liberalism more generally. Thus, it seems that some insurrectionary and subjugated knowledges ought to be subjugated, but to what end and by what means?

Another way of framing this would be to think of insurgent and subjugated knowledges as being, or at least emerging from, more local and personal histories than the discourse of experts.[8] In this sense, each person has an epistemic position that is subjugated—or mediated—by overarching discourse and objectification, such that what one knows is always qualified through what one is supposed to know, the reified "given" and its rigid boundaries. For those allowed to produce and who are typically favored by broader discourse, the colonizing subject and expert, this status quo often aligns with subjective experience by creating a sense of belonging, superiority, and various benefits that are now thought of in terms of privilege.[9]

For those typically objectified by discourse, however, the given world misaligns with lived experience, which subsequently affords a feeling of fragmentation or misalignment. Gloria Anzaldúa, Édouard Glissant, Edward Said, Sylvia Wynter, and W. E. B. Du Bois—to name only a few—all describe this interstitial modality and its affordant sight-beyond-sight in distinct ways, which Walter Mignolo frames as an "other thinking" or border thinking.[10] Yet, in abstraction, even this distinction between those who stand on the side of power and the wretched of the earth is consumed by an oppositional binary vortex, such that everyone claims to be a victim of the other in a constant war of position presently miscategorized as identity politics.[11] When everyone is a victim, then the term loses its meaning or the term only makes sense through the perpetual subjugation of another. The strategic appropriation of victimization poses distinct problems for liberatory approaches that center on what Walter Benjamin calls the "tradition of the oppressed."[12]

Consider, for example, Enrique Dussel's universal ethical assertion to "free the poor," where the poor are understood as those who are dominated within and thus by an evil social-political arrangement.[13] For Dussel, this capacity to hear the other and the universal ethical assertion that follows from that relation is preceded by a material encounter, but the material reality of conflict within systems of domination—that is, under the coloniality of power—is a state of all-against-all wherein actors from both poles understand themselves as dominated; thus, the material encounter is foreclosed or mediated by objectified preconceptions. This point is crucial in our contemporary because the centering of victimization often precedes and thus forecloses material encounters, as I discuss in Chapter 2.

Further, expert discourse often fails to offer a useful measure for differentiating legitimate normative demands from instrumental demands dressed up in moral language, in part because discourse is also driven by oppositional exchange, not reciprocal relationality, and it therefore operates as a continuation of the status quo—war by another means. Liberation will remain incomplete so long as it requires and thus depends on victimization as its motivation, which is not to discount victimization as a crucial motivating force; rather, the capacity to hear the voice of the other and thus our collective liberation from perpetual war requires something more.

Beyond discourse, the lived interstitial position serves an invaluable purpose insofar as the border subject is more likely to have to reconcile or make sense of opposing and contradictory positions. The interstitial conduit sheds light on the material and interpersonal conditions through which evaluative judgments can be legitimized. The interstitial subject remains embattled, however, despite having a clearer sense of the reconciliatory process involved in meaning-making, precisely because the overarching social-political world remains at war and the oppressor is unwilling to hear the plea of the oppressed.[14] Nevertheless, as I suggest in the remainder of this section and in the next, the material experience of those "in-between" exemplary figures and movements sheds light on the ideals, as well as tactics, that motivate a shift from critical awareness and abstract judgment to ethically grounded or legitimate transformation.

José Medina's work helps situate this tension between insurrectionary or insurgent knowledge in part because he too is offering a normative ideal, solidarity, and grappling with an ethical position that might demand certain modes remain silenced. Medina argues that within Foucault's genealogical approach,

> epistemic frictions are sought for their own sake, for the forms of resistance that they constitute. This is why I will call this more radical epistemic pluralism that can be found in Foucault a guerrilla pluralism. It is not a pluralism that tries to resolve conflicts and overcome struggles, but instead tries to provoke them and to re-energize them.[15]

On this reading, Foucault's version of the genealogical narrative is tasked with excavating, resurrecting or reviving, and producing or facilitating insurrectionary knowledges, "which are critical interventions that disrupt and interrogate epistemic hegemonies and mainstream perspectives (e.g., official histories, standard interpretations, ossified exclusionary meanings, etc.)."[16] This description might lead us to imagine the Foucaultian guerrilla in a wide range of ways, including as the student in the back of the classroom who challenges everything simply for the sake of challenging, not because they have any particular goal besides challenging, but because all authority and official doctrine ought to be challenged as such. And this sort of oppositional defiance can be quite useful, especially for the liberal subject who seeks to individuate and break free from the constraint of others.

But opposition simply for the sake of opposition affords repetition, not a break with the status quo, for at the heart of the liberal-colonial ethos is a fundamental opposition to others—unencumbered individualism of the kind described by J. S. Mill—especially a community grounded in tradition, which leads to *an embattlement without ends*.[17] Medina clarifies his notion of guerrilla pluralism as

> what we need when equitable and fair melioration for all is not yet possible, that is, when in a fractured society the conditions are not given for beneficial epistemic friction that results in mutual corrections and a collective process of learning in which all social groups can participate.[18]

In this passage, Medina reveals to some extent the ideal toward which his work is moving, namely, a society wherein the conditions are given for beneficial epistemic friction that is inclusive and affordant of collective learning (i.e., meaning-making).

Here, I generally agree with Medina, but a twofold concern lingers that I think requires a more explicit normative ideal: (1) the language of friction or resistance is easily co-opted by those who operate in a position of power precisely because said modes are integral to colonial power; (2) I think the use of the term *radical* in Medina's description of Foucault's method requires unpacking, especially given Medina's defense of solidarity that is common to leftist activists and scholars. Concerning (1), I do not think that Medina is advocating for the use of the master's tools; nevertheless—and this is the point of my advocating for a different normative ideal in this chapter—by centering agonism, Medina's normative goal is obfuscated, within his own work but more importantly in the way that the tactic of epistemic resistance can be taken up by anyone who understands themselves as oppressed and for radically divergent ends (i.e., the alt-right in the United States). Agonism or epistemic friction will certainly be crucial to solidarity, but when not treated as secondary to the collective demand for togetherness then "resistance" runs the risk of becoming the end itself, an end that can be taken up by anyone who understands themselves as marginalized (i.e., again, white supremacists under liberal power).

Concerning (2), the radical nature of Foucault's genealogical method, I think it is worth reassessing the term, as it emerged within the tradition through which Foucault is writing and responding. In left political thought, radicals suggest going to the "root" of things, which for Feuerbach, Marx, Foucault's teacher Althusser, and myself is the human person or meaning-making agents and their material relational experience.[19] From this social-material root, Marx offers a normative categorical imperative: "to overthrow all those conditions in which man is an abased, enslaved, abandoned, contemptible being,"[20] which is to say there is an obligation to transform those conditions that prevent people from making meaning together for themselves. Subsequently, for Foucault's guerrilla method to be radical in the left-meaning sense of the term, then it must also have ideals or normative ends-in-view that guide its processes—such as liberation—and thus certain knowledges and practices must remain subjugated insofar as they abase human life. Medina shares some version of this ideal, insofar as he argues "that in order to develop pluralistic democratic sensibilities, we need to cultivate a resistant imagination that is polyphonic and experimentalist."[21]

This sort of liberatory end also suggests a reconciliation of meaning, not merely its contestation, at the very least such that human persons can eventually declare their freedom—or at least declare what that requires—in a way that makes sense to other human persons. Of course, such declarations remain contestable, as I emphasize throughout this chapter that freedom is a laborious process, but contestation cannot be the only goal of liberatory movements. Liberation is the goal, and resistance, contestation, or agonism are tactics, means, or tools that ought to be carefully deployed toward the liberatory ideal.

Reframing my critique, the genealogical method can be radical insofar as it upends history such that knowledge/value are established or based in a material ground, rather than produced as a dream history that is imposed on life, as is the case with the liberal-colonial imaginary and its teleological cosmopolitanism. Medina's normative call for solidarity is at least partly motivated by a similar concern with disinterested expert utterance and top-down impositions, yet his position on solidarity stands in contrast to his concept of guerrilla pluralism, which defends agonism as the operative force in counter-historical meaning-making.

Ann Ferguson extends this point, arguing that Medina's project remains distant, much like Foucault's, from those central forces that keep the majority of the world's peoples in a state of conflict and absent from the discursive table.[22] Ferguson points to this distance by referencing two gaps in Medina's work:

> Capitalism as a structural cause of oppression (and epistemic ignorance) is nowhere mentioned; indeed the term "capitalism" does not even appear in the index! Class discrimination is mentioned only in passing, since the emphasis is on discrimination based on social identity locations: examples of epistemic privilege and oppression/silencing focus heavily on racial, ethnic, gender and sexual locations and social identity experiences/phenomenologies.[23]

Ferguson's critique is useful for distinguishing between the primary contradiction that prevents a unified liberation movement—which I have argued is social division produced through tactics of racialization that obfuscate the hypercomplexity of experience and thus prevent collective action—and the material conditions, as well as tactics, that maintain and afford the primary contradiction—exploitation and capitalist domination as the coloniality of power. Ferguson's point is crucial because the structures and habits of capitalist domination also rely on agonistic competition-based exchange, and this agonism is ideologically framed as a driving force, while history shows that opposition tends to leave us opposed and vulnerable to continuous domination. Guerrilla pluralism is framed much like capitalist competition, which alone ought to worry those interested in liberation, but at the very least the agonistic exchange advocated by Medina ought to be situated as one among various other possible epistemic means; thus, the problem of legitimacy is not one of means—perhaps agonistic exchange is sometimes good—but of ends or ideals—its goodness depends on how it is oriented.

Beyond making explicit the relationship between capitalism and the sort of war-for-the-sake-of-war that constitutes capitalism, Ferguson adds that Medina also problematizes his own claim by not taking seriously the various ways that solidarity might be realized across space-time by begging "the question against other views of solidarity that see it as uniting people around a common cause, and thus in that sense requiring unification."[24] Foucault and Medina's work are invaluable, and I understand the work of this chapter as extending their insights insofar as I maintain that the meaning of ideal concepts—an *anti-colonial solidarity*—must remain open in certain ways so as not to be overdetermined in discourse or by an oppressive state-apparatus, and to be organically emergent through face-to-face encounters in a living social world. Similarly, the means of that meaning-enactive relationality must also be open in that they are not reduced to one form, such as agonism.[25] The ideal of solidarity then might have variant forms depending on the ground-level means of organizing, but certain central qualities must remain in order to be legitimate, and that includes the ability to meaningfully contest said means while not reproducing the very problem being critiqued. Put simply, communities must be able to resist fascism without sacrificing value and meaning, but that might mean that certain performative modes are impermissible because they violate the foundational ideal of *anti-colonial solidarity*.

5.2. MYTH/FICTION AND EXEMPLARITY

To clarify this distinction between the open relationality that makes philosophy possible from the closed rigidity that has held philosophy captive for too long, and thus to justify reciprocity as the open-ended normative ideal that ought to guide our thought and action, I turn to myth/fiction and contemporary exemplarity. I first analyze the magical realism of Gabriel García Márquez. I then turn to the myth of Babel, and in the next chapter I discuss the exemplary cases of Cyprus and Rojava. I must begin, however, by making a methodological point concerning myth and history. History has a mythical element insofar as our retellings are never fully accurate because the events being described are fleeting, have come and gone, and are always recounted with some subjective influence. Of course, the mythical quality of historical analysis should not be understood as an opening for denial or complete fabrication—these sorts of false histories are transparent in their ideological production; rather, the myths of history ought to be understood as containing wisdom that is greater than empirical fact, meanings that ought to inform our individual and collective actions. Indeed, the worst aspect of historical denial, especially the denial of genocide, is that those who refuse to admit that such violence occurred are also failing to learn from those failures, which leaves the possibility of their repetition as an open and likely possibility. Whether or not the exact numbers of any given tragedy are accurate is not the point; what matters is that we ought to do everything in our power to prevent the repetition of historical tragedy, like genocide. Denial then is not merely denial of fact, but is also denial of wisdom and morality.

I focus on myth or ideals because it is through our interpretive starting points that we participate in co-creating the world, and thus my concern with a free-for-all of insurrectionary epistemologies is precisely those actors—philopolemical sociopaths, Machiavellians, or narcissists—who maintain a hermeneutic frame that encourages violent domination. An insurgent subjugated epistemic position can have radically different meanings depending on how the interpreting subject relates to its meaning. For example, those who are most suspicious of others, who think that people are generally bad and self-interested, tend to find those qualities in people with some accuracy and a lot of misunderstanding. The claim is not that the suspicious and Machiavellian type produces "bad" people—though they might also be generative in this way; rather, the conservative sees only the worst in people and, though sometimes correct, more often pushes away those who might otherwise be "good," which can have a range of meanings depending on the strategic ends of the interpreting actor. A fundamental quality of the philopolemical actor, the conservative, is what Hobbes describes as diffidence and anticipation, or a state of vigilance grounded in fear, that keeps subjects always "on guard" and ready for war.[26] The warrior is quick to react defensively, and the priest is quick to forgive, which is to say we co-create the world through our beliefs and habits. As Howard Zehr notes in a Hegelian fashion: "The lens we look through determines how we frame both the problem and the 'solution.'"[27]

Our "lens" is much more than a mere seeing, however, and changing that lens involves material transformations. Mary Midgley extends this critique to argue that myth often works as a non-reflective hermeneutic that permeates every aspect of our life:

> They [myths] are the matrix of thought, the background that shapes our mental habits. They decide what we think important and what we ignore. They provide the tools with which we organise the mass of incoming data. When they are bad they can do a great deal of harm by distorting our selection and slanting our thinking.[28]

The banal way that myth shapes life is precisely why it must be noticed, Midgley argues, and, as I am suggesting here, made explicit—that is, abandoned or made ideal. The goal of this section and its subsections is therefore to make myth explicit and thus establish a normative ideal that guides social-political action.

5.2.1. Melquíades in Macondo: Or, Appreciation versus Appropriation

I turn to García Márquez because he is producing myth that captures the meta-conditions that made isonomia possible in the pre-colonial ancient world, thus revealing the portability of those conditions for realizing other possible worlds. In other words, the value of the myth of history is the metatheory that structures the story and makes it meaningful to the present. The goal is not to reproduce the Ionian or Sumerian modality, but to learn what made those modes useful and also unstable. The Ionian modality is not often discussed because it does not clearly align with a world that is organized into nation-states, and we can speculatively claim that the Ionian way was partly lost precisely because it lacked the sort of security focus that accompanies a more rigid and reified approach (e.g., domination and its most recent extension as a nation-state).

Returning to the distinction between reciprocal relationality and domination, García Márquez's famous *One Hundred Years of Solitude* helps clarify Karatani's claim concerning the origins of philosophy and my own claim as concerns the reconciliatory modality that is needed to transcend colonial imposition. The argument I have built thus far suggests reconciliation and solidarity requires that identity be analytically centered and subjectively destabilized or deobjectified. This creates a bit of a rational paradox, which is to say in the sphere of disembodied thought, it does not make sense that our reconciliation requires some baseline togetherness in order to realize higher-order togetherness or solidarity. A similar concern might be raised in my previous critique of Foucault and to some extent Medina, insofar as togetherness cannot come before resistance when the other is working to annihilate difference. Our material starting point is divided, but those divisions are objectified and not necessarily material. Hence, the claim—that solidarity begins with togetherness—is only paradoxical in abstraction, as a disembodied statement, and on the presupposition that the binaries that divide us actually make us fully distinct from others. But, in material experience, people with wildly divergent positions make meaning and form friendships all of the time, including with imagined enemies, and their path to friendship, for lack of a better word, is not always (or even often) guided by oppositional exchange.

On this previous point, consider how García Márquez articulates the difference between (a) the colonial relation that is marked by nonencounters, chicken-wire, and a predetermined knowledge of the other that prevents epistemic modes that destabilize that objectification (i.e., racism and sexism) while creating a cyclical self-fulfilling experience, from (b) reciprocal relational encounters wherein outsiders are treated with hesitance and curiosity.

García Márquez's description of the colonial relation (a) adds to what I have already emphasized by situating the experience as distinctly spatial. In *One Hundred Years of Solitude*, García Márquez describes the relation between the foreigners that accompany the emergence of the banana company and the main characters of the book, the fictional life-world of Macondo. The relation between the Western colonizers and Macondo stands in stark contrast with the reciprocal encounter that defines the ancient or what I am describing as the anti-colonial principle through the encounter with Melquíades. The colonial relation is isolated, is hermetic, avoids emerging with certain others or, in other words, is incestual; yet, the colonial relation still emerges through others, in a nonreciprocal way, by consuming, exploiting, and imposing itself on those it refuses. The colonial relation is defined by appropriation and domination. García Márquez paints a detailed picture of the asymmetry between the colonizer and the colonized:

> When the banana company arrived, however, the local functionaries were replaced by dictatorial foreigners whom Mr. Brown brought to live in the electrified chicken yard so that they could enjoy, as he explained it, the dignity that their status warranted and so that they would not suffer from the heat and the mosquitoes and the countless discomforts and privations of the town. The old policemen were replaced by hired assassins with machetes.[29]

> The gringos, who later on brought their languid wives in muslin dresses and large veiled hats, built a separate town across the railroad tracks with streets lined with palm trees, houses with screened windows, small white tables on the terraces, and fans mounted on the ceilings, and extensive blue lawns with peacocks and quails. The section was surrounded by a metal fence topped with a band of electrified chicken wire which during the cool summer mornings would be black with roasted swallows. No one knew yet what they were after, or whether they were actually nothing but philanthropists, and they had already

caused a colossal disturbance, much more than that of the old gypsies, but less transitory and understandable. Endowed with means that had been reserved for Divine Providence in former times, they changed the pattern of the rains, accelerated the cycle of harvest, and moved the river from where it had always been and put it with its white stones and icy currents on the other side of the town, behind the cemetery. It was at that time that they built a fortress of reinforced concrete over the faded tomb of José Arcadio, so that the corpses smell of powder would not contaminate the waters.[30]

Here, the relation between the colonizer and the colonized is determined from beyond the social sphere and imposed on sociality. The colonized are supposed to be excluded from meaningful engagements, both interpersonal and political, and a system is imposed on them; but, at the same time, the colonizers exclude themselves from the possibility that operates in a reciprocal encounter.[31] Césaire describes this self-harm as the boomerang effect of colonization:

> Colonization, I repeat, dehumanizes even the most civilized man; that colonial activity, colonial enterprise, colonial conquest, which is based on contempt for the native and justified by that contempt, inevitably tends to change him who undertakes it; that the colonizer, who in order to ease his conscience gets into the habit of seeing the other man as *an animal,* accustoms himself to treating him like an animal, and tends objectively to transform *himself* into an animal.[32]

Decay begins with an objectification that forecloses possibility and, for the colonial relation, that objectification and rift in possibility is institutional in the sense that it is driven by an Orientalist-racist discourse that objectifies the world from beyond itself and in the sense that it is a structured and bureaucratic organization. The distinct institutional form of the Western colonizer becomes liberalism.

The various traditions that criticize liberalism emphasize the general historical concern that most liberal states were not established through agreement, despite the robust mytho-discourse of social contract theory, and do not represent the beliefs or values of most peoples. Historically speaking, the current social-political arrangement is the product of war, domination, and the exclusion of the majority of the world's peoples from participating and informing the emergence of the social and political situation. Charles Mills frames this critique with a razor: "A clear precedent exists in the Western contract tradition for the idea of an exclusionary manipulative contract deployed by the powerful to subordinate others in society under the pretext of including them as equals."[33] And, on the historical reality of the formation of our social-political existence, Mills adds,

Only some humans had effective causal input; only some humans had their moral equality recognized. In this fashion, it completely mystifies the creation (in the ongoing rather than ab initio sense) of society, denying or obfuscating the various structures of domination that are either transformed (class, gender), or that come into existence (race), in the modern period.[34]

The assumption within the tradition (conceptually and historically) is paternalistic; that is, it is believed that a liberal institutional order is the best situation, even for persons who are excluded or in conflict, because it will elevate those persons into a higher state of being/civilization—this belief has been critiqued as the "white Man's Burden."[35]

And, to be friendly, the ideal system is supposed to be a representative bureaucratic and legal enterprise that functions to negotiate the various demands and needs of peoples such that there is a general equilibrium or balance. The system is supposed to function as peacekeeper by guaranteeing and protecting certain rights, offering support when/where communities are destabilizing, and it is supposed to exist in a reciprocal relationship with the social sphere and its various worlds such that the distinction between the social world and the system is blurred. In other words, assuming historical practice accurately reflected liberal discourse, then its political systems ought to be direct representations of the people, but the ideal of liberalism is far from the reality of historical experience.

Positioning liberal political thought alongside the social reality of colonial experience illuminates a two-prong problematic. On the one hand, liberalism is supposed to "save" the unstable and backward states of society from themselves, as well as perpetual war, elevating the globe into an enlightened kingdom of ends.[36] On the other hand, sociality has been organized from outside of itself by liberal-colonial imposition such that those who are imposed on are presented with a false hierarchical dichotomy that includes an ideal of excellence toward which all should strive, but at the same time the possibility of achieving that status is foreclosed both materially, through electrified chicken wires, and also ideologically insofar as the coloniality that allows liberal societies to function cannot be undone without simultaneously shutting down the liberal project as such.[37]

On this point, García Márquez contrasts the colonial relation with Macondo's encounter with (b) Melquíades and the "ragged gypsies" with whom he arrives. Melquíades appears at the beginning of the book on the outskirts of the village at a time when "the world was so recent that many things lacked names, and in order to indicate them it was necessary to point."[38] The encounter between the family patriarch, José Arcadio Buendia, and Melquíades begins with a demonstration of magnets that inspires Buendia—or derails, from the perspective of his wife, Úrsula—opens possibility, and sparks a lasting friendship between the traveler, the Buendia family, and the village more generally. Further, this encounter elucidates a relational modality that both defines the book and also reveals how meaning emerges through experience when *allowed* to emerge. Césaire says, "For civilizations, exchange is oxygen,"[39] and the first encounter between Melquíades and Macondo elucidates this ideal exchange as an appreciative, not an appropriative, process. Part of what makes this open appreciation possible is the fact that the world was not yet named, not yet objectified, and thus not limited in its meanings. In other words, a central characteristic of the ancient/anti-colonial principle is that the relational world be seen as open, unfixed, and full of possibility. Throughout *I and Thou*, Martin Buber captures the significance of this open emergence, of which this quote is merely one example:

> Relation is reciprocity. My You acts on me as I act on it. Our students teach us, our works form us. The "wicked" become a revelation when they are touched by the sacred basic word. How are we educated by children, by animals! Inscrutably involved, we live in the currents of universal reciprocity.[40]

The modality captured in this example is akin to Buber's *I-you* relation insofar as it is marked by openness, flexibility, and a transformative quality that opposes a world that is rigidly defined and objectified. Buber's *I-you* tends toward the mystical, which I do not reject, but I prefer to remain grounded in material relations, specifically between living beings, and so the challenge raised by the ancient principle as distinct material iteration of the *I-you* mode is: How do we open ourselves to the material world as possibility such that the fabricated distinctions between our fleshy corpses and the sustaining and enriching externality is blurred? Given that the socialized embodied experience can feel solipsistic, the ancient principle as anti-colonial principle challenges us to shift our epistemic stance to know both ourselves and others as being grounded in an emergent relationality such that, impossible Cartesian certainty aside, personhood is always distinctly social and emergent through relations with others.[41] The challenge of the ancient principle is crucial for reconciliation processes between conflicting parties because friend-enemy relations are objectified relations, or negative relations that deny possibility and openness with the world.

Put another way, part of what made the encounter between the Buendia village and Melquíades possible is that both groups were indeed unknown to each other—their relations were unmediated—and thus they were allowed to engage in a face-to-face encounter driven by curiosity, not resistance or antagonism. The seeds of suspicion had not been fertilized by outside forces describing the evil of the other. The other and the self, Melquíades and Buendia, were allowed to know each other and thus themselves on their own terms. Isonomia and the relational modes of the pre-colonial world can be understood in a similar way. If Melquíades and Buendia had not been moved in their initial encounter, they were free to move on and live their own lives.

The ability to move and determine oneself freely with others is therefore a central component of a reconciliatory modality, especially in the higher-order sense of the concept that occurs when persons are not divided by already-existing conflicts. In our present, however, coloniality prevents us from having the sorts of raw encounters that are mythologized as defining the ancient world and the imagined world, especially as adults. We are all already infected with objectified knowledge of others, and our conflicts are entrenched such that certain social relations are nearly impossible or taboo. Thus, realizing the ancient principle or an isonomiac modality is an ideal end-in-view that should guide our processes—an anti-colonial principle—but at the end of the day, we have to be honest about our own corruption insofar as we will emerge as a *We* from within the liberal-colonial palimpsest.[42]

5.2.2. Finding Meaning on the Shores of Shinar: Normative Ideals in Myth and Practice

The reconciliatory position that I am defending throughout this book relies on a counter-ideal that heals and replaces the psychic space poisoned by the Euro-modern project. The myth or ideal of *anti-colonial solidarity* that I am developing inverts the liberal myth of a social contract that supposedly rescued us from a "state of nature," to bring us forward to the end of history—an end where meaning is fixed and other possible institutional arrangements are framed as impossibly utopian (i.e., communism) or failed relics (i.e., communism). And the social contract is clearly a farce that excuses domination, yet the general ideal of unity, wholeness, solidarity, or togetherness—not sameness, but the will and ability to engage, face-to-face, in creative meaning-making processes—can be preserved and recovered through a new myth.

Though not sufficient, the ideal of wholeness or a material togetherness that allows social groups to determine the meaning of their coexistence, for themselves, is nevertheless practically necessary for excavating those values and truths that ought to be upheld—that is, if the goal is to avoid the failure of social contract theory—and thus the question of how to envision the ideal requires a creative retelling of historical experience.

Countering the reified world and realizing a position from which value can ultimately be enacted therefore involves making explicit an ideal that diverges from the expectations contained within objectifying frames, while also changing oneself to account for the fact of possibility in nonobjectified life. In this sense, exceptional or exemplary cases—whether real or myth—serve an exigent purpose, not merely as a pedantic challenge to Orientalist and colonial resignation; rather, the exemplar acts as what Enrique Dussel calls an epiphany or a shock to our hermeneutic mode that demands we interpret that which is given in a new way and thus *be* different: "Epiphany is the beginning of real liberation."[43]

Adullah Öcalan is useful for rethinking the ideal through myth and example, especially as it concerns MENA solidarity, because Öcalan calls for the formation of a new ideological framework, a new identity, that affords a transition away from liberal-colonial capitalist domination.[44] In his rigorous study of world history, Öcalan rightly notes that previous world-systems emerged as the prevailing paradigms of thought and action through the dual deployment of a motivating ideology and material action.[45] Said's critique of Orientalism rests on a similar belief: Colonization of the extended east of the Americas and the Ottoman near-East was possible because of an attitude that afforded a robust narrative and eventually a formal discourse that moved, justified, and excused colonization. The Orientalist ideology was strategic and successfully facilitated the enactment of a new paradigm, coloniality, that persists. A decolonial shift requires a similar strategic foundation, but it must also resist the hermetic and authoritarian tendency of previous ideological frames, especially those top-down imaginaries that subsequently produce divisiveness as if it were an end in itself. The ideal that captures this framework is found on the shores of Shinar, through the myth of Babel, and that ideal is today carried out in the same general region through the living examples of Rojava and Cyprus.

5.2.3. Labor Precedes Language:
An Existential Reading of the Myth of Babel

The story of Babel (Genesis 11:1–9), for an example well known to many MENA peoples, can be treated as literal or as a metaphorical narrative that tragically captures a robust notion of solidarity as well as the ideal of resignation/domination.[46] Shinar, Sinjar, Shingal, or Singara, the territory wherein Babel was allegedly built, also happens to be a real place in the interstitial territories of present-day Kurdistan. On the plains of Shinar, the many peoples of the world successfully worked together to build a tower to the heavens, the tower of Babel. The unified tower-building unsurprisingly angered Old Testament god, and thus god responded by destroying the tower, making it so that the peoples of the world could no longer understand each other, and scattering or dividing them. I turn to Babel because, as Glissant suggests, "Myth

... contains a hidden violence that catches in the links of filiation and absolutely challenges the existence of the other as an element of relation."[47] The hidden violence in Babel is found in the fall of the tower and its aftermath, the naturalization of our disunity and the division of humanity as god's will.

When read with resignation, through a philopolemical lens, Babel simultaneously excuses humanity's failure to peacefully coexist and explains our submission to a dominating power—biblical discourse precedes present practice. But within the Babel myth are also all of the conditions of the possibility of reconciliation: The people trusted and respected each other enough to work together, and in that working together, their trust-respect strengthened. They worked together in a place, Shinar, and in a material face-to-face encounter, and they worked together toward a larger end, but, as is the case with all building projects, this larger end was only able to be accomplished through the completion of smaller, local tasks that would not always be clearly related to the larger goal and that would also shift the larger goal. Before we were divided, we were a collective that worked in common.

Another layer of meaning is excavated through Ted Chiang's retelling, "The Tower of Babylon," which follows the experience of a miner, Hillalum, who climbs the tower in order to break through the vault or barrier separating heaven and earth.[48] Chiang's retelling captures the optimism with which the unified peoples embarked on the Babylon project: "It had always seemed inspiring to Hillalum, a tale of thousands of men toiling ceaselessly, but with joy, for they worked to know Yahweh better."[49] The story emphasizes the labor, planning, collaboration, and patience such a project requires, and as the previous quote foreshadows, the epistemic relation to Yahweh is realized in the labor itself. When Hillalum finally reaches the vault and makes his way through, he finds himself somehow back on earth, befuddled:

> Somehow, the vault of heaven lay beneath the earth. It was as if they lay against each other, though they were separated by many leagues. How could that be? And then it came to him: a seal cylinder. When rolled upon a tablet of soft clay, the carved cylinder left an imprint that formed a picture. Two figures might appear at opposite ends of the tablet, though they stood side by side on the surface of the cylinder.... It was now clear why Yahweh had not struck down the tower, had not punished men for wishing to reach beyond the bounds set for them: for the longest journey would merely return them to the place whence they'd come. Centuries of their labor would not reveal to them any more of Creation than they already knew.[50]

Chiang's materialist reading of Babylon echoes other interpretations of the Abrahamic traditions more generally—god is within us, heaven is on earth—as well as Ludwig Feuerbach's materialist critique, which inspired Marx and various branches of the leftist tradition connected to Marx. Similarly, the emphasis on labor as the means of knowing the divine echoes many critical perspectives beyond the left, including the protestant movement that mutated into capitalism.[51]

The story of Babel has also received, at least, various forms of metaphorical attention from philosophers of language, with an emphasis on the written and verbal utterance component of the story, but not the embodied attributes.[52] And the general presumption persists that our lack of a shared language is a root cause of our divisiveness. The figures associated with the Vienna circle were concerned with a similar question of meaning and language, though they would likely reject the biblical homage, and given the historical context of early twentieth-century Western Europe, that focus was reactive to the violent potential that accompanies a world where meaning and value are not grounded in verifiable experience and thus common.[53] The overemphasis on written and spoken language, however, has overshadowed other aspects of meaning-making that are captured more fully in Chiang's telling and in the Marxist tradition: namely, labor. At the same time, the liberal rejection of materialism and the fetishization of utterance—both reflective of the general superficial tendency in the liberal-colonial tradition—presupposes that dialogue is the only or the preferred way for people to coordinate; but it turns out that speech can be both action and inaction, as anyone who has suffered through an infelicitous administrative meeting can verify, and something more than dialogue is required for cooperative action as well as a paradigm shift.

In other words, through Babel, certain tactical ideals become clear. Language matters, but that language is not merely linguistic, written, or even spoken; rather, as Di Paolo, Cuffari, and De Jaegher argue, language must always be understood as embodied, such that our being together and working together is itself a primal mode of communication that makes spoken utterance possible.[54] Labor, in the broadest sense, is primary to dialogue.

Abrahamic followers tend to read the story as a warning against challenging the highest power, but the story can also be read as a material motivation—there was a time before we were dominated when we were able to work together, and so we ought to remember how and try again. In other words, the myth and metaphor of Babel illuminates both the problem of our division and, as a normative ideal, the tactical and strategic (short- and long-term or means and ends) conditions of the possibility of reconciliation.

Babel is a metaphor for a historical reality, our divided present, but the myth also stands on its own insofar as it can be appealed to by those who lack historical memory or whose history is so corrupt that it seems impossible to move forward while tethered to that past. Babel is an abstract representation of the post-conflict experience. The "original position" from this imaginary perspective is collapse or apocalypse, thus raising the question: What do we do when our world, what we have built together, falls apart? How do we move forward when our collective identity, the known world, is rubble and ash?

5.2.4. From the Ruins, Hope (Not to Be Confused with Optimism)

The capacity to think beyond the divided and reified present is the core trait of the hermeneutic positioning I am defending. And, for many of the world's peoples who are already experiencing apocalyptic conditions, the motivation to think otherwise is almost reflexive insofar as the alternative, to stop imagining a different and better future beyond the violent-bound present, is to submit to death. Viktor Frankl emphasized this in his own experience of the end-time.[55]

Jonathan Lear makes related claims through the example of the transformation of the Crow nation in the face of the devastation they experienced in the colonial formation of the United States. He describes this same sort of resilience and survival instinct in terms of radical hope, which is "directed toward a future goodness that transcends the current ability to understand what it is."[56] The openness toward unknown possibility and a future that can be otherwise is a part of the same reconciliatory hermeneutic stance, one that is too often forced by the worst of situations, and one that is needed for the reconciliatory work that this book defends. Some will only think backward—what was done to me must be done to them, we will have our revenge—but solidarity and liberation require that subjects look back at the irreconcilable past while thinking forward toward a future where *We* are reconciled or able to make meaning together, despite our horrible history.[57]

Whatever the conceptual label, the hermeneutic of hope described above is a bracing stance that allows one to use relational tools in new and different ways. Just as a staggered and shortened riding stance is needed to chop wood, so too is an open positionality needed to reconcile and build solidarity.[58] To be clear, the ethical claim is not simply that hope is needed; rather, I am suggesting (1) that lived experience, especially the experiences of the wretched of the earth—the majority of the world's peoples—affords a hermeneutic potential that is reconciliatory in the sense that it envisions meanings and possibilities beyond the liberal-colonial imposition. In this sense, (2) experience functions in relation to but is not beholden to discourse because it is embodied, which is in many ways the opposite of discursivity, and it is formed through collective "labor" in the broadest sense. And (3) lived experience functions according to autopoietic normative constraints and also affords normative ideals from a naturalized foundation.[59] When cultivated and strengthened, these autopoietic norms are sufficient to reject certain modes of life because of the clear violence they propagate—that is, pre-liberal social worlds had no qualms with exiling the sociopath because of the clear threat such actors pose to the life of the community.

The iterations of Babel and the ideal contained therein can therefore be related to our present. There was a time when people, and MENA people in particular, coexisted in relative peace and even worked together toward common ends; there was an apocalypse—or multiple cataclysms—that created chaos and suffering, and now the peoples of the world live in division and disrepair, struggling to survive the lingering violence of the apocalyptic event by whatever means seem necessary, which too often includes reproducing the violence that has led to this collective disrepair. The act of domination that divided and thus conquered humanity in the case of Babel is a supernatural god, but in the material present that force has been imperialism and, since the fifteenth century, colonialism. The apocalyptic event, for most of the world's populations, arrived as a conquistador or crusader, and that persistent presence continues to be afforded through lingering top-down systemic forces.

My goal is not to romanticize the nostalgic pre-colonial mythoscape. Like Walter Benjamin's Angel of History or the Sankofa Bird, I am interested in how people move forward while looking backward and create something that truly diverges from the violence of written (i.e., colonial) history.[60] I draw on the mythical pre-colonial as inspiration especially as it emerges in stories like the tower of Babel—what once was could be again; the world as it is now is not how it always was; other worlds are possible—because such reflections help to clear the way for a grounded understanding of human interaction that, I think, will also help us move forward from our present circumstances.

Jean-Jacques Rousseau's *Discourse on the Origins of Inequality* is another example of this ideal reflection, insofar as his rational history is fabricated. Yet, through the storytelling process, Rousseau successfully reveals a flipside to human nature as the quality of pity, which we might now call sympathy or empathy.[61] The fact of Rousseau's story is not what matters. The discourse evokes a new way of thinking about ourselves that diverges from popular accounts that only focus on the self-interested aspect of human behavior. The fact of the Greeks did not matter for the Greek national movement; rather, it inspired and motivated such that downtrodden people were willing to die, and kill, for liberation. A similar claim can be made about all national collectives who organized around an imagined notion of the *We* for the purposes of liberation. Unfortunately, the nation now functions more often as a prison that we carry with us.[62]

Like Rousseau's reflection, the story of Babel similarly ought to evoke in us a rebellious curiosity to search for the truth in lived experience, even if the inspiring story is fabricated. Nationalism has failed, so a new myth is needed, but the new myth must resist the top-down form that other expert discourses, including Rousseau's, have enacted. In other words, history is fluid and open to interpretation, and when read through a hopeful frame, the past reveals possibility while simultaneously denaturalizing the state of things, and though it is not sufficient, an ideal is still necessary—solidarity, community, cooperative meaning-making—and that end-in-view is found on the plains of Shinar and in its living exemplary history, which I discuss in Chapter 6.

Chapter Six

Be Ready

Lessons from Cyprus and Rojava

If they attack you, wake me; I may be of some use.

—Ghassān Kanafānī[1]

I now turn from mytho-historical critique that clarifies how practice and discourse ought to relate, to two exemplary cases of bottom-up historical-material practice that are enacting *anti-colonial solidarity*. I begin with an analysis of the peace movement in Cyprus. I then look at the revolution in Rojava. I close by returning to the questions of legitimacy and possibility, framed at the start of Chapter 5, and thus reflect on the role these exemplary cases can play in building solidarity among the MENA diaspora. To be clear, these exemplary cases are not presented here as blueprints; rather, they are presented in order to demonstrate, as well as reaffirm, that collective meaning-making and the formation of new identities (i.e., reconciliation) is possible and affords solidarity, and that activity is best achieved through bottom-up labor.

Both the Rojava region of what is now northern Syria (Kurdistan) and the Island of Cyprus are conflicted interstitial spaces whose recent violent history is rooted in colonial imposition. Post-Ottoman Cyprus was divided into north and south along a line that was arbitrarily determined by British Major-General Peter Young in 1964 and that was impermeable from 1974 until 2003. Rojava and broader Kurdistan were similarly divided with equal disregard for the complexities of human sociality by the Sykes-Picot agreement in 1916 and the undermining of the 1920 Sévres treaty. The peoples of Cyprus and Rojava also maintain a comprehensive historical memory. A cursory examination of Öcalan's writings reveals hundreds of pages dedicated to the world-historical context within which present-day Rojava is situated, beginning with ancient Sumer. Yet, in both spaces, radical modalities are also being realized through reconciliatory processes—transcending status-quo divisions and defying discursive history that suggests MENA peoples are naturally violently opposed—that are affording a radical social-political collectivity, an *anti-colonial solidarity*.

Indeed, for those who know little about the broader MENA region, it seems especially striking that populations with such extensive and situated historical memory would shift their positionality and identity such that former "enemies" have become friends. But, in some ways, it is because of this extensive historical situatedness that MENA people are seemingly primed to reconcile. After all, we have done it many times before, changing names and practices over time because of our creative relationship with others, becoming something else while remaining ourselves, relational human persons who have survived, and thus making new meanings out of former meanings. From the ruins of empires, the peoples of the broader MENA world have rebuilt and thrived throughout history. We are survivors.

6.1. ETHOS FORMATION IN CYPRUS

In the case of Cyprus, a central concern of the ongoing peace movement has been to demonstrate that the oppositional worldview of the nationalist identities is neither natural nor necessary, and that Greek Cypriots (GCs), Turkish Cypriots (TCs), Greeks, and Turks can coexist, especially because their common and not-so-distant ancestors did coexist in relative peace for most of the historical period prior to the rise of nationalism.[2] The beginning of a reimagined and transformed world is marked by the capacity for, as Howard Gardner frames it, *changing minds*, or what Adam Curle calls "conscientization."[3] Hence, the first step in transforming the conflict in Cyprus required that persons on both sides of the divide be willing to risk seeing the world from another perspective and open themselves to difference. What is also realized in this transformative process is that social problems can be resolved through peaceful means.

Those who first attempted to bridge the intractable divide were aided by third-party organizations and experienced facilitators, mediators, and educators from the United States and the European Union. John Paul Lederach stresses that reconciliation requires a space—indeed, reconciliation is itself a place in Lederach's view—and this has also been true for Cyprus.[4] The third-party conflict and dispute-resolution activists would meet with both GCs and TCs on the island in the UN buffer zone—the unclaimed border space between north and south—in the village of Pyla, which is the last bicommunal village on the island.⁵ Harry Anastasiou describes these first meetings, which took place throughout the early 1990s:

> Through appropriate methods of facilitation, the implementation of specially designed processes of controlled communication during the first phases of all of these activities enabled the organizers to manage the conflict and render inter-ethnic interactions constructive and sustainable. . . . The bi-communal groups struggled through various critical aspects of the psychological, conceptual, historical, social, and political dimensions of the problem, some of which were not only complex and exceedingly difficult to deal with, but also extremely painful to encounter. . . . As communication matured and bonds of friendship and trust gradually became established, GCs and TCs moved to the next level of joint development of conceptual structures by which a range of issues pertaining to the conflict were reframed in an expanded and more inclusive perspective.⁶

With a space established wherein the bicommunal peace groups could meet and safely communicate, the movement began to transform the situation in Cyprus. These early meetings represent the beginnings of the dissolution of the preconceived binary scripts that accompany the nationalist identity through critical education about the conflict. In other words, it is in these early meetings that GCs and TCs really began to change their minds.

Though negotiations were still quite volatile and complex throughout the 1990s and early 2000s, the dual pressure of the bicommunal peace movement and the softening of tensions between Greece and Turkey, coupled with the desire of both Turkey and Cyprus to enter into the European Union, created a unique opportunity for the Cypriots interested in dissolving the green-line. In an effort to demonstrate a spirit of cooperation and also to aid Turkey's chance of entering into the EU system, the TC leader Rauf Denktash agreed to open the green-line in the capital city of Nicosia/Lefkosia, allowing GCs and TCs to "travel," provided that Cypriots from both sides return home the same day.⁷ Once the floodgates were opened, however, the demand from citizens for more border openings and longer periods of stay rapidly increased.⁸ GCs and TCs were able to visit their former villages and important religious sites, and beyond travel, opening the border also opened new economic opportunities. Similarly, opening the border allowed these supposedly natural enemies to be in direct contact and thus afforded the possibility of an increase in peaceful communication. Though the green-line still stands and the north still declares its independence as a state that is only recognized by Turkey, the south is now part of the European Union, and through various mediated peace talks, the identities of GCs and TCs have gone through a radical destabilization and transformation since the 1990s.

The peace movement in Cyprus has been effective for various reasons. One is the multilevel approach to the conflict; that is, leading officials in Cyprus, Greece, Turkey, and other EU countries have been forced to respond to grassroots peace efforts, meaning that the relational work is not solely occurring between representative statespersons or diplomats. International relations are not the appropriate framework for understanding the work in Cyprus, because the labor is not occurring primarily between states or state actors.

At the same time that the state has been deemphasized, Anastasiou points out, the reconciliation effort has been successful because it has redirected the focus on Greco-Turkic political relations from the big issues—namely, the problem in Cyprus and thus the state—to low-level political issues that are of greater significance to the everyday experience of Cypriot people: "Low-level politics signaled the beginning of a modest peace-building process that disclosed the historical possibility of changing interstate and intersocietal relationships between two traditional enemy countries."[9] Focusing on low-level political issues—tourism, economic development, combating terrorism, organized crime, drug trafficking, immigration, environmental protections, water access, and so on—on which both sides may be easily willing to agree, is important because it builds confidence and trust and has an immediate impact on the lives of Cypriots. "Low-level politics," Anastasiou says,

> give policy leaders the otherwise barred opportunity to become directly acquainted and familiar with their counterparts from the enemy camp, to work systematically together, to deepen understanding of each other, to become jointly focused and creative, to share successes, and to learn the merits and prospects of consensus-based cooperation.[10]

Through direct encounters and a focus on low-level politics, each side becomes familiar with the "other" as a person rather than an abstract idea, thus allowing for a more empathetic understanding and a concrete experience that undermines the myth that Greeks and Turks are essentially opposed. By establishing a potentially stable foundation of real and trusting relations, future diplomatic approaches to high-level disputes become increasingly possible.

It must be emphasized, however, that the peace movement was initiated by TC and GC citizens who imagined a different world and took steps to realize this vision through interethnic dialogue and collaborative projects to bring about a peaceful society that would emerge from the ground level. The peace movement in Cyprus was a citizen-initiated grassroots movement that received support from outside organizations like the United Nations, eventually the European Union, and other NGOs.

Though many external forces supported the peace movement, it is crucial that the movement was guided by "the long-term commitment and tireless determination of the local peace builders and their leaders in pursuing a peace-enhancing vision and peace-seeking options for Cyprus against much opposition."[11] In other words, the peace movement in Cyprus afforded a new and "organic" identity that emerged in response to much opposition from the nationalists on both sides of the divide. Despite heavy resistance, various citizen peace groups were formed, and an alternative identity has begun to emerge.[12]

The new identity is, Anastasiou suggests, based on two fundamental premises: first, the new identity disassociates citizen responsibility from the nationalist narrative that entrenches the Greco-Turkic people in opposition; secondly, the vision and future of the identity was left to the shared efforts of citizens from both sides, making it effectively their own and not an abstract concept that is violently imposed.[13] In this sense, the overwriting imposed by nationalism is gradually dissolved and replaced by a shared identity that emerges from the ground.

A unique condition—what some might call an "obstacle"—that the peace movement has had to navigate, besides the buffer zone that physically separates Cypriots, is that the Turkish Republic of Northern Cyprus is not officially recognized as a state by any country other than Turkey. On the one hand, some might call this an obstacle because contemporary international relations and politics is based on an interstate model; hence, because the north of Cyprus is not officially a state, UN support cannot be given on the macro-political level, and in fact, the north in general is closed off from most political and economic relations with the exception of Turkey. On the other hand, the fact that the northern republic lacks full state power has largely made it possible for the micro-political or grassroots level of politics to have more power than it might have otherwise had if macro-political institutions were fully functioning to block the ground-level movements.

In other conflict zones, where both sides of the divide are internationally recognized states, grassroots movements are blocked by upper-level political actors, ignored, demonized, or targeted, but in Cyprus, the peace movement and the UN development program (UNDP) circumnavigated the interstate barrier by empowering TC and GC citizen movements directly, rather than trying to mediate the movement through official and oppositional institutions. This allows for a dual pressure to be placed on official institutions to shift in reconciliatory directions. Internal pressure is generated by the peace movement, which effectively justifies external pressure from international organizations. One of the most striking examples of this is the UNDP's relation with the youth movement in Cyprus.

UNDP officials cite various projects they are working on with the citizens of both sides—such as the implementation of a standard emergency phone number, establishing a committee on cyber ethics, and teacher training in regard to "global education"—as well as its specific interaction with the youth movement. The youth projects center around training young leaders and activists, as well as setting up workshops in schools that focus on ways the students can develop their own campaigns to promote peace and work toward the millennium development goals. This direct engagement with the youth is important because it gives the students a sense of power and community by focusing their efforts on shared problems or goals; thus, the UNDP effectively does away with the traditional "banking model" of education and implements a problems-based approach.[14] The empowering of young Cypriots through problem-focused education solidifies practical knowledge through experience and further strengthens bonds in the social world. This model also coincides with the aforementioned two-part alternative identity framework.

An example of a project that was supported by the UNDP, but organized and deployed by the youth of Cyprus, is the "One StreetS Festival."[15] One StreetS was a multicultural street festival that was organized in 2010 and 2011 and brought together and celebrated the diverse cultures that exist in Cyprus. Various performances occurred along the main street of Nicosia, Ledras Street. This main street traverses the buffer zone and is separated by the main checkpoint in Nicosia. The divide has caused this main street to effectively become "two," much like the Cypriots themselves, and thus the goal of this festival—which is implied in the title—was to demonstrate and remind the people of Cyprus that it is One Street, just as they are one people, in all of their differences. In other words, the festival sought to celebrate a pluralist unity that is characteristic of the Middle East but has, in recent colonial history, operated as a reason for conflict. Similarly, the One StreetS Festival worked to reappropriate symbols that had previously been used to maintain an entrenched nationalist sentiment and refashion those very symbols as markers of peace and solidarity.

Another example of present grassroots reconciliatory efforts can be seen in the work of Maria Hadjipavlou, who has been integral to the women's peace movement in Cyprus.[16] Over several years, Hadjipavlou has worked to give the plurality of women in Cyprus their own voice, specifically because women in spaces of conflict are, at least, dually dominated. On the one hand, women are subjected to the consequences of the national conflict—being torn from their homes; losing husbands, children, siblings; being surrounded by nationalist violence—but, on the other hand, women are subjected to a second level of oppressive patriarchal violence that too often comes to a head in private home spaces—a situation that is often overshadowed by the national issue. The extra complications that mark the female situation in Cyprus made Hadjipavlou's research difficult, but by working to understand the various social histories of the communities in Cyprus, she persisted and has successfully established new community networks and helped give voice to many women in Cyprus.[17]

These are just a few examples of numerous grassroots movements that have emerged and are successfully transforming the Cypriot world, and they all reflect solidarity as a nonabstract end that takes many forms through direct meaning-making processes. The pressure from the peace movement also afforded several systemic shifts in Cyprus: the obvious continuous erosion of the buffer zone; the restoration of Hala Sultan Tekke and Apostolos Andreas Monastery, as well as various other significant cultural sites such as Turkish Baths; attaining EU membership; and various other pivotal changes, all of which would not have happened if not for the peace movement.

The force of the activities in Cyprus also have had a broader impact, as has been witnessed in the continuous warming of relations between Greece and Turkey. Similarly, officials from both countries began to offer support: Greece began to support Turkey being accepted into the EU; both sides have offered aid in response to disaster and combating the war on terror and other international criminal activity; they continue to collaborate on issues of tourism; and they have, at various points, offered support for reconciliation in Cyprus. In other words, a shift in identity that started out very small has rapidly begun to alter the course of history.

The broad implications of this identity shift are crucial, not just for the relations between Greek, Turkish, GC, and TC persons. The broader Middle Eastern identity, especially those peoples living in diaspora due to the very conflicts that need to be reconciled, can be reconceived in a similar fashion. The main problem, however, is that these identities must be willingly adopted and spread—oppositional national groups cannot be forced to abandon their nationalist identities; but those groups existing in conflict zones around the world that resist the nationalist vision and seek collaborative reconciliation can be empowered, the same way GCs and TCs are being empowered by various international organizations inside and outside of Cyprus. Being steeped in the conflict makes this sort of shift difficult, which is why the example set by Cyprus is so important.

6.2. RECONCILIATORY INSTITUTIONS AND SOLIDARITY IN ROJAVA

A similar example is found in the work being done in Rojava. The revolution in Rojava occurred at an opportune moment, after years of political repression at the hands of the Ba'ath regime's Arabization tactics and the Assad family's despotism, all committed in the name of "stabilizing" and unifying the state that was, like most nation-states, always splitting at its various imposed seams; the instability of domination politics was exposed, and protests turned to uprising, and then civil war erupted in 2011. In light of the instability of civil war, and cut off in various ways from state power in Damascus, the people of the three cantons of Rojava—Afrin, Jazira, and Euphrates—were left to fend for themselves.[18]

Rojavism therefore positions itself beyond the nation-state, despite its inspiration having origins in a nationalist movement, and yet it functions within the state as an autonomist project that has eroded the national power over the region. Rojava's primary intellectual inspiration is Abdullah Öcalan and by proxy Murray Bookchin.[19] Öcalan describes the social-political framework that has been taken up in Rojava as democratic confederalism, which responds to various Western theorists and is inspired by global grassroots struggles like the Zapatista movement in Chiapas. But Öcalan's thought is also distinctly indigenous, partly because he is a Kurd from the region and with the region in mind, but also because the aim of the project is to realize practices and relational modes that were standard for the region prior to the abovementioned colonial palimpsest. His aim is to recover these pre-colonial ways, and correct them where such amendment is needed, through consensual meaning-making activities. In other words, the relationality that is emerging throughout Rojava is reconciliatory in the sense that the space has been transformed to afford meaning-making, and the meaning of the space is emerging through meaning-making labors. Alongside other overlooked social-political movements, Rojava and Rojavism represent a third way that resists superficial liberalism and its Hobbesian conservative core, and that is working to transform the social-political landscape in ways that do not reproduce Western colonial norms.

In terms of the historical quality of Rojava's indigenous peacemaking, Öcalan emphasizes throughout his work that the Kurdish question must be understood in "the wider context of the history of civilization."[20] The historical context of the Kurds and Middle Eastern peoples more generally is crucial for analytic purposes, while at the same time this historical context is the wellspring from which the norms, values, and traditions of Middle Eastern peoples emerge. As I suggest in previous chapters, Kojin Karatani's *Isonomia and the Origins of Philosophy* elucidates some of these indigenous practices through an analysis of Ionian social-political thought. The politic of Ionia was marked by isonomia, or nonrule, which can be understood in the Rojava context as a direct and open democracy—open in the sense that all people have a right to come and go in all circumstances, including familial, but they have a responsibility to participate if they stay.[21]

Öcalan engages in a similar critical historical analysis, emphasizing the transformation of Sumerian thought by Babylonian patriarchal practices, which marks a pivotal shift away from a balanced relation between subjects, to the overdetermination and thus domination of feminine positionality that persists into the present. Through this historical counter-memory, Rojavism centers isonomiac forms through anti-patriarchal norms. I will first describe the general non-domination aspect of Rojavism before unpacking its anti-patriarchal component, which are obviously linked.

Öcalan argues,

> We did not believe that any ready-made political blueprints would be able to improve the situation of the people in the Middle East in a way that was sustainable. Had it not been nationalism and nation-states that had created so many of the problems in the Middle East?[22]

Öcalan views the modern colonial state as a monopolized hegemonic power with nationalism, positivism, sexism, and religion as its ideological foundation. To this end, Öcalan argues that the nation-state does not make sense for the Kurds. Rather, he says, "the solution to the Kurdish question . . . needs to be found in an approach that weakens capitalist modernity or pushes it back."[23] He recognizes that the geopolitical and historical peculiarity of the Kurdish situation also makes the emergence of a nation-state seem impossible—after all, the Kurds call home territory claimed by four other nation-states—which makes "a democratic solution indispensable."[24] He calls this democratic confederalism, a "non-state political administration, or a democracy without a state."[25]

As an example of the reconciliatory approach I am advocating, Rojavism's resistance to "blueprint" approaches makes way for a possible political system wherein the meaning and conditions of the social-political world are determined, as that system emerges, by the people who will be influenced by its processes. The sort of direct democracy required for a community-determined social-political project like that exemplified by Rojava—and of *anti-colonial solidarity* more generally—depends on inclusion or openness and transformation through difference, which I have described as emerging through an open hermeneutic stance and reconciliatory processes.

Rojava's non-domination as a democratic norm also emphasizes voluntary participation, feminism, ecology, and the formation of communes, which requires a strong reconciliatory ethos and solidarity. Among these various foundational values as an example of Rojava's struggle to correct for the failures of history through anti-patriarchal praxis, the most recognized sentiment associated with the uptake of Öcalan's thought in Rojava is that women must be centered in all activities. Indeed, if the goal is to resist domination, then empowering the longest-standing subjugated group is a sensible first step. The normative force of the feminist project is both an affront to an ethics and politics of domination and a reclamation of a historical mode that was corrupted. The centering of women in Rojava, however, becomes possible because of an already-established communal modality wherein difference, specifically racial or ethno-national difference, has been sufficiently eroded so that the gendered critique cannot be completely resisted through cultural relativism. One way that this reliance on cultural insularity is combatted within Rojava is through the banning of all homogenous religious political parties. As Robert Evans points out in his outstanding podcast *The Women's War*, "Under the constitution, political parties may not be founded on ethnic or religious lines."[26] The constitutional arrangement is crucial for the purposes emphasized above—namely, preventing the people of Rojava from hiding behind ethno-religious traditions as a means of justifying various forms of domination, especially against women.

Öcalan's critique of patriarchy begins by tracing the indigenous norms emphasized above through the various historical collectives that have existed throughout the region, beginning with the pre-Babylonian Sumerian society. Sumer is distinct insofar as it maintained a balance between maternalistic and paternalistic power, which is witnessed in the relationship between the god Enki and the goddess Tiamat. Here, Öcalan emphasizes that the shift away from ancient Sumerian to Babylonian patriarchal norms coincided with the emergence of class-based hierarchies: "Women initially held positions in the Sumerian temples that were equal to those of male priests, but females soon assumed subordinate roles in the households, which constituted the core units of the early stratified society."[27]

Like the Babel metaphor, the conditions of the possibility of colonial domination are rooted in previous historical movements—the naturalization and subjugation of difference—but the key to decolonial liberation can also be found in these early moments. Öcalan's broader social-political project therefore centers liberation from objectified hierarchical domination with an explicit focus on correcting for historical failures. For reconciliation to work and liberation to be realized, social stratification must be undone. Öcalan says, "The reality of women determines social reality to a large extent. . . . Therefore, no movement has a chance of creating a real and lasting, free society unless women's liberation is an essential part of its practice."[28]

Rojava has become famous largely because of images of its women's defense units (the YPJ) fighting and defeating ISIS, Al-Nusrah, and the Ba'ath loyalists. Unlike the liberal project, however, Rojavism's feminist empowerment is not merely a superficial representation or a limited inclusion (e.g., exclusively for white bourgeois women who are willing to "lean in" and behave like domineering men). Within the organizational structure and at every level, Rojavism demands dual or shared leadership that requires at least one of the two leaders to be female—a woman in every meeting, every decision-making process, defending the region alongside the other people of Rojava as equal participants directly impacting the emergence of the future world in which they hope to live. In other words, what makes Rojavism distinct and reconciliatory is that it has collectively instituted organizational forms that both bring people together as active and present social-political participants and empower their voices by grounding all decision-making in the collective work of the communities that comprise Rojava.

In this sense, a key to democratic confederalism's success is the formation of a democratic society, or an ethos that is oriented toward community and the face-to-face interactions that make us persons. Unlike the social world of the liberal West, which has been degraded by ideological and practical efforts to erode or annihilate communities, reducing politics to disengaged voting and a false representation by the least terrible option, the indigenous communities of the former Ottoman world already have a strong communal orientation, and thus the real issue within Rojava has been how to redirect "culture" in liberatory ways, specifically away from nationalist thinking that defines itself through nearby enemies (while the issue for Westerners trying to learn from Rojava will be cultivating a strong communal ethos in light of anti-social norms that are habituated through Western institutions, which is an especially difficult task in the absence of historical memory).

Again, Öcalan has emphasized that this cultural shift begins with how women are treated, and since Rojava's revolution in 2012, various patriarchal practices have been banned alongside the general inclusion and empowerment described above (e.g., circumcision, child marriages, honor killings, and swap marriages, to name a few). In other words, Rojava has not merely "caught up" with Western standards of humane treatment—not that the Western standard is the standard we ought to look to, because it is not. Rather, Rojava is exceeding the West on all fronts.

Along with a more radical feminist realignment, another important shift that has strengthened Rojava's communal ethos is an unwavering acceptance of diverse identities and experiences. The openness to the other or the embrace of a reciprocal relationality is not new to the region—indeed, prior to the rise of religious nationalism and colonialism, most communities in the former Ottoman world were "mixed" in various ways—and the Kurds have not lost sight of this fact. Rojava is already a highly diverse region, and it has become one of the primary stops for refugees fleeing the Syrian civil war, adding to its diversity. Throughout his writing, Öcalan laments the reification of the Middle East through the expulsion and annihilation of difference, especially as it is perpetrated against the various indigenous non-Muslim communities.[29] Among those who do flee through Rojava, some continue on, though some stay and become active participants in the social-political structure.

The social-political structure is in flux as the people of Rojava try to figure out how to put theory into practice, running into problematic details that no theorist could account for. But the basic structure is fairly straightforward: Everything comes from the grassroots, beginning with the communes where peoples meet, face-to-face, and discuss all of the issues that are exigent to their lives. The Democratic Autonomous Administration (DAA) was established in January of 2014 in an attempt to have the UN take Rojava and the Kurds seriously. All three cantons of Rojava independently declared their democratic autonomy and cosigned a "social contract" and simultaneously enacted a transitional administration that acts instead of a state to formalize the decisions made by the People's Council of West Kurdistan (MGRK). The relationship between the MGRK and the DAA is still being worked out—moving from a merely social democratic project to a formal legal-institutional democracy that is nested within an authoritarian and floundering state that rejects its existence, with an openly hostile state (Turkey) encroaching at every moment.

The social contract that has been enacted through this formalization process details the standards of life in Rojava. In other words, a radical form of consent has been realized in Rojava that has been elevated into a social contract that informs the way that the societies involved emerge into the future through bottom-up or grassroots action. There are a lot of structural details that define the emerging political system that I am unable to clarify, for various reasons, so I want to move to discuss the conditions that made Rojava possible and reflect on the complexity of things in the region.

Rojava is positioned in a defensive state, and they are surviving while doing everything they can to remain consistent with their own values in the process. The exigent nature of Rojava's emergence is therefore remarkable and also raises the question as to whether or not Rojavism will sustain when things stabilize, or if their unity is the byproduct of what I call "the independence day fallacy": the presence of a common enemy—ISIS, Al-Nusra, and the Ba'ath regime (Arab nationalists)—makes unification necessary. It is nearly impossible to retreat into private life and consumerism when caught in the vortex of war, especially when the power is out, so what has made the residents of Rojava willing and able to engage in direct democratic processes—to seriously invest the time and energy—is an existential question. I take this to be important because in a society like the United States that is caught up in a low-intensity conflict, a conflict that is still repressed or managed by the state and not yet in a full-blown civil war, the motivation to engage and participate is largely lacking from those who are not directly impacted by state violence.

However, the beauty of Rojavism is that it does not require that we wait for others to be ready; rather, the strategy of the Kurds and the other residents of Rojava has been one of perpetual vigilance. Michael Knapp and his coauthors emphasize this in the following:

> On July 18, 2012, armed Syrian Opposition forces launched an offensive on Damascus and Aleppo. The MGRK and YPG expected that the FSA and others would enter Rojava soon, to attack the state there. The next day, the revolution started in Kobani. In just over a year, from March 2011 to July 19, 2012, Rojava had established its new direct-democratic social order. This lead time was very short, but on July 19 it was ready. *The revolution succeeded because the people in the cities and villages had organized themselves in advance.*[30]

Those who had not been organizing with the Kurdish revolution and who stuck around have been welcomed into the communal processes, but what matters is that the general ethos was already being cultivated such that when everything fell apart, the Kurds were ready.

Extending this point, Öcallan says:

> The classification of society into categories and terms following a certain pattern is produced artificially by capitalist monopolies. Such societies do not exist. Their propaganda does. However, societies are essentially political and moral. Economic, political, ideological, and military monopolies are constructions which contradict the nature of society by merely striving for the accumulation of surplus. *They do not create values. Nor can a revolution create a new society. It can only play a positive role in restoring the moral and political fabric of the society that has been eroded.* The rest is determined by the free will of moral and political society.[31]

The restoration of the moral and political fabric, as seen in these examples, begins with raw social encounter and the labor involved in getting to know others, as if for the first time. Reconciliatory tactics, coupled with the appropriate material-political climate, afford this possibility between embattled actors, and central to this process is an upheaval of discursive forces that otherwise prevent the social encounter.

At the same time, within the encounter there is a dire need to facilitate and in some ways police the interaction such that certain types of utterance are blocked or treated as illegitimate. Educators perform this mediating task all of the time in their classrooms, not to stifle persons, but to afford circumstances where all involved parties can grow and emerge together in various ways.

Further, the mediating actor's objective ought to be to maintain the emergent sociality, keep the peace, such that participants can determine the meaning of their experiences for themselves.

Beyond the above examples, there are various other MENA communities who are seeking similar reconciliations and are of equal importance.[32] Yet the problem of other nationalist forces, especially institutional forces, lingers. This problem is seen most clearly in the United States, where MENA Americans are constantly brought under the gaze of suspicion. In other words, the need for reconciliation in the Middle Eastern identity extends beyond imagined geographical boundaries. It is the recognition of a common history and a common desire for this recognition and the peace that comes with it. Greeks, Turks, Armenians, Israelis, Palestinians, Lebanese Christians and Muslims, Baha'is and Persians, and so on, all emerged from a shared history and culture. These identities depend on each other, in various ways, and have much more in common than not; thus, as I have worked to demonstrate throughout this chapter with the cases of Cyprus and Rojava, reconciliation requires a deeper shift. It requires altering the way we understand ourselves and our relation to the world.

6.3. EXEMPLARITY AND POSSIBILITY

Returning to the problems of legitimacy and possibility that I introduced in Chapter 5, the problem remains as to what power these exemplary cases can have for those beyond the shores of Shinar, especially the MENA diaspora in the United States. Beyond representing the opposite of what MENA peoples are supposed to be, the exemplary cases of Cyprus and Rojava also inspire in forceful ways. Alessandro Ferrara eloquently captures the depth of this point:

> Historical change of great magnitude is often spurred by the capacity, possessed by exemplary figures, actions, and events, to illuminate new ways of transcending the limitations of what is and expanding the reach of our normative understandings. Over and beyond providing us with a sense of our possibilities for transformation, the force of the example often provides us with anticipatory prefigurations of reconciliation—in the first place, a reconciliation of the tragic rift of necessity and freedom reverberated by a world shaped only by the force of what exists or the force of things, on one hand, and the force of ideas or of what ought to be, on the other hand.[33]

It is in this spirit of "what is as it should be"—neither status quo nor utopian dream—that Cyprus and Rojava represent a modality that is simultaneously ancient in the pre-colonial sense, but also beyond the given or status quo of

Euro-modern politics (i.e., state liberalism) and thus a new path. The problem then becomes how to follow a similar path of *anti-colonial solidarity*, as witnessed in Cyprus and Rojava, without reverting back to coloniality.

Here, it is helpful to reflect on Foucault's genealogical works in relation to his ethical writings. Specifically, Foucault discusses two normative concepts—parrhesia and the struggle to discover pleasure—that are crucial constraints on his historical method. Foucault notes that in those previous historical moments of which Western civilization is mythologized as a by-product, there was a space wherein nonexperts could speak truth to power, literally facing the political elites and speaking with them, thus performing a parrhesiatic speech act. And yet present liberal-colonial institutions lack this space or openness to others.

The lack of connection between the social world and the institutional actors who impose on that world is (part of) what makes our current systemic iteration both illegitimate and also highly unstable. Consensus is required for legitimacy—that much is clear—but consensus is not sufficient, as the qualitative world is overdetermined by colonial power. After all, as Sidanius and Pratto clarify, people make decisions and identify with groups based on perceived opportunities and likenesses, not because of shared interests, such that they will act against their own interests in the name of maintaining an in-group status.[34] Consensus, then, without critique is not necessarily legitimate. Nevertheless, by reflecting on the example of parrhesia, a possibility is revealed that was not previously clear, and that mechanism can itself be inspirational. But at the heart of Foucault's analysis of parrhesia is a more general concern with meaning-making, which is more obvious in his writings on pleasure.

Hence, Foucault's work on pleasure is also revealing, especially when coupled with the parrhesiatic writings, because he suggests that persons who seek pleasure for themselves work to find its meaning outside of what they are told is pleasurable. At one point, Foucault describes finding pleasure in being hit by a car![35] These concepts help contextualize Foucault's "insurrection of subjugated knowledges" as those experiential meanings that emerge against or in response to discursive objectification, leading to an openness to difference and possibility, and Foucault's engagement with them, as well as his general abolitionist activism, act as a normative declaration: Howard Zinn said it best: *You Can't Be Neutral on a Moving Train.*[36] In other words, Foucault maintains a certain materialist assumption in his ethical writing that presupposes that meaning emerges in experience, and thus it is through encounters and social self-cultivation—our missives are always written for and to someone—that we find our power to transform the surrounding world, even when that world makes no parrhesiatic space for transformation.

In other words, the question of possibility—specifically enacting a legitimate arrangement through direct action, labor, or experience—involves moving beyond discourse and structure, toward the making of new meanings. And, to reiterate in slightly different form, part of what makes Cyprus and Rojava so forceful is that they are "live" or emergent and thus not yet stagnant remnants to only be addressed in discourse. The meaning of these movements remains critically open, and it is precisely this openness that is needed to sustain a legitimate enactive political project that does not revert to domination.

In other words, when knowledge is viewed from a social ground, the problem is no longer one of deciding which insurgent knowledges are valuable and worth empowering; rather, the question becomes, how do we deal with the philopolemical actor in a way that does not reproduce the forms of domination that oppose the radical imperative? How do we uphold the anticolonial principle of non-domination and continue to strive toward *anti-colonial solidarity* when confronted by hostile forces? This is a far more difficult task in our present experiential landscape, wherein we are disconnected from other persons and all knowledge claims have been destabilized by massive propaganda machines—that is, not all of us are there yet, so the question remains abstract. Still, my humble suggestion is that we unplug and engage, and in those material encounters, solidarity will emerge through collective sense-making, and the future *We* can decide how best to heal the remnants of coloniality that linger in ourselves and the bodies of our potential neighbors.

Conclusion

MENA America and the Future

As I write this closing reflection, while simultaneously editing these various chapters, global politics continues to change while also remaining the same. Joe Biden won the 2020 presidential election, and his domestic policies have appeased enough liberals that the protest movements that defined the Trump presidency have been given less attention. So far, however, Biden's foreign policy is nearly identical to Trump's, especially on the issue of Israel.[1]

In September of 2020, before power transitioned back to the liberal right, Trump facilitated a historic treaty between Israel and the United Arab Emirates. This was a diplomatic treaty, a top-down cease-fire that did not really address the underlying issues that I have emphasized throughout this text. Still, I reference this moment because Trump made a point in a press conference that revealed exactly what the colonial overlords think of MENA peoples and thus how colonial domination is justified. He said, "And this is peace in the Middle East without blood all over the sand. I say it: Right now, it's been blood all over the sand for—for decades and decades and decades. That's all they do, is they fight and kill people, and nobody gets anything."[2] In other words, it is clear that, at least within elite governing circles and expert discourse, the Orientalist position remains unwavering.

I have worked to combat the Orientalist-racist narrative that is found throughout Trump's many performances, and well beyond Trump, and I have illuminated other possible social-political arrangements, a third way, that can be drawn on by MENA Americans who are interested in enacting a possible future that does not replicate the failure of colonial power and that comes from a shared historical-material ground. Still, the question of building a movement or working with already-existing movements, realizing an *anti-colonial solidarity* in the U.S. context, or wherever the MENA diaspora finds itself in proximity and resistant to the colonial leviathan, remains open-ended.

And, this has been intentional at least in part because there are many ways to be MENA and thus many ways for our solidarity to emerge. Certainly it is not just blood all over the sand for countless generations.

Still, the conditions of the possibility of the emergence of a MENA collective within the United States are unique precisely because the space of our engagement is differently overdetermined. Though some MENA Americans remember the violence that creates the diaspora in an ongoing manner, that violence is also, in some ways, distant by comparison to the immediate violent domination that demarcates the United States. Put in more concrete but also anecdotal terms, in the United States, I can enter a store that is operated or frequented by Arabs and Jews, for example, and their base-level coexistence is obvious, as well as unexceptional. Just as distance from the territorial nation can breed a rabid form of nationalism, that same distance can also be capitalized on for the purposes of reclaiming historical relationality and working toward something new.

Of course, as I argue in Chapter 3, this work cannot be done if MENA people remain isolated in hermetic and homogeneous communities. We must engage with each other, and despite the failures of institutional recognition, I nevertheless maintain that social recognition is at least one avenue for beginning this creative process. Many of our MENA siblings already do this work, as I argue in Chapter 6, but also unintentionally, out of curiosity, and in passing moments of conversation. The problematic question—*Where are you from?*—takes on a different meaning when performed by an actor who is looking for commonality, friendship, or connection.

On this point, there is immediate work to do, to save ourselves, and that involves unlearning those interventions that turn our imagined differences into the points of our opposition. The world of representation and malicious intervention—that is the negativity of colonial mediation—will try to tell you who you are, or more precisely *what* you are, as well as how the world of others is and always will be, working to limit through these false narratives.

If, somehow, we are able to see beyond rigid and overdetermined objectifications, then the world of possibility is radically opened—that is, uprooted, or re-rooted, to emerge in new ways and under new circumstances. Though I offer no blueprint, I do still dream of worlds beyond, but not detached, from this one. I imagine there are other folks like me, who dream of better worlds too, and once we can relearn how to be, together, perhaps we can share those dreams.

I do not know what crisis is next, but with every crisis, I hope that the potential such catastrophe affords will be seized in better ways, toward a cooperatively-determined future and the commons, and not simply capitalized on by corporate overlords. I worry, with each crisis, that the failure to appropriately respond brings us closer and closer to a point of no return. In this sense, cooperative-determination—or what I have idealized as *anticolonial solidarity*—is not merely one theory among others, but a necessary strategic and tactical effort, a movement for a future and against resignation to the status quo of apocalyptic time.

On this point, I return to Gloria Anzaldúa's claim from the beginning of this book:

> Devastating events can help us overcome our desconocimientos, which dehumanize other people and deny their suffering, prompting us to realize our common humanity. As we see beyond what divides us to what connects us, we're compelled to reach out beyond our walls of distrust, extend our hands to others, and share information and resources. The human species' survival depends on each one of us connecting to our vecinos (neighbors), whether they live across the street, across national borders, or across oceans. A calamity of the magnitude of 9/11 can compel us to think not in terms of "my" country or "your" nation but "our" planet.[3]

While working on ourselves, with each other, it is crucial that the tendency to create new boundaries is related to with critical care. Blind cosmopolitanism is not what I am advocating. Of course, it would be nice if humans could just suddenly forget their various rigid allegiances and a system of global solidarity spontaneously generated, but this is the gaseous work of ideal theory, to presuppose collectivity before it has actually emerged, and that tendency replicates the sort of domination that this text is hoping to transcend. So, as I hope I have made clear throughout this text, thinking in terms of our planet and enacting a broader future collectivity must include an appreciation of the complexity of boundary in order to understand what is needed for its dissolution.

Notes

PREFACE AND ACKNOWLEDGMENTS

1. Tijoux 2014. Also see Akar and Cárdenas 2017; Cárdenas, Akar, and Tijoux 2018; Drury 2017.
2. Rivera Berruz 2014.
3. Ibid.
4. Anzaldúa 2012.

INTRODUCTION

1. Harfouch 2021.
2. Ibid., 4.
3. "The Palestinian Resistance & Sheikh Jarrah" 2021.
4. Buber 1997.
5. See the classic case captured in Sandy Tolan's work (2007), also the more recent example found in Apkon, Hale, and Reconsider (2016)—many thanks to Bar Kolodny for this reference and many critical discussions around the question of MENA solidarity.
6. For a useful overview of the contested idea of "Europe," see Dainotto 2007.
7. Khatibi 2019, 3.
8. Ibid.
9. Perhaps at this point Hitler's claims about the Armenian genocide can be treated as common knowledge, for those who are invested in knowing, but anti-Armenian sentiment has a more extensive history among the Germanic people that has been thoroughly documented and critiqued by Stefan Ihrig (2016). Lesser known, however, is that some of the key figures in the early Palestinian resistance were also Orthodox Christians who would have been systematically murdered under Ottoman rule and

are now being threatened by the Israeli state (e.g., George Habash and Constantine K. Zurayk).

10. Examples of these tensions persisting are countless, but as I am writing this introduction, Armenian and Azeri Americans are facing off in the streets of Los Angeles over the ongoing Turkish and Azerbaijani offense against Armenia and Armenians, specifically in the Artzakh. See, e.g., "Armenian & Azerbaijani/Turkish Protestors" 2020.

11. Quijano 2007; Wynter 2003.

12. See, e.g., Said 1993; 1994; 2000; 2019.

13. See Koppes 1976; Lockman 2010; 2016.

14. See Mack 2017.

15. On John Brown, see DeCaro 2002. On the port workers, see The New Arab Staff 2021. On the International Peoples' Assembly, see https://ipa-aip.org/.

16. Allen 2006.

17. Ibid., 17.

18. Historical liberal-capitalism as distinct from the immaterial ideal theories of liberalism and capitalism. Liberal theory, for example, is often a panacea that responds to historical-material fact with reforms to theory but not practice. Historical liberalism, however, is an entrenched system that is held by some at the expense of most, and is largely unresponsive to its theoretical apologists beyond giving thanks for said ongoing justification.

19. I defend a variant of this argument in previous work (Fourlas 2015b).

20. See, e.g., Kant 1970.

21. Li 2020.

22. Fanon 2004, 1. I maintain the older translation, *phenomenon*, but in the version cited the term is changed to *event*.

23. Di Paolo, Cuffari, and De Jaegher 2018, esp. 139–45.

24. See, e.g., Fourlas 2014; 2015a; 2015b.

25. I say *ideally* here because we can unintentionally influence the consequence of experience, or at least our interpretation of it, and I think this is the more common way that meaning-making occurs among coordinating participants. Indeed, the coordination takes on a "givenness" or ease that makes it seem natural, beyond intentional control.

26. On social or moral accounts of trust, see, e.g., Baier 1994; Bernstein 2011; Helm 2013. On the political elements of trust, see, e.g., Rosanvallon 2008.

27. Silva 2018.

28. There are, of course, still those who defend notions of "race" without the moral and political hierarchy that accompanied its insidious original forms (see, e.g., Spencer 2016; 2018b; 2018a), and others who defend the hierarchical form of race that I refuse to validate through citation. I am mainly concerned with this latter bio-moral/political concept, but for the sake of clarity, I am not a biological realist, and I am skeptical that the moral/hierarchical components of the concept can be removed such that we are only discussing population similarities. For a thorough debunking of racial pseudo-science, see Zack 2002.

29. Alcoff 2006. Also, I borrow the language of race/racism/racialization from Omi and Winant 2015. Further, it is worth emphasizing that the notion of "visibility" is not exclusively a reference to the ocular and, at least for my purposes, is also a reference to the possibility of being objectified or captured by the colonial gaze as a distinct racial type. John Harfouch (2017) draws out the significance of this point in an essay that traces the emergence of orientalism through philology, but this type of institutional racialization was also apparent in Nazi Germany.

30. Here and throughout this book, I move between a descriptive critique of race as the primary contradiction and normative accounts of how we must transcend or overcome institutionally backed objectified forms like race, which is what I take to be the force of intersectional critique, as well as creolization.

31. Crenshaw 1991; Hill Collins 2018. Many thanks to Tess Greenwood for bringing Pauli Murray to my attention.

32. McClintock 1995, 5.

33. Curry 2021, 132.

34. Wagner, Macaya, and Hayes 2021; Hagen 2021.

35. See, e.g., Horkheimer and Adorno 1992; Midgley 2011; Sorel 2008.

36. Benjamin 2018.

37. Ibid., 2019.

CHAPTER ONE

1. The performance could have been made by any person in a similar position of power. J. L. Austin's *How to Do Things with Words* (1975) emphasizes that the success or failure of a performative utterance is determined by the conditions of their operation, and Michel Foucault, in *The Archaeology of Knowledge* (1972), adds to this critique by noting that the meaning of an author's claims is not solely determined by the individual author, but are the emergent byproduct of a discursive situation. Hence, though the predatory actor is a vile being, their villainy is only possible within a context that affords, expects, and empowers that activity, and the performative was ultimately just the reproduction of an already-existing objectification and power that subjugates racialized populations.

2. Said 1994.

3. Consider Rayna Green's (1975) analysis of the Pocahontas story as it mirrors an older tale, "Young Beichan" or "Lord Beichan and the Turkish King's Daughter," in "The Pocahontas Perplex: The Image of Indian Women in American Culture." Many thanks to my colleague Susan Tracy for bringing this article to my attention. "Young Beichan" describes an almost-identical experience as that commonly said to have defined the relationship between John Smith and Pocahontas: a white Anglo-Saxon man ventures into the dark unknown to meet a beautiful, melanin-rich, and non-Catholic princess, and the pair fall in love such that the man is driven to save the princess from her backward existence by converting her and marrying her. The key differences, however, are that "Young Beichan" takes place in the Ottoman world,

before John Smith colonized the Americas, and the princess is indigenous to the lands now generally reduced to the Middle East, while in the Pocahontas story, the extended East affords the American princess Pocahontas. Another key difference between the stories is that one is known to have happened—Pocahontas and John Smith were real figures, and their story is somewhat grounded in real events—while "Young Beichan" was written prior to Smith's conquests and is not clearly grounded in historical fact. Nonetheless, Green reflects on the relation between the stories:

> The frame story was printed before 1300 and was, no doubt, well distributed in oral tradition before then. Whether or not our rakish adventurer-hero, John Smith, had heard the stories or ballad, we cannot say, but we must admire how life mirrors art since his story follows the outlines of the traditional tale most admirably. What we do know is that the elements of the tale appealed to Europeans long before Americans had the opportunity to attach their affection for it onto Pocahontas. (699–700)

Beyond exemplifying how the colonial imaginary extends the objectification of the East into the objectification of the Americas and thus creates a transatlantic phenomenal bridge, the "Pocahontas Perplex" reveals the powerful connection between the Orientalist attitude and the teleological quality of colonial practice.

4. There are endless examples of Middle Eastern people being racialized and targets of violent domination, only some of which make headlines: the Christchurch massacre, the Quebec City mosque shooting, the Wisconsin Sikh temple shooting, countless orthodox churches and synagogues vandalized, but also the more complex cases, like that of Cameron Mohammed, a young man from Florida with Trinidadian roots who, before being shot, was asked, "Are you Middle Eastern?" Erik Love in *Islamophobia and Racism in America* (2017) notes in reference to this latter example that "the shooter . . . saw Cameron Mohammed's physical features and then placed a racial identity upon him" (2). These macro-level cases are only the tip of the experiential iceberg, as many who are seen as Middle Eastern are constantly mistreated in local and less obvious ways. Childhood denied, always assumed guilty, and blamed when things "blow up," the Middle Eastern object is a target of violence in every sphere.

For other critical analysis of the racialization of Middle Eastern Americans, see, e.g., Amaney A. Jamal and Nadine Christine Naber, *Race and Arab Americans before and after 9/11: From Invisible Citizens to Visible Subjects* (2008); Sarah Gualtieri, *Between Arab and White* (2009); George N. Fourlas, "Being a Target: On the Racialization of Middle Eastern Americans" (2015b); Neda Maghbouleh, *The Limits of Whiteness: Iranian Americans and the Everyday Politics of Race* (2017); Helen Samhan, "Not Quite White: Race Classification and the Arab-American Experience" (1999); and John Tehranian, *Whitewashed: America's Invisible Middle Eastern Minority* (2009).

5. Naber 2014, 1107.

6. Omi and Winant 2015.

7. Alcoff 2006. My understanding here also aligns with Aníbal Quijano's critique of coloniality; see, e.g., Quijano 2007.

8. Mamdani 2012.

9. I use the problematic term *Middle Eastern* or *MENA* in two ways: (1) affirmatively, as a general reference to those populations who, through what Jorge J. E. Gracia (2000) frames as familial-historical commonality, associate or are associated with the interstitial and continuously contested territories of Afro-Eurasia, though my more specific focus centers on the former Ottoman territories that were forcefully divided by colonial tactics; and (2) in a negative sense to describe the racial experience that anyone who seems to be Middle Eastern might experience. I am largely defending my second usage in racial terms and in response to critics like Ron Sundstrom (2013), David Kim and Ron Sundstrom (2014), José Jorge Mendoza (2017), and Eduardo Bonilla-Silva (2018), each of whom offers a different interpretation of how MENA folks ought to be understood in the present.

10. My normative position on historical conflict and its possible transformation through reconciliatory processes coincides with Charles Mills's (1997; Pateman and Mills 2007) descriptive or nonideal analysis, which he frames as a racial and domination contract. Mills rightly argues that "a clear precedent exists in the Western contract tradition for the idea of an exclusionary manipulative contract deployed by the powerful to subordinate others in society under the pretext of including them as equals" (Pateman and Mills 2007, 82).

11. Mills 2003a. Also, I am indebted to Lewis Gordon's (2013) critique of modernity in my use of the term *Euro-modernity*.

12. The day after Barack Obama was elected president, the front page of the *New York Times* declared "Racial Barrier Falls in Decisive Victory" (2008). For more on the civil rights era as post-racial monument, see Frankowski 2015.

13. For a detailed critique of scientific racism, see, e.g., Zack 2002; Appiah 1985; 1996.

14. "Blue Racism" 2017.

15. Ibid.

16. In Alfred Frankowski's comments on a draft of this manuscript, he makes a crucial point in relation to post-racial thought and action, as well as the "Blue Lives Matter" effort, that is best kept in its original form. He says,

> Post-raciality functions discursively, even if it does not link to a social reality of any sort. Because of this I think it important to think of things that follow as more than language, but as strategies. Notice, individually, these are ineffective. Blue Lives never gained as much steam as Black Lives Matter (or even Say Her Name or I Can't Breathe.) However, as one leg of a larger strategy it does not need to undermine BLM completely, it just needs to hang on and give folks an excuse not to confront the reality of the racial violence of their institution or social position in any real sense.

17. *Saturday Night Live*, Season 42, Episode 6, November 12, 2016.

18. Fields and Fields 2014.

19. Ibid., 18–19.

20. See Dussel 1995; Erickson 2016; Mariscal 1998; Bernasconi and Lott 2000; Hannaford 1996; Frederickson 2002.

21. Dussel 2013, 34.

22. Ibid., 48.

23. Even if las Casas did not believe in the language of barbarism used in his appeal, his use reveals the norms and popular sentiment of the time and people with whom he was engaging. In other words, that las Casas thought making distinctions among barbarians would be a useful argumentative position is revealing. Also, for a more detailed analysis of the role that the Ottoman world played in the formation of the Americas, see Mikhail 2020.

24. Sheth 2009.

25. Key selections in the emergence of racial discourse are collected in Eze 1997.

26. See, e.g., Sundstrom 2008; Omi and Winant 2015; Bonilla-Silva 2018.

27. In Northern Ireland, I would argue that the Irish Catholics remain racialized, even though the conflict is described through religious terminology, because Catholic subjectivity is objectified in a sanguineous way, such that one can be an "atheist" and still be Catholic if one's ancestors were Catholic.

28. Haney López 2006.

29. "In re Najour, 174 F. 735 (1909)."

30. Gualtieri 2009, 53.

31. Ibid.

32. Haney López 2006, 48–49.

33. Ibid.

34. Gualtieri 2009, 60.

35. *Takao Ozawa v. United States,* 260 U.S. 178 (1922).

36. *United States v. Bhagat Singh Thind,* 202 (1923).

37. As Haney López (2006) notes, the judge went on to say, "It may be true that the blond Scandinavian and the brown Hindu have a common ancestor in the dim reaches of antiquity, but the average man knows perfectly well that there are unmistakable and profound differences between them today" (x). See also *U.S. v. Baghat Thind* (1923), 63.

38. And after WWII, scientific racism lost favor, partly because the United States wanted to superficially distance itself from the German Nazis.

39. Gualtieri 2009, 74.

40. The experts, as experts, constantly revise their beliefs, and the public gets stuck in past expert belief (e.g., that the earth is flat).

41. See, e.g., Taylor 2016; Davis 2003; Murakawa 2014; Alexander 2010.

42. Bonilla-Silva 2018.

43. Sundstrom 2013; Kim and Sundstrom 2014.

44. For more on the way that nonbinary people of color are perceived, especially MENA people, in a context that is overdetermined by a Black-white modality, see, e.g., Chaney, Sanchez, and Saud 2020.

45. Kim and Sundstrom 2014, 166.

46. And part of the persistence of racialization across generations is likely connected to the metaphysical commitments of Western racism, which maintains that racialized actors are barbarians, nonagents/incomplete agents, or—as John Harfouch (2018) puts it—"non-beings."

47. For a detailed analysis of Islamophobia, see, e.g., Beydoun 2018.

48. Mamdani 2004.
49. Al-Saji 2010.
50. For more on the various ways Middle Eastern people "cover," or relate to the ambiguity and complexity of racialization in the present, see, e.g., Beydoun 2017; Alsultany and Shohat 2012.
51. Recent shifts in macro-institutional policy have broadened the formal usage of the terrorism charge to include white supremacists in the United States, but I stand by the racialized understanding of the term because of how it is deployed in mainstream discourse and what the term evokes when it is deployed—that is, the terrorist remains a racialized image in broader discourse, even if white actors might eventually be formally classified as terrorists for committing atrocious violence. More importantly, the presumed innocence that accompanies whiteness is not shared by MENA people such that the terrorist charge is determined before birth. For an outstanding analysis of the deployment of terrorism and its relation to Euro-modern power, see Erlenbusch-Anderson 2018.
52. "Enrique Marquez Jr. Agrees" 2017.
53. A similar argument can be made regarding the language of anti-Semitism. Anti-Semitism often accompanies racism against Middle Eastern people, especially when the hateful gaze is directed against those who are presumed to be Middle Eastern and non-Muslim; but anti-Semitism is also alive within Middle Eastern communities such that one can be racialized as Middle Eastern and be anti-Semitic. Again, we ought to be able to address both in their distinct functioning.
54. Also, my claim is not that all nonbinary racialized bodies are always judged in relation to the Middle Eastern racial stereotype. I think the nonbinary racialized comparison group shifts depending on what Western war tactics need to be justified at the time. The racialized Latinidad figure can also be centered, as it was throughout the cold war in order to justify war against communists in the broader Middle East and East Asia.
55. See, e.g., the example in this chapter of Cameron Mohammed's experience.
56. Buber 1970.
57. Giovanni and Baldwin 2019. The point is not that the police are only a problem because of a few bad apples; rather, the point is that the uniform, gun, and thus positionality of the police is one of violent domination no matter how great the person is behind the badge. The police play a role, and it is one that they could stop playing under the right conditions.
58. Here, an anonymous reviewer raises a critique leveled by Frantz Fanon in *Black Skin, White Masks* (2008), on the ambiguous status of Jewishness. A key element of the noted text is that the "Jew is not liked as soon as he has been detected" (Fanon 2008, 95). It is true that the capacity to detect the racialized subject as non-white might vary with MENA people, and this is a unique element of MENA racialization. The MENA world is phenotypically pluralistic. My emphasis has been on those who cannot simply pass and for those who are mistaken. Nevertheless, the ability to pass raises an additional moral problem: Does one have a moral responsibility not to pass if that is an option? I think the answer is yes, but plenty of passing

people—MENA and non-MENA—choose to live in bad faith, raising further questions about their sleep habits.

59. For the history of the emergence of the police, see, e.g., Balko 2014.

CHAPTER TWO

1. 1993, 18.

2. On social or moral accounts of trust, see, e.g., Baier 1994; Bernstein 2011; Helm 2013. On the political elements of trust, see, e.g., Rosanvallon 2008.

3. On how social relations are structured by predation, specifically under racial-capitalism, see Hall 2021; Gilmore 2007. Specifically, Hall notes:

> Each level of the social formation requires its own independent "means of representation"—the means by which the class structured mode of production appears, and acquires effectivity at the level of the economic, the political, the ideological class struggle. Race is intrinsic to the manner in which the black laboring classes are complexly constituted at each of these levels. It enters into the way black labor, male and female, is distributed as economic agents at the level of economic practices, and the class struggles which result from it; and into the way the fractions of the black laboring classes are reconstituted, through the means of political representation (parties, organizations, community action centers, publications and campaigns) as political forces in the "theatre of politics"—and the political struggles which result; and the manner in which the working class is articulated as the collective and individual "subjects" of emergent ideologies—and the struggles over ideology, culture and consciousness which result. This gives the matter or dimension of race, and racism, a practical as well as theoretical centrality to all the relations which affect black labor. The constitution of this fraction as a class, and the class relations which ascribe it, function as race relations. Race is thus, also, the modality in which class is "lived," the medium through which class relations are experienced, the form in which it is appropriated and "fought through." This has consequences for the whole class, not specifically for its "racially defined" segment. It has consequences in terms of the internal fractioning and division within the working class which, among other ways, are articulated in part through race. This is no mere racist conspiracy from above. For racism is also one of the dominant means of ideological representation through which the white fractions of the class come to "live" their relations to other fractions, and through them to capital itself. Those who seek, with effect, to disarticulate some of the existing syntaxes of class struggle (albeit of a corporatist or social reformist kind) and to rearticulate class experience through the condensed interpellations of a racist ideological syntax are, of course, key agents in this work of ideological transformation. (Hall 2021, 239)

4. 1999, 4.

Notes

5. The general critique of social policing that I am alluding to here was captured by Foucault (1995) in his description of the panopticon, which is to say that various disciplinary mechanisms cooperate in the production of docile bodies or those actors who know how to behave when they are potentially being surveyed, while also acting as surveillance and thus witness to others. Benjamin Stumpf (2020) more recently extended this critique in his excellent essay, "The Whiteness of Watching: Surveillant Citizenship and the Carceral State."

6. For two recent examples of right-leaning politicians denying racism and thus advocating for a certain version of post-racialism, see Linly 2021; Miller 2021.

7. Buber 1996; Quijano 2007; Wynter 2003.

8. Quijano 2007, 177.

9. Rueb and Taylor 2019.

10. Monahan 2021; Silva 2019; 2021.

11. X 2020, 118.

12. See, e.g., Andone 2019; Garvey 2019; Itzkoff 2019; NPR 2019.

13. Anderson 2015, 6.

14. Andone 2019; Garvey 2019.

15. See, e.g., Zhou 2019.

16. Davis 2003.

17. For an extended, extensive, and invaluable critique of social death, see Patterson 1985.

18. Murakawa 2014, 15.

19. Ibid., 17

20. Ibid., 127

21. Alexander 2016.

22. Flores 2016.

23. Stumpf 2020.

24. Braithwaite 2000.

25. Braithwaite 1989, 101.

26. Ross 2019

27. Foucault 2012, 12–13.

28. Of course, academics are concerned by the students, but the concern often becomes detached from the events themselves—objects of discussion. For example, Shannon Sullivan (2015) writes about a call-out experience in her own classroom, thus using an actual event to introduce an entire monograph, but it is unclear if those involved in the catalytic event are aware of the analysis or were engaged after the call-out event. Of course, this abstract form of concern is important, especially for playing the academic game, but the more immediate concern for those who are directly polarized by call-outs is my point of focus.

29. And retreating to whiteness is ontologically foundation to the false category—after all, to admit being wrong would admit to non-supremacy. Often, accompanying, backing, or driving the retreat to whiteness is what Carol Anderson aptly describes as *White Rage* (2020).

30. Baer 2018.

31. For an analysis of this lingering resentment, see Brudholm 2008.

144 *Notes*

32. Fourlas, 2014. Also, for another affirmative defense of anger, see Srinivasan 2018.

33. See, e.g., Braithwaite and Brathwaite 2010.

34. Or, if not dismissal, then the racialization will be coupled to another category depending on one's phenotypic proximity to other racialized groups.

35. For a defense of in-the-heart racism, see Garcia's (1999) volitional model; for a response to Garcia, see Mills 2003b and more recently Urquidez 2017.

36. Harfouch 2021.

37. Dussel 1988, 9.

38. Dussel 2013, 45.

CHAPTER THREE

1. 2002, 16.

2. This claim has, at least, a dual meaning: On the one hand, institutional norms are not organized to afford recognition of MENA peoples, specifically in the United States; on the other hand, however, even where institutional acknowledgment exists (i.e., Canada, to some extent) the hyperpluralism that is obscured by the categorical status is not appreciated, and the status seems to only make this worse for recognized peoples.

3. Maghbouleh 2012.

4. For an argument that mirrors some of the claims I am making about the race-nation conflation, see Michaels 1995.

5. Anderson 1991.

6. Minh 1945.

7. Lorde 1984.

8. Khatibi 2019, 3.

9. Ibid.

10. Here I think it is worth noting an additional critique of ethnicity as a post-racial or politically correct replacement category for "race." So when racial science is formally abandoned (see Chapter 1), ethnicity appears to carry the justifying burden of exclusion that was previously carried by race. I hold onto race because I do not think that it is meaningfully distinct from ethnicity even if the formal institutional claim is that ethnicity does not equate to race.

Naomi Zack emphasizes a similar concern in our correspondence about an earlier version of this chapter. She says:

> Seeing Anglos as white and themselves as not white is not limited to MENA people in the history of US immigrants. For instance, Polish Americans regularly distinguished between themselves and whites in the early 20th century, before they assimilated to dominant Anglo culture. And yet, there is something about MENA groups, and also Latinx groups, which despite their white categorization, prevents them from being accepted as white by whites. It is interesting that US census allows for Latinx to indicate whether they are white or black,

and so forth. Although, the same census insists that Latino/Hispanic identity is not a race, but an ethnicity and everyone has to indicate whether they are Latino/Hispanic or not. And, many Latinx experience racism, purely on the grounds of being Latinx, even though they could check Latino and white on the census. (Naomi Zack, personal correspondence, 2021)

My claim is simply that the thing that prevents MENA and Latinidad peoples from being accepted is racialization and the language of ethnicity is introduced to obscure this fact that creates another layer of divisiveness among racialized peoples. At the same time, MENA nationalists are overdetermining the bounds of racial experience by appealing to the recently created MENA boundaries to determine who is or is not MENA, thus reproducing the nationalist exclusion that I am critiquing throughout.

11. There are many outstanding critical texts on the creation of the modern MENA world, some of which I have cited throughout this book, but a useful starting point would be Lockman's work from 2010 and 2016.

12. Tehranian 2009.

13. Ibid., 79.

14. Ibid., 26.

15. Sicily and Malta, for example, are strategic points of territorial conflict, claimed by various groups throughout history, creating the mixed, ambivalent, and often-victimized circumstances I am associating with Middle Eastern experience.

16. Friedman 2011; Stoiciu 2012; Lindner 2012.

17. Landress, Grey, and Chase 2000.

18. For critiques of the language of degeneration in racial thought, see, e.g., Park 2014; Harfouch 2018.

19. Under Ottoman rule, the space that would become the Middle East operated under a millet system that taxed non-Islamic communities at higher rates in exchange for religious-political autonomy. It was not uncommon for persons to convert for the sake of lower taxes, protection under Islam, love, or out of a genuine belief in Islam. Deringil 2012.

20. Ibid.

21. James 1981.

22. Öcalan 2007, 247.

23. Feuerbach 2012, 228.

24. See, e.g., Nagy 2013; Fourlas 2015b; Valandra and Yazzie 2020.

25. Antonius 1965, 90.

CHAPTER FOUR

1. Said 1993, 35.

2. Dainotto 2007, 12.

3. See, e.g., Hill Collins 2018; Crenshaw 1991; Curry 2021. Also, I think the way that I am using intersectionality as a normative ideal through which the hypercomplexity of life is appreciated also aligns with the notion of creolization illuminated by

Jane Gordon (Gordon 2014). It is possible that creolization would be a more accurate and helpful term, especially given Curry's concerns, but at the moment I hold on to intersectionality for purely instrumental reasons (that is, the term is enjoying a certain popularity at the moment that is largely accompanied by a lack of critical understanding, and my hope is to extend the concept or build bridges with it and other concepts).

4. Dussel 2014.
5. Bernal 2020.
6. Harfouch 2021, 10.
7. The divide is also discussed in relation to Egypt (see, e.g., James 2017), though the popular and false imaginary of European continental distinction is in relation to Asia, not Africa, hence my emphasis on Turkey. See also Gordon 2013. Here, Gordon offers a powerful accompanying critique to Dussel's "Anti-Cartesianism," from which I borrow the language of multiple modernities, or the distinction that Euro-modernity stands in relation to other modern eras (in the cases of my own work here, the height of power prior to Euro-modernity was seated in the Ottoman world (Istanbul/Constantinople). It is also worth pointing out that the most infamous Orientalists and white nationalists who defend various versions of the "clash of civilizations" hypothesis hold on to a more rigid notion of Europe that excludes much of the southern and Eastern regions. Common knowledge, however, is of the cartographic Europe, and so my critique stands. I imagine this division aligns with right versus liberal political ideology as well, but that is something to be argued in a separate place/time.
8. And Euro-modern power is being challenged, as the boundary between its imaginary birthplace and the Eastern other is unraveling through various crisis.
9. Dussel 2014, 1.
10. Lewis 1982.
11. Said 1979, 342.
12. Carastathis 2014; Gourgouris 1996; Koundoura 2007.
13. Gourgouris 1996.
14. Hegel is infamous for this narrative, as Peter K. J. Park (2014) argues. Of course, as both Park and Emmanuel C. Eze (1997) point out, Hegel was not alone in his racism, as in fact most of the canonical figures from the Euro-modern tradition were not merely racist but built their theories around racist values.
15. Dainotto 2007.
16. Park 2014, 2.
17. One visit to the British Museum reveals a few of the fruits of this appropriative activity.
18. Koundoura 2007, 20. See also Gourgouris 1996.
19. Carastathis 2014, 6.
20. Constantine 2011.
21. Ibid., xiii.
22. Ibid., xiii–xiv.
23. For more on cartographic production in relation to the Ottoman world, see, e.g., Palmira Brummett's *Mapping the Ottomans* (2020).
24. Here too are traces of the emergence of archaeology as a distinct field that is grounded in recovery, excavation, and the production of evidence, thus becoming a

bizarre empirical necromancy where tombs and other markers are forced to do the impossible and speak.

25. See, e.g., Cuffari, Di Paolo, and De Jaegher 2015; Di Paolo, Cuffari, and De Jaegher 2018.

26. See, e.g., Melissaropoulou 2016. Similar linguistic "purification" occurred in Turkey as part of the Kemalist movement, in Spain under Franco, and numerous other conservative nationalist contexts.

27. Ibid., xiii–xiv.

28. Ibid.

29. Of course, the fetishization of the imagined Athenian past is not limited to the Germans. Indeed, in the United States, for example, there is a robust appropriative social system of fraternities and sororities found in many universities with minimal regard for what "Greek life" is or means to the history of coloniality.

30. On Catherine II's "Greek project," see, e.g., Davies 2016.

31. Fromkin 2000.

32. Said 1979, 54.

33. See Molos 2019. Also, Catherine II 2018, especially letter 52, which ends with the following expectation: "We certainly expect that you will apply all means and force to sustain it in the name of and in association with the Greek peoples" (126).

34. See, e.g., Clark 2006; Iğsız 2018.

35. Panourgiá 2009.

36. Bargu 2014.

37. Carastathis 2014, 11.

38. Mamdani 2012.

39. To be clear, this pluralism was not equitable—the Ottoman millet system coupled with its forced conscription of young boys and men from non-Muslim populations afforded a largely second-class status for many.

40. The split between ideological approaches persists, but violent universalism has become a common non-Western response to colonial efforts, and this is seen clearly as the West continues demanding liberalism for all and certain groups, such as ISIS, are embattled and have taken up a similar universalist mentality.

41. James 2017; Bernal 2020; and, accompanying the material erasure of the relational and appreciative modes that undergird and drive pre-colonial Hellenism, there is the discursive or epistemic erasure described by Reiland Rabaka (2010) as "epistemic apartheid" and Lewis Gordon (2021) as "citational," as well as "ontological," apartheid.

42. I use the term Arabic philosophy to denote the linguistic element of the figures associated with this tradition, not a national designation. There was no Arab nation as it is presently imagined in the pre-colonial world wherein Arabic philosophy formed and functioned.

43. Along with the previously mentioned James (2017) and Bernal (2020), who emphasize the conditions and traditions that afforded pre-colonial Hellenism, there is also an extensive history of that same Hellenism then being recirculated throughout Eastern Eurasia and Africa; see, e.g., Mairs 2014; Parker 2017. And, of course, the exchange of tradition and habit, as well as the remembrance of that connectedness,

throughout the broader MENA world, remains in various ways, some minor—the shared language of baklava, which transcends many ethno-national barriers (Abu-Jaber 2005)—to more substantial forms such as the solidarity between Kurds, Armenians, and Greeks, to name only a few, in resistance to neo-Ottoman aspirations.

44. Thucydides 1954.

45. See James 2017. We see a similar critique being made in relation to the theft of indigenous land, which is also misleading because that which is common, shared, and belonging to all can only be stolen once it has first been made property. The pre-colonial world was largely held in and as common, and the Western project begins with the denial of communality (ontologically and materially, as Dussel [2014] also suggests).

46. Said 1993, 15–16.

47. To be clear, I am not making a strong normative claim here; rather, I am clarifying what is needed for normativity to emerge as an ethos grounded in reciprocity. The call for an anti-colonial universalism is present throughout many decolonial projects—see, especially, Khader 2019—and even some critical theorists are concerned with the decolonial critique of universalism (see, e.g., Allen 2016).

48. Said 1993, 35.

49. Karatani 2017.

50. Ibid., 18. As Emiliano Zapata put it, "Tierra y libertad!"

51. Karatani 2017.

52. Ibid.; also Mauss 2002; Hyde 2007; Marx 1990.

53. Karatani 2017, 6–14.

54. Again, see Quijano 2007; Wynter 2003.

55. See Moraña, Dussel, and Jáuregui's (2008) introduction, "Colonialism and Its Replicants."

56. Gordon 2006.

57. Césaire 2000, 33.

CHAPTER FIVE

1. 1997, 17.

2. 2004, 2.

3. Horkheimer and Adorno 1992; Midgley 2011; Sorel 2008.

4. Sayegh 1958; Öcalan 2007. I could and likely will write an essay engaging Sayegh and Öcalan, and commenting on the means, as well as ideals, of unity within these figures. I certainly have more to say, and I hope my audience will read said future essay when it is ready.

5. I have said a bit about this in previous chapters, specifically my use of MENA instead of Arab, but it is not a hill I am willing to die on. If the term *Arab* can indeed include all MENA peoples, and I am skeptical that it can, then I am happy to have that term operate in place of MENA for organizational purposes. My worry, and thus my reason for appealing to myth rather than language or culture, is that the tendency to exclude those who might otherwise be family can creep back into thought and prac-

tice if sufficient distance is not placed between our historical present and the ideas through which we become ourselves. Myth has greater power, too, insofar as it does not require verification. Consider how quickly capitalists appeal to the myth of competitive and self-interested nature to justify their ongoing domination and destruction of life. There are, of course, many counterexamples that reveal the capitalist myth for the fabrication that it is (see, e.g., Tsing 2015), but the capitalists are unmoved by evidence to the contrary because that position is baked into their myth—the self-interested element is therefore a supremacist element for the capitalist. So the myth or ideal that guides *anti-colonial solidarity* must have its own fundamental values, and those might include the celebration of difference, non-domination (isonomia), cooperation, and a critical historical awareness that corrects for the sort of supremacy that drives capitalist ideologues.

Further, though I disagree with Sayegh on the usefulness of nationalism—which, I think, is only possible because of the difference in historical moment within which I write—I certainly agree with the sentiment expressed in the full version of the passage quoted at the beginning of this book:

> Like the other national aspirations for freedom and for progress, which animate the Arab national movement and to which the Arab peoples at large are ardently dedicated, the longing for unity cannot be indefinitely frustrated, whether by outside intervention or by domestic suppression, with impunity. To the degree to which such legitimate, vital, and popularly appealing aspirations are obstructed, to that degree the indignation and wrath of the peoples concerned is incurred, and the counsel of moderation is resultantly discarded in favor of extremism and fanaticism. The alternative to Arab unity, and to dynamic Arab nationalism in general, is not eternal submissiveness by Arabs, nor their perpetual acquiescence in fragmentation, outside domination, and obsolete patterns of socio-economic organization—but a violent revolutionary reaction in the direction of extreme self-assertion. (Sayegh 1958, 212)

Unity is the ideal path, especially for those who are tired of the violence warned against in this quote, and my concern throughout this text are the means of that collective mode.

6. Foucault 2003, 7.

7. For example, in discussing the emergence of disciplinary power, Foucault describes the role of reformers who wanted to make punishment more humane. Foucault does not seem to care whether these reformers were right or wrong; rather, his point is that the reformist position has been central to the ongoing emergence of our current disciplinary systems. He seems to treat the moral position—that is, public corporeal punishment is wrong—as a neutral, not "progressive," historical force.

8. Spivak uses the language of subaltern, which is borrowed from Gramsci, to capture this more normative version of subjugated knowledge forms (see Spivak 2010).

9. For a useful critique of the language of white privilege, see Zack 2015. For an analysis of the complex dynamics of group privilege and preference, see Sidanius and Pratto 1999.

10. Mignolo 2000.

11. The initial deployment of the language of "identity politics" is typically attributed to the "The Combahee River Collective Statement," which has since been misunderstood and warped in various ways (Taylor 2017). On this point, Barbara Smith summarizes the specific meaning of the concept as follows:

> But however the right wing got ahold of identity politics and began using it as their whipping boy and their whipping girl, what we meant by identity politics when we originated the terminology was wholly different. What we were saying is that we have a right as people who are not just female, who are not solely Black, who are not just lesbians, who are not just working class, or workers—that we are people who embody all of these identities, and we have a right to build and define political theory and practice based upon that reality. That was all we were trying to say. That's what we meant by identity politics. We didn't mean that if you're not the same as us, you're nothing. We were not saying that we didn't care about anybody who wasn't exactly like us. One of the things I used to say, and of course I've had so many speaking engagements I have taglines at this point [laugh] of things that I've said more than once, is that it would be really boring only to do political work with people who are exactly like me. (Taylor 2017, 61)

12. Benjamin 2019, 200.

13. Dussel 1988, 56.

14. I clarify the definition of *meaning* in my introduction, but recall that for my purposes, *meaning* includes the functional or pragmatic position, which is consequences in experience, and the not so explicitly functional transcendence that accompanies what Martin Buber describes as an *I-you* relation. I expand on the nonrational and nonfunctional nature of meaning in previous work, specifically through Harry Frankfurt's reflections on love (Fourlas 2014, 76–108).

15. Medina 2011, 24.

16. Ibid., 11.

17. Mill 2015.

18. Medina 2013, 283.

19. Feuerbach 2008.

20. Marx and Engels 2013, 60.

21. Medina 2013, 26.

22. Ferguson 2013. And the similar point is made in the famous essay "Can the Subaltern Speak?" (Spivak 2010).

23. Ferguson 2013.

24. Ibid.

25. I develop this point in a slightly different way in my other writings (see, e.g., Fourlas 2018). The general point is focused on the idea of play, which I take to be a central component to free meaning-making, but that process is open to various possible relational modes (i.e., not limited to agonism, though agonism is one possible modality that can and should occasionally afford meaning)—unlike play, however,

which requires a vulnerability that is not immediately available, if it ever becomes so, to conflicted parties, meaning there must be normative limits to these engagements.

26. Hobbes 2016, 87–88.
27. Zehr 2005, 178.
28. Midgley 2011, 5.
29. García Márquez 2003, 237.
30. Ibid., 226–27.
31. I say "supposed to exclude" because, despite the rigidity of colonial boundaries, persons find a way to engage and be together from all sides of division. The walls will always have cracks through which human sociality will flow. As Buber (1996) puts it: "Love is a cosmic force" (66). For a crucial analysis of how people find a way through the colonial cracks, specifically within academic philosophy, see Dotson 2011.
32. Césaire 2000, 41.
33. Pateman and Mills 2007, 82.
34. Ibid., 88
35. See Curry 2018 for a powerful and damning analysis of the "White Man's Burden" in the U.S. context.
36. Kant 1970.
37. Of course, certain tactics and strategies will be similar to those advocated for by ideal liberal thinkers, as well as nonideal radical liberals—the idea of social agreement and collective determination as a societal starting point, for example—but the guiding ideals of liberalism inform those modes such that even the basic shift in ideological framing would at the very least afford a different social-political future distinct from liberalism. In this case, social agreement cannot be taken as granted and must be enacted in an ongoing way—collective determination is a generational project.
38. García Márquez 2003, 1.
39. Césaire 2000, 33
40. Buber 1996, 67.
41. For a more extensive critique of the impossible certainty Descartes demands, see Wittgenstein 1975.
42. And the difficulty of this honesty in the U.S. context around the primary contradiction was made clear by the experiences George Yancy had after publishing "Dear White America" in the *New York Times*, captured and critiqued in *Backlash: What Happens When We Talk Honestly about Racism in America* (Yancy 2018).
43. Dussel 2003, 16.
44. Öcalan 2007, 247–54.
45. Ibid.
46. I am not contesting whether or not the story of Babel is historical fact because part of my project is to destabilize the role that historical fact plays in how we relate to our present and future. Much of history is simultaneously fact and fiction, and what matters is how we relate to that history and what that history does to us or for us. As I suggest, Babel acts to naturalize and excuse our division, but it also offers an alternative possible world wherein people once were able to unite in common.
47. Glissant 1997, 50.

48. Chiang 2016.
49. Ibid., 6.
50. Ibid., 28.
51. Weber and Parsons 2014.
52. See, e.g., Steiner 1998.
53. For a fun read on the history of the Vienna Circle, see, e.g., Edmonds 2020.
54. Di Paolo, Cuffari, and De Jaegher 2018.
55. Frankl 2020.
56. Lear 2006, 103.

57. Jean Améry (2009) is particularly helpful on this point, as he demands that the horrors of the past cannot be reconciled, but we must live forward anyway, perhaps even in spite of the past.

58. This is at least part of the reason that figures like W. E. B. Du Bois (2004; 2008) and Anzaldúa (2012) emphasize the ease with which their interstitial existence affords an alternative epistemic mode, an other thinking or border thinking, as Mignolo frames it (2000).

59. See, e.g., Maturana and Varela 1980; 2008.
60. Benjamin 2018.
61. Rousseau 2002.

62. Of course, for those subjugated peoples who identify with a nation, in the absence of a state, or with a nominal state apparatus (a state without teeth), then the modality might still orient toward a liberatory end, but here I think the ideal "nation" is a stand-in for a descriptive liberatory solidarity that is necessary because the alternative is death. Many of the reified nationalisms that I am critiquing were once similarly oriented—recall, Arab, Armenian, and Greek nationalism were all initially formulated in response to Ottoman domination. Nationalism was a useful tool for transcending Ottoman rule, but it has outlived its usefulness, and that tendency to linger beyond its functionality is implicit to the project—after all, how could the eternal nation be merely a temporary organizing force to be abandoned once the colonial/imperial domination has been transcended?

CHAPTER SIX

1. 1999, 23.
2. My analysis of Cyprus is deeply indebted to Harry Anastasiou and Maria Hadjipavlou, who I cite throughout. Their guidance and support remain invaluable to my thinking.
3. Gardner 2006; Curle 1971.
4. Lederach 1997, 27.
5. Anastasiou 2008, 177–83.
6. Ibid., 177–78.
7. "Emotion as Cyprus Border Opens" 2003.
8. "Cyprus Contacts Gather Pace" 2003.
9. Anastasiou 2008, 32.

10. Ibid., 34.
11. Ibid., 37.
12. Ibid., 40. Here, Anastasiou presents an excellent account, which he originally wrote in 1996, of this "new hope."
13. Ibid., 41.
14. Freire 2000.
15. Youth Power 2012; "(1) One StreetS" n.d.
16. Hadjipavlou 2010.
17. Ibid.
18. For an invaluable overview of the Rojava revolution, see Knapp, Flach, and Ayboga 2016.
19. A founding member of the Kurdistan Workers Party (the PKK), Öcalan was arrested in Nairobi and extradited to Turkey, where he was treated as a terrorist and sentenced to life in prison. From 1999 to 2009, he was the only occupant of an island prison, Imrali, in the Mamara Sea. His isolation has only increased over time, and since 2014, information on the situation in the Imrali prison has been severely limited. Nevertheless, Öcalan (Apo) managed to publish several prison notebooks and pamphlets that detail a social-political framework that is centered around liberation; thus, coupled with his involvement in the PKK throughout the 1970s, 1980s, and 1990s, Apo's influence has been crucial to the movement.
20. Öcalan 2007, 1.
21. The obvious exception here are Daesh prisoners, a problem that imploded when the United States betrayed Rojava in 2019.
22. Öcalan 2017, 31.
23. Ibid., 39.
24. Ibid.
25. Öcalan 2011.
26. In *The Women's War* (2020), Evans captures the nuances of how this gender shift has impacted the people of Rojava. In episode 5, "Grandma Law and Revolutionary Sacrifice," Evans interviews people throughout one of the towns in Rojava, and voices of disagreement are present. Evans notes that this is a useful marker for the political state in Rojava, namely, as one that is not dictatorial—otherwise, ordinary citizens would be unlikely to voice dissent.
27. Öcalan 2007, 13.
28. Originally in Öcalan 2015, 266, but quoted from Knapp, Flach, and Ayboga 2016, 43.
29. See, e.g., Öcalan 2017, 55–56.
30. Knapp, Flach, and Ayboga 2016, 86.
31. Öcalan 2017, 41.
32. This is especially true on the ground in Greece, where various grassroots community organizations are working to integrate refugees while experiencing violent opposition from the fascist front. See Omnes 2021; Thornhill 2018. In Israel/Palestine, consider Friends of Roots 2021 and Apkon et al. 2016.
33. Ferrara 2008, 3–4.
34. Sidanius and Pratto 1999.

35. Foucault 2000, 129.
36. Zinn 2018.

CONCLUSION

1. Polychroniou 2021.
2. "President Trump Participates" 2020.
3. Anzaldúa 2015, 20.

Bibliography

"(1) One StreetS." n.d. *Facebook.* Accessed June 1, 2021. www.facebook.com/on estreets.

Abu-Jaber, Diana. 2005. *The Language of Baklava.* 1st ed. New York: Pantheon Books.

Akar, Hiba Bou, and Roosbelinda Cárdenas. 2017. "Writing about Violence: A Joint Reflection from Latin America and the Middle East." *Middle East Report* 47 (284/285): 46–51.

Alcoff, Linda. 2006. *Visible Identities: Race, Gender, and the Self.* Studies in Feminist Philosophy. New York: Oxford University Press.

Alexander, Michelle. 2010. *The New Jim Crow: Mass Incarceration in the Age of Colorblindness.* New York: New Press.

———. 2016. "Why Hillary Clinton Doesn't Deserve the Black Vote." *The Nation*, February 10. www.thenation.com/article/archive/hillary-clinton-does-not-deserve-black-peoples-votes.

Allen, Amy. 2016. *The End of Progress: Decolonizing the Normative Foundations of Critical Theory.* New Directions in Critical Theory. New York: Columbia University Press.

Allen, Danielle S. 2006. *Talking to Strangers: Anxieties of Citizenship Since Brown v. Board of Education.* Chicago: University of Chicago Press.

Al-Saji, Alia. 2010. "The Racialization of Muslim Veils: A Philosophical Analysis." *Philosophy & Social Criticism* 36 (8): 875–902. https://doi.org/10.1177/0191453710375589.

Alsultany, Evelyn, and Ella Shohat. 2012. *Between the Middle East and the Americas: The Cultural Politics of Diaspora.* Ann Arbor: University of Michigan Press.

Améry, Jean. 2009. *At the Mind's Limits: Contemplations by a Survivor on Auschwitz and Its Realities.* Bloomington: Indiana University Press.

Anastasiou, Harry. 2008. *The Broken Olive Branch: Nationalism, Ethnic Conflict, and the Quest for Peace in Cyprus.* Vol. 1, *The Impasse of Ethnonationalism.* 1st ed. Syracuse, NY: Syracuse University Press. http://catdir.loc.gov/catdir/toc/fy0903/2008032776.html.

Anderson, Benedict R. O'G. 1991. *Imagined Communities: Reflections on the Origin and Spread of Nationalism*. Rev. and extended ed. London: Verso.

Anderson, Carol. 2020. *White Rage*. New York: Bloomsbury.

Anderson, Luvell. 2015. "Racist Humor." *Philosophy Compass* 10 (8): 501–9. https://doi.org/10.1111/phc3.12240.

Andone, Dakin. 2019. "Andrew Yang Still Says SNL Should Not Have Fired Comedian for Racist Comments." *CNN*, September 21. www.cnn.com/2019/09/21/politics/andrew-yang-van-jones-cancel-culture/index.html.

Antonius, George. 1965. *The Arab Awakening: The Story of the Arab National Movement*. New York: Capricorn Books.

Anzaldúa, Gloria. 2012. *Borderlands/La Frontera: The New Mestiza*. 25th anniversary, 4th ed. San Francisco: Aunt Lute Books.

———. 2015. *Light in the Dark = Luz En Lo Oscuro: Rewriting Identity, Spirituality, Reality*. Latin America Otherwise. Durham, NC: Duke University Press.

Apkon, Stephen, Marcina Hale, and Reconsider, Inc. 2016. *Disturbing the Peace: A Reconsider Film*. Oley, PA: Bullfrog Films.

Appiah, Anthony. 1985. "The Uncompleted Argument: Du Bois and the Illusion of Race." *Critical Inquiry* 12 (1): 21–37. https://doi.org/10.1086/448319.

———. 1996. *Color Conscious: The Political Morality of Race*. Princeton, NJ: Princeton University Press.

"Armenian & Azerbaijani/Turkish Protestors Face Off at Azerbaijani Consulate in Los Angeles." 2020. *Zartonk Media*, July. https://zartonkmedia.com/2020/07/21/breaking-news-armenian-azerbaijani-turkish-protestors-face-off-at-azerbaijani-consulate-in-los-angeles.

Austin, John Langshaw. 1975. *How to Do Things with Words*. 2nd ed. Edited by J. O. Urmson and Marina Sbisà. William James Lectures 1955. Cambridge: Harvard University Press.

Baer, Hannah. 2018. "Malefragility." *Instagram*. www.instagram.com/malefragility.

Baier, Annette. 1994. *Moral Prejudices: Essays on Ethics*. Cambridge: Harvard University Press. www.gbv.de/dms/bowker/toc/9780674587151.pdf.

Balko, Radley. 2014. *Rise of the Warrior Cop: The Militarization of America's Police Forces*. 1st ed. New York: PublicAffairs.

Bargu, Banu. 2014. *Starve and Immolate: The Politics of Human Weapons*. New Directions in Critical Theory. New York: Columbia University Press. www.hnet.org/reviews/showrev.php?id=43513.

Bayoumi, Moustafa. 2009. *How Does It Feel to Be a Problem? Being Young and Arab in America*. New York: Penguin Books.

———. 2015. *This Muslim American Life: Dispatches from the War on Terror*. New York: University Press.

Benjamin, Walter. 2018. *Illuminations*. Boston: Mariner Books.

———. 2019. *Illuminations*. Edited by Hannah Arendt. Translated by Harry Zohn. Boston: Mariner Books, Houghton Mifflin Harcourt.

Bernal, Martin. 2020. *Black Athena: The Afroasiatic Roots of Classical Civilization*. Vol. 1, *The Fabrication of Ancient Greece 1785–1985*. New Brunswick, NJ: Rutgers University Press.

Bernasconi, Robert, and Tommy Lee Lott. 2000. *The Idea of Race*. Hackett Readings in Philosophy. Indianapolis: Hackett.

Bernstein, J. M. 2011. "Trust: On the Real but Almost Always Unnoticed, Ever-Changing Foundation of Ethical Life." *Metaphilosophy* 42 (4): 395–416. https://doi.org/10.1111/j.1467-9973.2011.01709.x.

Beydoun, Khaled A. 2017. "Being a Muslim under Trump Is Risky. That's Why Many Are Hiding Their Identity." *The Guardian*, March 30. www.theguardian.com/commentisfree/2017/mar/30/being-muslim-under-trump-risky-many-hiding-identity.

———. 2018. *American Islamophobia: Understanding the Roots and Rise of Fear*. Oakland: University of California Press.

"Blue Racism." 2017. *YouTube*, August 20. Accessed August 3, 2019. www.youtube.com/watch?v=8IjjdBNfhW0&feature=youtu.be.

Bonilla-Silva, Eduardo. 2018. *Racism without Racists: Color-Blind Racism and the Persistence of Racial Inequality in America*. 5th ed. Lanham, MD: Rowman & Littlefield.

Braithwaite, John. 1989. *Crime, Shame, and Reintegration*. Cambridge: Cambridge University Press.

———. 2000. "Reintegrative Shaming." http://johnbraithwaite.com/wp-content/uploads/2016/05/2000_Reintegrative-Shaming.pdf.

Braithwaite, John, and Valerie Brathwaite. 2010. *Anomie and Violence: Non-Truth and Reconciliation in Indonesian Peacebuilding*. Canberra, Australia: ANU Press.

Brudholm, Thomas. 2008. *Resentment's Virtue: Jean Améry and the Refusal to Forgive*. Politics, History, and Social Change. Philadelphia: Temple University Press. http://catdir.loc.gov/catdir/toc/ecip0718/2007018931.html.

Brummett, Palmira. 2020. *Mapping the Ottomans: Sovereignty, Territory, and Identity in the Early Modern Mediterranean*. Cambridge: Cambridge University Press.

Buber, Martin. 1970. *I and Thou*. New York: Charles Scribner's Sons.

———. 1996. *I and Thou*. 1st Touchstone ed. New York: Touchstone.

———. 1997. *On Zion: The History of an Idea*. 1st Syracuse University ed. Syracuse, NY: Syracuse University Press.

Carastathis, Anna. 2014. "Is Hellenism an Orientalism? Reflections on the Boundaries of 'Europe' in an Age of Austerity." *Critical Race & Whiteness Studies* 10 (1): 1–17.

Cárdenas, Roosbelinda, Hiba Bou Akar, and Ana Tijoux. 2018. "Desde El Sur: ¡hasta La Victoria Siempre! (Interview)." *NACLA Report on the Americas* 50 (4): 430–34. https://doi.org/10.1080/10714839.2018.1551467.

Catherine II, Empress of Russia. 2018. *Selected Letters*. Oxford World's Classics. Oxford: Oxford University Press.

Césaire, Aimé. 2000. *Discourse on Colonialism*. New York: Monthly Review Press.

Chaney, K. E., D. T. Sanchez, and L. Saud. 2020. "White Categorical Ambiguity: Exclusion of Middle Eastern Americans from the White Racial Category." *Social Psychological and Personality Science*. https://doi.org/10.1177/1948550620930546.

Chiang, Ted. 2016. *Stories of Your Life and Others*. 1st Vintage Books ed. New York: Vintage Books.

Clark, Bruce. 2006. *Twice a Stranger: The Mass Expulsions That Forged Modern Greece and Turkey.* Cambridge: Harvard University Press.
Constantine, David. 2011. *In the Footsteps of the Gods: Travellers to Greece and the Quest for the Hellenic Ideal.* Revised paperback ed. London: Tauris Parke Paperbacks.
Crenshaw, Kimberlé. 1991. "Mapping the Margins: Intersectionality, Identity Politics, and Violence against Women of Color." *Stanford Law Review* 43 (6): 1241–99.
Cuffari, Elena Clare, Ezequiel Di Paolo, and Hanne De Jaegher. 2015. "From Participatory Sense-Making to Language: There and Back Again." *Phenomenology and the Cognitive Sciences* 14 (4): 1089–1125. https://doi.org/10.1007/s11097-014-9404-9.
Curle, Adam. 1971. *Making Peace.* London: Tavistock.
Curry, Tommy J. 2018. *Another White Man's Burden: Josiah Royce's Quest for a Philosophy of White Racial Empire.* SUNY Series in American Philosophy and Cultural Thought. Albany: State University of New York Press.
———. 2021. "Decolonizing the Intersection: Black Male Studies as a Critique of Intersectionality's Indebtedness to Subculture of Violence Theory." In *Critical Psychology Praxis,* edited by Robert K. Beshara. New York: Routledge.
"Cyprus Contacts Gather Pace." 2003. *BBC News,* April 29. http://news.bbc.co.uk/2/hi/europe/2985991.stm.
Dainotto, Roberto M. 2007. *Europe (in Theory).* Durham, NC: Duke University Press. http://site.ebrary.com/id/10217159.
Davies, Brian L. 2016. *The Russo-Turkish War, 1768-1774: Catherine II and the Ottoman Empire.* London: Bloomsbury Academic.
Davis, Angela Y. 2003. *Are Prisons Obsolete?* Open Media Book. New York: Seven Stories Press.
DeCaro, Louis A. 2002. *"Fire from the Midst of You": A Religious Life of John Brown.* New York: New York University Press. http://site.ebrary.com/lib/siouxfalls/Doc?id=10137138.
Deringil, Selim. 2012. *Conversion and Apostasy in the Late Ottoman Empire.* Cambridge: Cambridge University Press.
Di Paolo, Ezequiel A., Elena Clare Cuffari, and Hanne De Jaegher. 2018. *Linguistic Bodies: The Continuity between Life and Language.* Cambridge: The MIT Press.
Dotson, Kristie. 2011. "Concrete Flowers: Contemplating the Profession of Philosophy." *Hypatia* 26 (2): 403–9.
Drury, Meghan. 2017. "Counterorienting the War on Terror: Arab Hip Hop and Diasporic Resistance." *Journal of Popular Music Studies* 29 (2). https://doi.org/10.1111/jpms.12210.
Du Bois, W. E. B. 2004. *Darkwater: Voices from within the Veil.* 1st Washington Square Press trade pbk. ed. New York: Washington Square Press. http://catdir.loc.gov/catdir/enhancements/fy0640/2003069067-s.html.
———. 2008. *The Souls of Black Folk.* Edited by Brent Hayes Edwards. New edition. Oxford World's Classics. Oxford: Oxford University Press.
Dussel, Enrique. 1988. *Ethics and Community.* Liberation and Theology Series. Maryknoll, NY: Orbis Books.

———. 1995. *The Invention of the Americas: Eclipse of "the Other" and the Myth of Modernity*. Translated by Michael D. Barber. New York: Continuum.

———. 2003. *Philosophy of Liberation*. Translated by Aquilina Martinez. Eugene, OR: Wipf. & Stock.

———. 2013. *Ethics of Liberation in the Age of Globalization and Exclusion*. Durham, NC: Duke University Press.

———. 2014. "Anti-Cartesian Meditations: On the Origin of the Philosophical Anti-Discourse of Modernity." *Journal for Culture and Religious Theory* 13 (1): 11–52.

Edmonds, David. 2020. *The Murder of Professor Schlick: The Rise and Fall of the Vienna Circle*. Princeton, NJ: Princeton University Press.

"Emotion as Cyprus Border Opens." 2003. *BBC News*, April 23. http://news.bbc.co.uk/2/hi/europe/2969089.stm.

"Enrique Marquez Jr. Agrees to Plead Guilty to Plotting Violent Attacks and Buying Firearms for Shooter in San Bernardino Terrorist Attack." 2017. *U.S. Department of Justice*, February 14. www.justice.gov/usao-cdca/pr/enrique-marquez-jr-agrees-plead-guilty-plotting-violent-attacks-and-buying-firearms.

Erickson, Bruce A. 2016. "Gender and Violence: Conquest, Conversion and Culture on New Spain's Imperial Frontier." In *Gender, Race and Religion in the Colonization of the Americas*, edited by Nora E. Jaffary, 29–38. Women and Gender in the Early Modern World. New York: Routledge.

Erlenbusch-Anderson, Verena. 2018. *Genealogies of Terrorism: Revolution, State Violence, Empire*. New York: Columbia University Press.

Evans, Robert. 2020. "The Women's War." www.thewomenswar.com.

Eze, Emmanuel Chukwudi. 1997. *Race and the Enlightenment: A Reader*. Cambridge, MA: Blackwell.

Fanon, Frantz. 2004. *The Wretched of the Earth*. New York: Grove Press.

———. 2008. *Black Skin, White Masks*. 1st new ed. Edited by Charles Lam Markmann. New York: Grove Press.

Ferguson, Ann. 2013. "The Epistemology of Resistance: Gender and Racial Oppression, Epistemic Injustice, and Resistant Imaginations." *Notre Dame Philosophical Reviews*. https://ndpr.nd.edu/reviews/the-epistemology-of-resistance-gender-and-racial-oppression-epistemic-injustice-and-resistant-imaginations.

Ferrara, Alessandro. 2008. *The Force of the Example: Explorations in the Paradigm of Judgment*. New Directions in Critical Theory. New York: Columbia University Press. http://catdir.loc.gov/catdir/toc/ecip085/2007047003.html.

Feuerbach, Ludwig. 2008. *The Essence of Christianity*. Translated by George Fielding Eliot. Dover Philosophical Classics. Mineola, NY: Dover.

———. 2012. *The Fiery Brook: Selected Writings*. Radical Thinkers. London; New York: Verso.

Fields, Karen E., and Barbara Jeanne Fields. 2014. *Racecraft: The Soul of Inequality in American Life*. London: Verso.

Flores, Reena. 2016. "Hillary Clinton on 'Superpredators' Remark: 'I Shouldn't Have Used Those Words.'" *CBS News*, February 25. www.cbsnews.com/news/hillary-clinton-on-superpredators-remark-i-shouldnt-have-used-those-words.

Foucault, Michel. 1972. *The Archaeology of Knowledge; and, the Discourse on Language*. New York: Pantheon Books.

———. 1995. *Discipline and Punish: The Birth of the Prison*. 2nd Vintage Books ed. New York: Vintage Books.

———. 2000. *Ethics: Subjectivity and Truth: the Essential Works of Michel Foucault, 1954–1984*. Edited by Paul Rabinow and Robert Hurley. London: Penguin.

———. 2003. *"Society Must Be Defended": Lectures at the Collège de France, 1975–76*. 1st ed. New York: Picador.

———. 2012. *The Courage of Truth (the Government of Self and Others II): Lectures at the Collège de France, 1983–1984*. 1st Picador ed. New York: Picador.

Fourlas, George N. 2014. *Justice as Reconciliation: Political Theory in a World of Difference*. Ph.D. dissertation. University of Oregon. https://scholarsbank.uoregon.edu/xmlui/bitstream/handle/1794/18506/Fourlas_oregon_0171A_11088.pdf?sequence=1&isAllowed=y.

———. 2015a. "A Politics of Reconciliation: Trust, Legitimacy, and the Need for Truth Commissions." *Journal for Peace & Justice Studies* 25 (2): 29–55. https://doi.org/10.5840/peacejustice201525213.

———. 2015b. "Being a Target. On the Racialization of Middle Eastern Americans." *Critical Philosophy of Race* 3 (1): 101–23. https://doi.org/10.5325/critphilrace.3.1.0101.

———. 2015c. "No Future without Transition: A Critique of Liberal Peace." *The International Journal of Transitional Justice* 9 (1): 109–26. https://doi.org/10.1093/ijtj/iju029.

———. 2018. "The Ants and the Elephant: Martial Arts and Liberation Philosophy in the Americas." In *Comparative Studies in Asian and Latin American Philosophies*, edited by Stephanie Rivera Berruz and Leah Kalmanson, 201–16. London: Bloomsbury Academic.

Frankl, Viktor E. 2020. *Man's Search for Meaning*. Classic Editions. London: Rider Books.

Frankowski, Alfred. 2015. *The Post-Racial Limits of Memorialization: Toward a Political Sense of Mourning*. Lanham, MD: Lexington Books.

Fredrickson, George M. 2002. *Racism: A Short History*. Australia: Scribe Publications.

Freire, Paulo. 2000. *Pedagogy of the Oppressed*. 30th anniversary ed. New York: Continuum. http://hdl.library.upenn.edu/1017.12/366263.

Friedman, Thomas L. 2011. "Can Greeks Become Germans?" *New York Times*, July 19. www.nytimes.com/2011/07/20/opinion/20friedman.html.

"Friends of Roots." n.d. Friends of Roots. Accessed November 9, 2021. https://www.friendsofroots.net.

Fromkin, David. 2000. *A Peace to End All Peace: Creating the Modern Middle East*. London: Phoenix Press.

Garcia, J. L. A. 1999. "Philosophical Analysis and the Moral Concept of Racism." *Philosophy & Social Criticism* 25 (5): 1–32. https://doi.org/10.1177/0191453799025005001.

García Márquez, Gabriel. 2003. *One Hundred Years of Solitude*. Translated by Gregory. Rabassa. 1st HarperCollins ed. New York: HarperCollins. http://hdl.library.upenn.edu/1017.12/498375.

Gardner, Howard. 2006. *Changing Minds the Art and Science of Changing Our Own and Other People's Minds*. Boston: Harvard Business School Press.

Garvey, Marianne. 2019. "Shane Gillis' 'SNL' Firing for Racist Remarks Splits the Comedy Community." *CNN*, September 17. www.cnn.com/2019/09/17/entertainment/shane-gillis-reaction/index.html.

Gilmore, Ruth Wilson. 2002. "Fatal Couplings of Power and Difference: Notes on Racism and Geography." *The Professional Geographer* 54 (1): 15–24. https://doi.org/10.1111/0033-0124.00310.

———. 2007. *Golden Gulag: Prisons, Surplus, Crisis, and Opposition in Globalizing California*. Berkeley: University of California Press. http://catdir.loc.gov/catdir/enhancements/fy0642/2006011674-t.html.

Giovanni, Nikki, and James Baldwin. 2019. "James Baldwin & Nikki Giovanni—Soul! A Conversation (1971)." *YouTube*, February 8. www.youtube.com/watch?v=4Jc54RvDUZU.

Glissant, Édouard. 1997. *Poetics of Relation*. Ann Arbor: The University of Michigan Press.

Gordon, Jane Anna. 2014. *Creolizing Political Theory: Reading Rousseau through Fanon*. 1st ed. New York: Fordham University Press.

Gordon, Lewis R. 2006. *Disciplinary Decadence: Living Thought in Trying Times*. Radical Imagination Series. Boulder, CO: Paradigm.

———. 2013. "Thoughts on Dussel's 'Anti-Cartesian Meditations.'" *Human Architecture* 11 (1): 67–71.

———. 2021. *Freedom, Justice, and Decolonization*. New York: Routledge.

Gourgouris, Stathis. 1996. *Dream Nation: Enlightenment, Colonization, and the Institution of Modern Greece*. Stanford, CA: Stanford University Press. http://catdir.loc.gov/catdir/toc/cam026/95050865.html.

Gracia, Jorge J. E. 2000. *Hispanic/Latino Identity: A Philosophical Perspective*. Malden, MA: Blackwell.

Green, Rayna. 1975. "The Pocahontas Perplex: The Image of Indian Women in American Culture." *The Massachusetts Review* 16 (4): 698–714.

Gualtieri, Sarah M. A. 2009. *Between Arab and White: Race and Ethnicity in the Early Syrian American Diaspora*. American Crossroads 26. Berkeley: University of California Press.

Hadjipavlou, Maria. 2010. *Women and Change in Cyprus*. London: Tauris Academic Studies.

Hagen, Lisa. 2021. "'Sex Addiction' Cited as Spurring Spa Shooting, But Most Killed Were Of Asian Descent." *NPR*, March 17. www.npr.org/2021/03/17/978288270/shooter-claimed-sex-addiction-as-his-reason-but-most-victims-were-of-asian-desce.

Hall, Stuart. 2021. *Selected Writings on Race and Difference*. Edited by Paul Gilroy and Ruth Wilson Gilmore. Durham, NC: Duke University Press.

Haney López, Ian. 2006. *White by Law: The Legal Construction of Race*. 10th anniversary ed. New York: University Press.

Hannaford, Ivan. 1996. *Race: The History of an Idea in the West*. Washington, DC: Woodrow Wilson Center Press. http://catdir.loc.gov/catdir/bios/jhu051/96004162.html.

Harfouch, John. 2017. "The Arab That Cannot Be Killed." *Radical Philosophy Review* 20 (2): 219–41. https://doi.org/10.5840/radphilrev201712067.

———. 2018. *Another Mind-Body Problem: A History of Racial Non-Being*. Albany: State University of New York Press.

———. 2021. "Anti-Colonial Middle Eastern and North African Thought: A Philosopher's Introduction." *Radical Philosophy Review*, June. https://doi.org/10.5840/radphilrev202163117.

Helm, Bennett. 2013. "Trust as a Reactive Attitude." In *Oxford Studies in Agency and Responsibility*, edited by David Shoemaker and Neal A. Tognazzini, 187–215. Oxford: Oxford University Press.

Hill Collins, Patricia. 2018. "Pauli Murray's Journey toward Social Justice." *Ethnic and Racial Studies* 41 (8): 1453–67. https://doi.org/10.1080/01419870.2018.1445270.

Hobbes, Thomas. 2016. *Leviathan*. 2nd ed. Cambridge: Cambridge University Press.

Horkheimer, Max, and Theodor W. Adorno. 1992. *Dialectic of Enlightenment*. Edited by John Cumming. Stanford, CA: Stanford University Press.

Hyde, Lewis. 2007. *The Gift: Creativity and the Artist in the Modern World*. 25th anniversary ed. New York: Vintage Books.

Iğsız, Aslı. 2018. *Humanism in Ruins: Entangled Legacies of the Greek-Turkish Population Exchange*. Stanford, CA: Stanford University Press.

Ihrig, Stefan. 2016. *Justifying Genocide: Germany and the Armenians from Bismarck to Hitler*. Cambridge: Harvard University Press.

"In Re Najour, 174 F. 735 (1909) | Caselaw Access Project." 1909. https://cite.case.law/f/174/735.

Itzkoff, Dave. 2019. "Shane Gillis Dropped from 'S.N.L.' Cast Amid Criticism of Racist Slurs." *New York Times*, September 16. www.nytimes.com/2019/09/16/arts/television/shane-gillis-snl.html.

Jamal, Amaney A., and Nadine Christine Naber. 2008. *Race and Arab Americans before and after 9/11: From Invisible Citizens to Visible Subjects*. 1st ed. Syracuse, NY: Syracuse University Press. http://catdir.loc.gov/catdir/toc/fy0803/2007039522.html.

James, George G. M. 2017. *Stolen Legacy: The Egyptian Origins of Western Philosophy*. Reprint edition. [Place of publication not identified]: Allegro Editions.

James, William. 1981. *The Principles of Psychology*. Edited by Frederick Burkhardt, Fredson Bowers, and Ignas K. Skrupskelis. Cambridge: Harvard University Press. http://babel.hathitrust.org/cgi/pt?id=mdp.39015025117477.

Kanafānī, Ghassān. 1999. *Men in the Sun & Other Palestinian Stories*. Translated by Hilary Kilpatrick. Boulder, CO: Lynne Rienner.

Kant, Immanuel. 1970. *Kant's Political Writings*. Edited by Hans Reiss. Cambridge Studies in the History and Theory of Politics. Cambridge: Cambridge University Press. https://bac-lac.on.worldcat.org/oclc/1032906857.

Karatani, Kōjin. 2017. *Isonomia and the Origins of Philosophy*. Durham, NC: Duke University Press.

Khader, Serene J. 2019. *Decolonizing Universalism: A Transnational Feminist Ethic*. New York: Oxford University Press.

Khatibi, Abdelkebir. 2019. *Plural Maghreb: Writings on Postcolonialism*. London; New York: Bloomsbury Academic.

Kim, David Haekwon, and Ronald R. Sundstrom. 2014. "Xenophobia and Racism." *Critical Philosophy of Race* 2 (1): 20–45.

Knapp, Michael, Anja Flach, and Ercan Ayboga. 2016. *Revolution in Rojava: Democratic Autonomy and Women's Liberation in Syrian Kurdistan*. Translated by Janet Biehl. London: Pluto Press.

Koppes, Clayton R. 1976. "Captain Mahan, General Gordon, and the Origins of the Term 'Middle East.'" *Middle Eastern Studies* 12 (1): 95–98. https://doi.org/10.1080/00263207608700307.

Koundoura, Maria. 2007. *The Greek Idea: The Formation of National and Transnational Identities*. London: Tauris Academic Studies.

Landress, Ilene S., Brad Grey, and David Chase. 2000. *The Sopranos. The Complete First Season*. New York: HBO Video.

Lear, Jonathan. 2006. *Radical Hope: Ethics in the Face of Cultural Devastation*. Cambridge: Harvard University Press.

Lederach, John Paul. 1997. *Building Peace: Sustainable Reconciliation in Divided Societies*. Washington, DC: U.S. Institute of Peace Press.

Lewis, Bernard. 1982. "The Question of Orientalism." *The New York Review*, June. www.nybooks.com/articles/1982/06/24/the-question-of-orientalism.

Li, Darryl. 2020. *The Universal Enemy: Jihad, Empire, and the Challenge of Solidarity*. Stanford, CA: Stanford University Press.

Lindner, Fabian. 2012. "Europe Is in Dire Need of Lazy Spendthrifts." *The Guardian*, February 18. www.guardian.co.uk/commentisfree/2012/feb/18/europe-lazy-spendthrifts-germany.

Linly, Zack. 2021. "Mississippi Gov. Tate Reeves Says 'There Is Not Systemic Racism in America.'" *The Root*. www.theroot.com/mississippi-gov-tate-reeves-says-there-is-not-systemic-1846804247.

Lockman, Zachary. 2010. *Contending Visions of the Middle East: The History and Politics of Orientalism*. 2nd ed. Cambridge, UK; New York: Cambridge University Press.

———. 2016. *Field Notes: The Making of Middle East Studies in the United States*. Stanford, CA: Stanford University Press.

Lorde, Audre. 1984. *Sister Outsider: Essays and Speeches*. Trumansburg, NY: Crossing Press.

Love, Erik. 2017. *Islamophobia and Racism in America*. New York: New York University Press. https://search.ebscohost.com/login.aspx?direct=true&scope=site&db=nlebk&db=nlabk&AN=1367251.

Mack, Mehammed Amadeus. 2017. *Sexagon: Muslims, France, and the Sexualization of National Culture.* New York: Fordham University Press.

Maghbouleh, Neda. 2012. "'Shahs of Sunset': The Real Iranians of Los Angeles?" *Salon*, December 1. www.salon.com/2012/12/01/shahs_of_sunset_the_real_iranians _of_los_angeles.

———. 2017. *The Limits of Whiteness: Iranian Americans and the Everyday Politics of Race.* Stanford, CA: Stanford University Press.

Mairs, Rachel. 2014. *The Hellenistic Far East: Archaeology, Language, and Identity in Greek Central Asia.* Oakland: University of California Press.

Mamdani, Mahmood. 2004. *Good Muslim, Bad Muslim: America, the Cold War, and the Roots of Terror.* 1st ed. New York: Pantheon Books.

———. 2012. *Define and Rule: Native as Political Identity.* 1st ed. Cambridge: Harvard University Press.

Mariscal, George. 1998. "The Role of Spain in Contemporary Race Theory." *Arizona Journal of Hispanic Cultural Studies* 2 (1): 7–22. https://doi.org/10.1353/hcs.2011.0018.

Marx, Karl. 1990. *Capital: A Critique of Political Economy.* London; New York: Penguin Books, in association with New Left Review.

Marx, Karl, and Friedrich Engels. 2013. *The Marx-Engels Reader.* Edited by Robert C. Tucker. New York: Princeton.

Maturana, Humberto R., and Francisco J. Varela. 1980. *Autopoiesis and Cognition: The Realization of the Living.* Dordrecht, Holland: D. Reidel. http://catdir.loc.gov/catdir/enhancements/fy0814/79024724-t.html.

———. 2008. *The Tree of Knowledge: The Biological Roots of Human Understanding.* Rev. ed. Boston: Shambhala.

Mauss, Marcel. 2002. *The Gift: The Form and Reason for Exchange in Archaic Societies.* London: Routledge.

McClintock, Anne. 1995. *Imperial Leather: Race, Gender, and Sexuality in the Colonial Contest.* New York: Routledge.

Medina, José. 2011. "Toward a Foucaultian Epistemology of Resistance: Counter-Memory, Epistemic Friction, and Guerrilla Pluralism." *Foucault Studies*, 9–35. https://doi.org/10.22439/fs.v0i12.3335.

———. 2013. *The Epistemology of Resistance: Gender and Racial Oppression, Epistemic Injustice, and Resistant Imaginations.* Oxford: Oxford University Press. www.oxfordscholarship.com/view/10.1093/acprof:oso/9780199929023.001.0001/acprof-9780199929023.

Melissaropoulou, Dimitra. 2016. "Variation in Word Formation in Situations of Language Contact: The Case of Cappadocian Greek." *Language Sciences* 55: 55–67. https://doi.org/10.1016/j.langsci.2016.02.005.

Mendoza, José Jorge. 2017. "Philosophy of Race and the Ethics of Immigration." In *The Routledge Companion to Philosophy of Race*, edited by Linda Martín Alcoff, Paul C. Taylor, and Luvell Anderson, 507–19. New York: Routledge.

Michaels, Walter Benn. 1995. *Our America: Nativism, Modernism, and Pluralism.* Durham, NC: Duke University Press. https://doi.org/10.1215/9780822397434.

Midgley, Mary. 2011. *The Myths We Live By.* London: Routledge.

Mignolo, Walter. 2000. *Local Histories/Global Designs: Coloniality, Subaltern Knowledges, and Border Thinking*. Princeton, NJ: Princeton University Press. http://catdir.loc.gov/catdir/toc/prin032/99032342.html.

Mikhail, Alan. 2020. *God's Shadow: Sultan Selim, His Ottoman Empire, and the Making of the Modern World*. Illustrated ed. New York: Liveright.

Mill, John Stuart. 2015. *On Liberty*. Peterborough, Ontario: Broadview Press.

Miller, Hayley. 2021. "Lindsey Graham Says There's 'No' Systemic Racism in U.S., Citing Kamala Harris as VP." *HuffPost*, April 25. www.huffpost.com/entry/lindsey-graham-no-systemic-racism_n_60856dece4b003896e052dc6.

Mills, Charles W. 1997. *The Racial Contract*. Ithaca, NY: Cornell University Press.

———. 2003a. *From Class to Race: Essays in White Marxism and Black Radicalism*. Lanham, MD: Rowman & Littlefield.

———. 2003b. "'Heart' Attack: A Critique of Jorge Garcia's Volitional Conception of Racism." *The Journal of Ethics* 7 (1): 29–62.

Minh, Ho Chi. 1945. "Declaration of Independence." *Embassy of the Socialist Republic of Vietnam in the United States*. http://vietnamembassyusa.org/vietnam/politics/declaration-of-independence.

Molos, Vasilis. 2019. "New Horizons of Political Possibility: Greek Political Imagination after the Russo-Ottoman War of 1768–1774." In *European Revolutions and the Ottoman Balkans*, 37–64. London: Bloomsbury; I. B. Tauris.

Monahan, Michael J. 2021. "Racism and 'Self-Love': The Case of White Nationalism." *Critical Philosophy of Race* 9 (1): 1–15. https://doi.org/10.5325/CRITPHIL RACE.9.1.0001.

Moraña, Mabel, Enrique D. Dussel, and Carlos A. Jáuregui. 2008. *Coloniality at Large: Latin America and the Postcolonial Debate*. Durham, NC: Duke University Press.

Murakawa, Naomi. 2014. *The First Civil Right: How Liberals Built Prison America*. Oxford; New York: Oxford University Press.

Naber, Nadine Suleiman. 2014. "Imperial Whiteness and the Diasporas of Empire." *American Quarterly* 66 (4): 1107–15. https://doi.org/10.1353/aq.2014.0068.

Nagourney, Adam. 2008. "Obama Elected President as Racial Barrier Falls." *New York Times*, November 5. www.nytimes.com/2008/11/05/us/politics/05elect.html.

Nagy, R. L. 2013. "The Scope and Bounds of Transitional Justice and the Canadian Truth and Reconciliation Commission." *The International Journal of Transitional Justice* 7 (1): 52–73. https://doi.org/10.1093/ijtj/ijs034.

New Arab Staff. 2021. "Pro-Palestine Italian Port Workers Refuse Arms Shipment to Israel." *The New Arab*, May 15. http://english.alaraby.co.uk/news/propalestine-italian-port-workers-refuse-arms-shipment-israel.

NPR. 2019. "Comedian Shane Gillis Fired from 'Saturday Night Live' for Racist Remarks." *NPR*, September 16. www.npr.org/2019/09/16/761367838/comedian-shane-gillis-fired-from-saturday-night-live-for-racist-remarks.

Öcalan, Abdullah. 2007. *Prison Writings: The Roots of Civilization*. Translated by Klaus Happel. London: Transmedia Publications.

———. 2011. *Democratic Confederalism*. 2nd ed. Neuss, Germany: Mezopotamien-Verl. https://d-nb.info/1019002808/04.

———. 2015. *Jenseits von Staat, Macht und Gewalt*. Translated by Reimar Heider. Neuss, Germany: Mezopotamien Verlags GmbH.

———. 2017. *The Political Thought of Abdullah Öcalan: Kurdistan, Women's Revolution and Democratic Confederalism*. International Initiative ed. Translated by Havin Güneşer. London: Pluto Press. www.tcd.ie/library/using-library/eLD/#PDA.

Omi, Michael, and Howard Winant. 2015. *Racial Formation in the United States*. 3rd ed. New York: Routledge/Taylor & Francis Group.

"Omnes." n.d. Omnes.Gr. Accessed November 9, 2021. https://www.omnes.gr/en.

Ozawa v. United States. 1922, 260 US 178. Supreme Court.

"Palestinian Resistance & Sheikh Jarrah, The." 2021. *Groundings*, May 17. https://groundings.simplecast.com/episodes/sheikh-jarrah.

Panourgiá, Neni. 2009. *Dangerous Citizens: The Greek Left and the Terror of the State*. 1st ed. New York: Fordham University Press.

Park, Peter K. J. 2014. *Africa, Asia, and the History of Philosophy: Racism in the Formation of the Philosophical Canon, 1780–1830*. Syracuse: State University of New York Press.

Parker, Robert. 2017. *Greek Gods Abroad: Names, Natures, and Transformations*. Oakland: University of California Press. http://media.library.ku.edu.tr/BookCover Images/greek_gods_abroad.jpg.

Pateman, Carole, and Charles W. Mills. 2007. *Contract and Domination*. Cambridge: Polity.

Patterson, Orlando. 1985. *Slavery and Social Death: A Comparative Study*. Cambridge: Harvard University Press.

Polychroniou, C. J. 2021. "Noam Chomsky: Biden's Foreign Policy Is Largely Indistinguishable from Trump's." *Truthout*, March. https://truthout.org/articles/noam-chomsky-bidens-foreign-policy-is-largely-indistinguishable-from-trumps.

"President Trump Participates in Bilateral Meeting with Israeli Prime Minister Benjamin Netanyahu—Video and Transcript." 2020. *The Last Refuge* (blog), September 15. https://theconservativetreehouse.com/2020/09/15/president-trump-participates-in-bilateral-meeting-with-israeli-prime-minister-benjamin-netan yahu-video-and-transcript.

Quijano, Aníbal. 2007. "Coloniality and Modernity/Rationality." *Cultural Studies* 21 (2–3): 168–78. https://doi.org/10.1080/09502380601164353.

Rabaka, Reiland. 2010. *Against Epistemic Apartheid: W.E.B. Du Bois and the Disciplinary Decadence of Sociology*. Lanham, MD: Lexington Books.

"Racial Barrier Falls in Decisive Victory." 2008. *New York Times*, November 5.

Rivera Berruz, Stephanie. 2014. "The Quest for Recognition: The Case of Latin American Philosophy." *Comparative Philosophy* 10 (2). http://search.proquest .com/pqdtlocal1007354/docview/1627780797/abstract/ADD679290D9249B9PQ/ 1?accountid=14169.

Rosanvallon, Pierre. 2008. *Counter-Democracy: Politics in an Age of Distrust*. Cambridge, UK; New York: Cambridge University Press.

Ross, Loretta. 2019. "I'm a Black Feminist. I Think Call-Out Culture Is Toxic." *New York Times*, August 17. www.nytimes.com/2019/08/17/opinion/sunday/cancel-culture-call-out.html.

Rousseau, Jean-Jacques. 2002. *The Social Contract and the First and Second Discourses*. New Haven, CT: Yale University Press.

Rueb, Emily S., and Derrick Bryson Taylor. 2019. "Obama on Call-Out Culture: 'That's Not Activism.'" *New York Times*, October 31. www.nytimes.com/2019/10/31/us/politics/obama-woke-cancel-culture.html.

Said, Edward W. 1993. *Culture and Imperialism*. 1st ed. New York: Knopf. www.gbv.de/dms/bowker/toc/9780394587387.pdf.

———. 1994. *Orientalism*. 25th anniversary ed. New York: Vintage Books.

———. 2000. *The Edward Said Reader*. Edited by Moustafa Bayoumi and Andrew Rubin. New York: Vintage Books. http://catdir.loc.gov/catdir/bios/random052/00034947.html.

———. 2019. *The Selected Works of Edward Said, 1966–2006*. Edited by Moustafa Bayoumi and Andrew N. Rubin. 2nd Vintage Books ed. New York: Vintage Books.

Samhan, Helen. 1999. "Not Quite White: Race Classification and the Arab-American Experience." In *Arabs in America: Building a New Future*, edited by Michael W. Suleiman, 209–26. Philadelphia: Temple University Press.

Sayegh, Fayez A. 1958. *Arab Unity: Hope and Fulfillment*. New York: Devin-Adair Company.

Sheth, Falguni A. 2009. *Toward a Political Philosophy of Race*. Albany, NY: SUNY Press.

Sidanius, Jim, and Felicia Pratto. 1999. *Social Dominance: An Intergroup Theory of Social Hierarchy and Oppression*. Cambridge: Cambridge University Press. http://catdir.loc.gov/catdir/samples/cam032/98044356.html.

Silva, Grant J. 2018. "'The Americas Seek Not Enlightenment but Liberation': On the Philosophical Significance of Liberation for Philosophy in the Americas." *Pluralist* 13 (2): 1–21. https://doi.org/10.5406/pluralist.13.2.0001.

———. 2019. "Racism as Self-Love." *Radical Philosophy Review* 22 (1): 85–112. https://doi.org/10.5840/radphilrev201913193.

———. 2021. "On 'Ur-Contempt' and the Maintenance of Racial Injustice: A Response to Monahan's 'Racism and "Self-Love": The Case of White Nationalism.'" *Critical Philosophy of Race* 9 (1): 16–26.

Sorel, Georges. 2008. *Reflections on Violence*. Edited by Jeremy Jennings. Cambridge: Cambridge University Press.

Spencer, Quayshawn. 2016. "Do Humans Have Continental Populations?" *Philosophy of Science* 83 (5): 791–802.

———. 2018a. "Racial Realism I: Are Biological Races Real?" *Philosophy Compass* 13 (1). https://doi.org/10.1111/phc3.12468.

———. 2018b. "Racial Realism II: Are Folk Races Real?" *Philosophy Compass* 13 (1). https://doi.org/10.1111/phc3.12467.

Spivak, Gayatri Chakravorty. 2010. *Can the Subaltern Speak? Reflections on the History of an Idea*. Edited by Rosalind C. Morris. New York: Columbia University Press.

Srinivasan, Amia. 2018. "The Aptness of Anger." *Journal of Political Philosophy* 26 (2): 123–44. https://doi.org/10.1111/jopp.12130.

Steiner, George. 1998. *After Babel: Aspects of Language and Translation*. 3rd ed. Oxford: Oxford University Press.

Stoiciu, Victoria. 2012. "Lazy Greeks, a Neo-Liberal Cliché." *VoxEurop*, February 13. https://voxeurop.eu/en/lazy-greeks-a-neo-liberal-cliche.

Stumpf, Benjamin. 2020. "The Whiteness of Watching: Surveillant Citizenship and the Carceral State." *Radical Philosophy Review* 23 (1): 117–36. https://doi.org/10.5840/radphilrev2020225105.

Sullivan, Shannon. 2015. *The Physiology of Sexist and Racist Oppression*. Oxford: Oxford University Press. www.gbv.de/dms/bowker/toc/9780190250614.pdf.

Sundstrom, Ronald R. 2008. *The Browning of America and the Evasion of Social Justice*. Albany, NY: SUNY Press.

———. 2013. "Sheltering Xenophobia." *Critical Philosophy of Race* 1 (1): 68–85. https://doi.org/10.5325/critphilrace.1.1.0068.

Taylor, Keeanga-Yamahtta. 2016. *From #BlackLivesMatter to Black Liberation*. Chicago, IL: Haymarket Books.

———. 2017. *How We Get Free: Black Feminism and the Combahee River Collective*. Chicago, IL: Haymarket Books.

Taylor, Paul Christopher. 2004. *Race: A Philosophical Introduction*. Cambridge, UK; Malden, MA: Polity Press.

Tehranian, John. 2009. *Whitewashed: America's Invisible Middle Eastern Minority*. New York: University Press.

Thornhill, Teresa. 2018. *Hara Hotel: A Tale of Syrian Refugees in Greece*. London: Verso.

Thucydides. 1954. *History of the Peloponnesian War*. Melbourne, Australia; Baltimore, MD: Penguin Books.

Tijoux, Ana. 2014. *Vengo*. [Place of publication not identified]: Nacional Records.

Tolan, Sandy. 2007. *The Lemon Tree: An Arab, a Jew, and the Heart of the Middle East*. 1st paperback ed. New York: Bloomsbury.

Tsing, Anna Lowenhaupt. 2015. *The Mushroom at the End of the World: On the Possibility of Life in Capitalist Ruins*. Princeton, NJ: Princeton University Press.

United States v. Thind. 1923, 261 US 204. Supreme Court.

Urquidez, Alberto G. 2017. "Jorge Garcia and the Ordinary Use of 'Racist Belief.'" *Social Theory and Practice* 43 (2): 223–48.

Üstündağ, Nazan. 2016. "Self-Defense as a Revolutionary Practice in Rojava, or How to Unmake the State." *South Atlantic Quarterly* 115 (1): 197–210. https://doi.org/10.1215/00382876-3425024.

Valandra, Edward Charles, and Robert Yazzie. 2020. *Colorizing Restorative Justice: Voicing Our Realities*. 1st ed. St. Paul, MN: Living Justice Press.

Varela, Francisco J. 1999. *Ethical Know-How: Action, Wisdom, and Cognition*. Stanford, CA: Stanford University Press.

Wagner, Meg, Melissa Macaya, and Mike Hayes. 2021. "March 17 Atlanta Spa Shootings News." *CNN*, March 17. www.cnn.com/us/live-news/atlanta-area-shootings-03-17-21/index.html.

Weber, Max, and Talcott Parsons. 2014. *The Protestant Ethic and the Spirit of Capitalism*. Angelico Press reprint ed. Kettering, OH: Angelico Press.

Wittgenstein, Ludwig. 1975. *On Certainty*. Oxford: Blackwell.
Wynter, Sylvia. 2003. "Unsettling the Coloniality of Being/Power/Truth/Freedom: Towards the Human, After Man, Its Overrepresentation—an Argument." *CR* (East Lansing, MI) 3 (3): 257–337. https://doi.org/10.1353/ncr.2004.0015.
X, Malcolm. 2020. *The End of White World Supremacy: Four Speeches*. Edited by Benjamin Karim. 1st Arcade ed. New York: Arcade Publishing. www.sky horsesupplements.com/malcolmx.
Yancy, George. 2018. *Backlash: What Happens When We Talk Honestly about Racism in America*. Lanham, MD: Rowman & Littlefield.
Youth Power. 2012. *One StreetS Festival 2011*. www.youtube.com/watch?v=hJxrFBeXJBY.
Zack, Naomi. 2002. *Philosophy of Science and Race*. New York: Routledge.
———. 2015. *White Privilege and Black Rights: The Injustice of U.S. Police Racial Profiling and Homicide*. Lanham, MD: Rowman & Littlefield.
Zehr, Howard. 2005. *Changing Lenses: A New Focus for Crime and Justice*. 3rd ed. Scottdale, PA: Herald Press. http://search.ebscohost.com/login.aspx?authtype=ip,s hib&custid=s1123049&direct=true&defaultdb=nlebk&AN=28157.
Zhou, Li. 2019. "Andrew Yang's Use of Asian Stereotypes Is Reinforcing Toxic Tropes." *Vox*, September 17. www.vox.com/policy-and-politics/2019/9/17/20864861/andrew-yang-debate-asian-stereotype-model-minority-myth.
Zinn, Howard. 2018. *You Can't Be Neutral on a Moving Train: A Personal History*. Boston: Beacon Press.

Index

activism, 40, 55–56
Africa, 64, 67–68. *See also* Middle East and North African people
Alexander, Michelle, 44–45
Allen, Danielle S., 6
Améry, Jean, 152n57
Anastasiou, Harry, 117, 119
Anderson, Carol, 143n29
Anderson, Luvell, 42
anti-colonialism. *See* colonialism; decolonization
anti-racist posturing: colonialism and, 13; praxis compared to, 35–40, 50; systemic posturing, 40–46
Antonius, George, 71
Anzaldúa, Gloria, 74, 133
appreciation, 89–92, 102–7
appropriation, 102–7
Arabs: for Greece, 82–83; Islam for, 30; Jews and, 132; MENA people compared to, 148n5; philosophy of, 147n41; terrorism for, 29; in United States, 20; for Western culture, 2–3; for white supremacists, 63–64
The Archaeology of Knowledge (Foucalt), 137n1
Are Prisons Obsolete? (Davis), 43
Armenians, 69–70, 82–83, 135n9, 136n10

Asians, 11, 61–62
Assad family, 121–22
Atatürk, Kemal, 64–65
Austin, J. L., 137n1
Austria, 81
autonomy, 16–17

Babel, 94–95, 108–13, 124, 151n46
Backlash (Yancy), 151n42
Baer, Hannah, 49
Baldwin, James, 33
Bargu, Banu, 83
BDS. *See* Boycott, Divest, and Sanction
Benjamin, Walter, 16, 96, 112
Bernal, Martin, 75, 88
Biden, Joe, 131
Bin Laden, Osama, 29
Black Athena (Bernal), 75, 88
Black Lives Matter movement, 139n16
Black men, 11
Blackness, 56, 73–74
Black Skin, White Masks (Fanon), 141n58
Bookchin, Murray, 122
Boycott, Divest, and Sanction (BDS), 1
Braithwaite, John, 45–46
Buber, Martin, 2, 33, 39, 74, 106, 150n14

call-out culture, 40, 46–47, 143n28
capitalism, 7, 100, 136n18, 142n3
Carastathis, Anna, 78, 83–84
Catholic Church, 23–24, 62, 140n27
Caucasians, 27. *See also* whiteness
Césaire, Aimé, 92, 104, 106
Chapelle, Dave, 22–23
Chiang, Ted, 109–10
citizenship, 25, 27–29
civic-national identity, 66
civilization, 92
Clinton, Bill, 44
Clinton, Hillary, 44–45, 46–47
coded language, 45
Cold War, 83
colonialism: anti-racist posturing and, 13; boundaries in, 151n31; for Catholic Church, 23–24; colonial relations, 105–6; for Europe, 91; in fiction, 103–7; in globalization, 90; for Greece, 75–77; Hellenism before, 147n41; history of, 31–32, 71; for identity, 69; liberal-colonialism, 37–38, 52; mediation in, 132; for MENA people, 7, 15, 56–58, 112; in modernity, 91–92; objectification in, 32–33; Orientalist-racism from, 59; post-racial anxieties after, 19–21; power of, 6, 10–11, 37–38, 58, 96; racialization for, 24–25; racism and, 47–48; reciprocity for, 148n47; for Said, 77–80, 86; self-preservation in, 15–16; solidarity against, 7–8, 17, 131–33; for Spain, 25; for United States, 137n3; violence in, 16; for Western culture, 4, 60–61. *See also* imperialism
compassion, 49–50
conflict, 8–9, 23–28, 38–39, 70, 127, 139n10
Constantine, David, 78–79
cooperative-determination, 2, 5, 9, 17, 58, 92, 132–33
cosmopolitanism, 133

counter-historical narratives, 95
Crenshaw, Kimberlé, 10–11, 74
creolization, 10, 137n30, 145n3
Crow nation, 111
Culture and Imperialism (Said), 88–89
Curle, Adam, 116
Curry, Tommy J., 11, 74
Cyprus, 16–17, 94, 101, 115–21, 128–30

DAA. *See* Democratic Autonomous Administration
Dangerous Citizens (Panourgiá), 83
Davis, Angela, 43
"Dear White America" (Yancy), 151n42
decolonization: for Fanon, 93; for Hellenism, 75–77; philosophy of, 89–92; for Said, 84–89; violence of, 8, 81–84; for Western culture, 73–75
Democratic Autonomous Administration (DAA), 126
Denktash, Rauf, 117
Dianotto, Roberto M., 73
diaspora groups, 81, 94, 115
Discourse on the Origins of Inequality (Rousseau), 112–13
discrimination, 10
domination, 5
Du Bois, W. E. B., 96
Dussel, Enrique, 24, 52–53, 74–76, 96, 108

East/West divide, 14, 63–64, 75–77, 79–84, 89, 93–95
education, 36, 48–49, 127–28
Egypt, 146n7
enaction, enactivism, 68, 70, 100, 130, 131, 133; meaning-making, 5, 8–9, 13, 36, 50, 66, 97–99, 107, 111, 115, 122, 136n25, 150n25. *See also* reconciliation
the Enlightenment, 75, 85
ethnicity, 144n10
ethno-national identity, 59–61

ethos formation, 116–21
EU. *See* European Union
Europe: Africa and, 67–68; colonialism for, 91; Egypt for, 146n7; the Enlightenment for, 85; Germany for, 80; Greece and, 77–78, 81–83, 121; Hellenism for, 77; Middle East and, 2–3; modernity for, 84; religion in, 110; United States and, 15, 23–24. *See also* Western culture
European Union (EU), 82–84, 118, 121
Evans, Robert, 124, 153n26
exemplarity, 100–102, 128–30

face-to-face encounters, 35–36
Fanon, Frantz, 93, 141n58
fascism, 100
feminism, 124–25, 153n26
Ferguson, Ann, 99–100
Feuerbach, Ludwig, 70, 110–11
fiction, 100–107, 151n46
Fields, Barbara, 23
Filiki Eteria, 81
First Nations, 23, 25, 52–53, 111
Floyd, George, 38–39
foreign policy, 51
Foucault, Michel, 47, 95, 97–100, 102–3, 129, 137n1, 149n7
France, 5
Frankl, Viktor, 111
Frankowski, Alfred, 139n16

Gardner, Howard, 116
gaslighting, 58
GCs. *See* Greek Cypriots
gender politics, 16
genocide, 2
Germany, 80
Gillis, Shane, 41–43, 45
Glissant, Édouard, 93, 96
globalization, 20, 23–28, 70–71, 74, 90
Gordon, Jane, 145n3
Gordon, Lewis, 92
Gourgouris, Stathis, 77

Gracia, Jorge J. E., 139n9
grassroots reconciliation, 120–21
Greece: Arabs for, 82–83; colonialism for, 75–77; for EU, 82–84; Europe and, 77–78, 81–83, 121; identity for, 86–87; nationalism for, 84; philosophy from, 87–88; Turkey and, 65, 75–77, 81, 117, 152n62; for Western culture, 88–89. *See also* Hellenism
Greek Cypriots (GCs), 116–21
Green, Rayna, 137n3
Gualtieri, Sarah M. A., 26–27
guerrilla pluralism, 98–99

habituated experience, 8–9
Hadjipavlou, Maria, 120–21
Haney López, Ian, 25–26, 140n37
Harfouch, John, 1, 75–76, 137n29
Hegel, Georg Wilhelm Friedrich, 146n14
Hellenism: before colonialism, 147n41; decolonization for, 75–77; history of, 85–86, 88–89, 147n43; identity, 72; Orientalist-racism and, 77–80, 83–84; reciprocal, 84–89; in United States, 147n29; for Western culture, 78–80, 87
history: for Améry, 152n57; of colonialism, 31–32, 71; of conflict, 139n10; counter-historical narratives, 95; of Cyprus, 116–21; of ethno-national identity, 60–61; exemplarity in, 100–102; of Hellenism, 85–86, 88–89, 147n43; of hierarchies, 136n28; historical lens, 101–2; of identity, 94; language for, 80; of liberalism, 111–12; of MENA people, 128–30, 144n10; myth as, 93–95, 151n46; of Orientalist-racism, 19–20, 68, 75–77, 85–87; of Ottoman empire, 25–26, 79; of racialization, 137n29; religion and, 109–10; of resistance, 16; for Said,

73, 90; of solidarity, 15; of Turkey, 64–65
History of the Peloponnesian War (Thucydides), 86
Hitler, Adolf, 135n9
Hobbes, Thomas, 101
Hobsbawm, Eric, 88
hope, 111–13
How to Do Things with Words (Austin), 137n1
humanity, 9–10
human rights, 28

I and Thou (Buber), 106, 150n14
identity: civic-national, 66; colonialism for, 69; ethno-national, 59–61; for Greece, 86–87; Hellenism, 72; history of, 94; for MENA people, 67–72; in Middle East, 128, 139n9; nationalism for, 58, 117; in Ottoman empire, 64–65; politics, 150n11; racial, 63; racialization for, 56
ideology, 40–41, 83, 92, 98–99, 107–8
Ihrig, Stefan, 135n9
imperialism, 20, 88–89
India, 2
Indigenous Americans. *See* First Nations
institutional racism, 38–39
intersectionality, 11
In the Footsteps of the Gods (Constantine), 78
The Invention of Tradition (Hobsbawm and Ranger), 88
Ioannidis, Dimitrios, 83
Iran, 57, 61–63
Ireland, 140n27
ISIS, 31, 124, 126, 147n40
Islam: for Arabs, 30; in France, 5; Islamophobia, 12, 20–21, 28–31, 32; Jihadism for, 8; for MENA people, 32; for non-Muslims, 125–26; stereotypes of, 4; for Western culture, 65, 79–80
isonomia, 89–92

Isonomia and the Origins of Philosophy (Karatani), 90–92, 122
Israel. *See* Palestine

James, William, 67
Jersey Shore (TV show), 64
Jews, 132
Jihadism, 8

Kanafānī, Ghassān, 115
Karatani, Kojin, 90–92, 122
Katherine the Great, 82
Keane, A. H., 27
Khatibi, Abdelkebir, 2–3, 60
Kim, David, 28–29
Knapp, Michael, 127
knowledge, 95–100
Koundoura, Maria, 78
el-Kurd, Mohammed, 2
Kurdistan, 68, 108, 115, 122–23, 126, 153n19. *See also* Rojava
Kurds, 122–27

labor, 108–11, 142n3, 153n19
language, 94–95, 108–13; coded, 45; for history, 80; in nationalism, 86–87, 147n26; power of, 110; of racism, 21–22; religion and, 65
las Casas, Bartolomé de, 23–24, 32, 140n23
Latin America, 60, 68
Lear, Jonathan, 111
Ledarch, John Paul, 116
legitimacy, 93–100
Levinas, Emmanuel, 52–53
Lewis, Bernard, 76–77
Li, Darryl, 8
liberalism: history of, 111–12; liberal-capitalism, 7, 136n18; liberal-colonialism, 37–38, 52; liberal niceties, 40–46; Marx for, 110; for MENA people, 95; racist guilt and, 50–53; radical liberals, 151n37; social politics in, 104–5; in United States, 38–39

liberation, 9, 11–12, 98–99, 108
Ludwig, Otto Friedrich, 83

Mack, Mehammed Amadeus, 5
Maghbouleh, Neda, 29, 57
magical realism, 100–101
male fragility, 49
Malta, 145n15
Mamdani, Mahmood, 20
marginalization, 3, 48–49
Marquez, Enrique, 30–31
Márquez, Gabriel García, 100–107
Marx, Karl, 91, 98, 110–11
Mauss, Marcel, 91
McClintock, Anne, 11
meaning-making. *See* enaction/
  enactivism; reconciliation
media, 40–42, 64
mediation, 70–71, 127–28, 132
Medina, José, 16, 94–95, 97–100, 102–3
men, 11, 49
MENA people. *See* Middle East and
  North African people
MGRK. *See* People's Council of West
  Kurdistan
Middle East: Europe and, 2–3; identity
  in, 128, 139n9; for Iran, 62–63;
  Islamophobia in, 32; Latin America
  and, 60, 68; for MENA people,
  51–52; Ottoman empire for, 3,
  145n19; racialization in, 12, 141n53;
  reification of, 125–26; religion in,
  81; solidarity in, 121–28; stereotypes
  of, 57, 62, 141n54; violence in, 131;
  for Western culture, 67–68. *See also
  specific topics*
Middle East and North African (MENA)
  people: Arabs compared to, 148n5;
  autonomy for, 16–17; BDS for, 1;
  colonialism for, 7, 15, 56–58, 112;
  communities for, 128; as diaspora
  groups, 94, 115; history of, 128–30,
  144n10; identity for, 67–72;
  Islam for, 32; liberalism for, 95;
  marginalization for, 3; Middle East

for, 51–52; nationalism for, 55–56;
  Orientalist-racism for, 1–2, 63; peace
  for, 2–3; POC and, 73; race-nation
  conflation for, 59–67; racialization
  of, 25–26, 137n4, 141n50; racism
  against, 19–21, 28–31, 36–37, 38,
  50–53; reconciliation for, 11–12;
  for Said, 4–5; solidarity for, 13–14,
  71–72, 108; stereotypes of, 41; in
  United States, 17, 23, 50–51, 65–66,
  131–33, 144n2; violence against,
  116; for Western culture, 12, 31–34,
  46; whiteness for, 29–30, 141n51,
  141n58
Midgley, Mary, 101–2
Mill, J. S., 97–98
Mills, Charles, 21, 104–5, 139n10
modernity, 76, 84, 91–92, 139n11
Monahan, Michael J., 41
Murakawa, Naomi, 44
Murray, Pauli, 10
Muslims. *See* Islam
myth: of appreciation, 102–7; as
  history, 93–95, 151n46; hope in,
  111–13; myth/fiction, 100–107;
  of nationalism, 112–13; normative
  ideals in, 107–8; power of, 148n5;
  of Shinar, 106–11, 113; subjugated
  knowledge and, 95–100; of Tower
  of Babylon, 94–95, 108–13, 124,
  151n46; in Western culture, 129

Naber, Nadine, 20
Najour, Costa George, 25–28
nationalism: for Armenians, 69–70;
  civic-national identity, 66; ethno-
  national identity, 59–61; for Greece,
  84; for identity, 58, 117; language in,
  86–87, 147n26; for MENA people,
  55–56; myth of, 112–13; politics of,
  56–58, 67–72; race and, 16; race-
  nation conflation, 59–67; racialized,
  13–14; reification for, 152n62;
  solidarity and, 6; for Turkey, 119; in
  United States, 62

non-Black populations of color, 14, 28
non-Muslims, 125–26, 147n39
normative ideals, 107–8
Northern Ireland, 140n27

Obama, Barack, 21, 40, 139n11
objectification, 32–34, 103–4
Öcalan, Abdullah, 16–17, 68, 94, 108, 115–16, 122–26, 153n19
One Hundred Years of Solitude (García Márquez), 102–7
oppression, 22
optimism, 111–13
Orientalism (Said), 75–77
Orientalist-racism: from colonialism, 59; conflict from, 23–28; Hellenism and, 77–80, 83–84; history of, 19–20, 68, 75–77, 85–87; for MENA people, 1–2, 63; objectification in, 104; in Western culture, 4–5
Ottoman empire, 3; history of, 25–26, 79; identity in, 64–65; for Middle East, 145n19; non-Muslims in, 147n39; power for, 72; racism in, 62; religion in, 84–85, 89, 135n9; for Turkey, 81–82; for Western culture, 83, 140n23
Ozawa, Takao, 27–28

Pakistan, 2
Palestine, 1–3, 61–62, 92
Panourgiá, Neni, 83
Papadopoulos, Giorgos, 83
Park, Peter, 78
partisan racial criminalization, 44–45
Pasha, Mustafa Kemal, 64
patriarchy, 123–24
Patterson, Orlando, 43
peace, 2–3
people of color (POC), 48–49, 73
People's Council of West Kurdistan (MGRK), 126
Persians. *See* Iran
phenotypes, 69–70

philosophy: of Arabs, 147n41; of decolonization, 89–92; of the Enlightenment, 75; ethos formation, 116–21; of Foucault, 98–99; from Greece, 87–88; of Hobbes, 101; of Mill, 97–98; of Said, 75–76
PIC. *See* prison-industrial complex
Plato, 88
POC. *See* people of color
Pocahontas, 137n3
police, 22, 32–34, 139n16, 141n57
politics: of appropriation, 102–7; of call-out culture, 46–47; call-out culture in, 40; of citizenship, 27; of EU, 118; gender, 16; identity, 150n11; labor, 142n3; of legitimacy, 93–100; of liberation, 9, 98–99; of nationalism, 56–58, 67–72; partisan racial criminalization in, 44–45; of patriarchy, 123–24; of race, 136n28; of reconciliation, 8; of religion, 62; social, 93–95, 104–5; of solidarity, 7, 16–17, 129–30; systemic posturing in, 36–37; in Turkey, 126; of violence, 19–20; in Western culture, 25
possibility, 128–30
post-racial anxieties, 19–23
poverty, 96
power: of colonialism, 6, 10–11, 37–38, 58, 96; from discrimination, 10; domination and, 5; of genocide, 2; of language, 110; of myth, 148n5; for Ottoman empire, 72; of police, 32–33; racism and, 12–13; reciprocity for, 1, 90–91; for reconciliation, 9; for Turkey, 3–4, 71–72; of war, 85–86; for Western culture, 14
praxis, 25, 35–40, 43, 46–50, 67
prison-industrial complex (PIC), 43–44
prisons, 43, 153n19
propaganda, 22
Prussia, 82
punishment, 43–46, 49, 149n7

Al Qaeda, 31
Quijano, Aníbal, 4, 39–40

race: citizenship and, 25; ethnicity and, 144n10; for humanity, 9–10; human rights and, 28; liberation and, 11–12; nationalism and, 16; for non-Black populations of color, 14; partisan racial criminalization, 44–45; for POC, 48–49; politics of, 136n28; race-nation conflation, 59–67; racial hierarchies, 31–32; racial identity, 63; racial stereotypes, 41–43; racist guilt, 50–53; religion and, 30; in United States, 25; violence against, 21; whiteness as, 26
racial-capitalism, 142n3
racialization: for colonialism, 24–25; hierarchies from, 10; history of, 137n29; for identity, 56; of MENA people, 25–26, 137n4, 141n50; in Middle East, 12, 141n53; objectification compared to, 33–34; oppression and, 22; racialized nationalism, 13–14; of terrorism, 30–31; in United States, 12; in Western culture, 140n46; of whiteness, 57–58, 62; for white supremacists, 61–62
racism: anti-racist posturing for, 37–38; colonialism and, 47–48; in education, 48–49; globalization for, 23–28; hierarchies for, 55; institutional, 38–39; language of, 21–22; against MENA people, 19–21, 28–31, 36–37, 38, 50–53; in Ottoman empire, 62; for police, 33–34; power and, 12–13; racist praxis, 25; for Said, 24; on social media, 36; stereotypes for, 9–10. *See also* Orientalist-racism
radical liberals, 151n37
Ranger, Terence, 88
reciprocity: for colonialism, 148n47; objectification and, 103; for power, 1, 90–91; reciprocal Hellenism, 84–89; victimization for, 96
reconciliation, 8–9, 11–12, 120–28
reification, 19, 39–40, 125–26, 152n62
religion: in Europe, 110; history and, 109–10; language and, 65; in Middle East, 81; in Ottoman empire, 84–85, 89, 135n9; politics of, 62; race and, 30. *See also specific religions*
the Renaissance, 81
resistance, 16
Rojava, 16–17, 94, 101, 115–16, 121–30
Ross, Loretta, 46–47
Rousseau, Jean-Jacques, 112–13

Said, Edward, 96; colonialism for, 77–80, 86; decolonization for, 84–89; history for, 73, 90; imperialism for, 88–89; Lewis for, 88; MENA people for, 4–5; philosophy of, 75–76; racism for, 24; reification for, 19
Al-Saji, Alia, 30
Sayegh, Fayez A., 94
scholarship, 55–56, 143n28
self-preservation, 15–16
Serbia, 81
el-Shabazz, El Hajj Malik, 41
Shahs of Sunset (TV show), 57
Sheth, Falguni, 24
Shinar, 106–11, 113
Sicily, Italy, 145n15
Silva, Grant, 41
Smith, Barbara, 150n11
Smith, John, 137n3
social conflict, 8–9, 66
social interactions, 37–38
social media, 36
social policing, 143n5
social politics, 93–95, 104–5
social posturing, 35–36, 46–50
Socrates, 87–88
solidarity. *See specific topics*
The Sopranos (TV show), 64

South Africa, 50
Spain, 23, 25
Starve and Immolate (Bargu), 83
stereotypes: of Islam, 4; of Jihadism, 8; for media, 64; of MENA people, 41; of Middle East, 57, 62, 141n54; phenotypes and, 69–70; racial, 41–43; for racism, 9–10; of terrorism, 21; of Turkey, 79–80; in Western culture, 15, 42–43
subjugated knowledge, 95–100
Sundstrom, Ron, 28–29
Sykes-Picot agreement, 115
Syria, 60, 121–22, 124, 126, 127. *See also* Rojava
systemic posturing, 36–37

TCs. *See* Turkish Cypriots
Tehranian, John, 61
terrorism, 21, 29–31, 124, 126, 147n40
Thucydides, 86
Tolan, Sandy, 135n5
Tower of Babylon (myth), 94–95, 108–13, 124, 151n46
"The Tower of Babylon" (Chiang), 109–10
Trump, Donald, 131
Turkey: Armenians for, 82–83; for EU, 121; Greece and, 65, 75–77, 81, 117, 152n62; history of, 64–65; nationalism for, 119; Ottoman empire for, 81–82; politics in, 126; power for, 3–4, 71–72; stereotypes of, 79–80; Syria and, 60
Turkish Cypriots (TCs), 116–21
Tutu, Desmond, 50

United Nations development program (UNDP), 118–20
United States: Arabs in, 20; Armenians in, 136n10; Asians in, 61–62; colonialism for, 137n3; conflict in, 38–39, 127; Europe and, 15, 23–24; Hellenism in, 147n29; for immigrants, 65; Indigenous Americans in, 111; Iranian-Americans, 57; Israel and, 3; liberalism in, 38–39; MENA people in, 17, 23, 50–51, 65–66, 131–33, 144n2; nationalism in, 62; non-Black populations of color in, 28; post-racial anxieties in, 20–23; punishment in, 43–46; race in, 25; racialization in, 12; *United States v. Bhagat Singh Thind*, 27–28; whiteness in, 25–27; white supremacists in, 141n51. *See also* Western culture

Varela, Francisco, 37
victimization, 96
violence: against Armenians, 135n9; in colonialism, 16; of decolonization, 8, 81–84; in foreign policy, 51; gaslighting for, 58; against MENA people, 116; in Middle East, 131; by police, 141n57; politics of, 19–20; praxis and, 67; against race, 21; in social conflict, 66; in Syria, 127; in Western culture, 29; by white supremacists, 67; by Young Turks, 84–85

war, 85–86, 100
Western culture: Africa for, 64; Arabs for, 2–3; colonialism for, 4, 60–61; decolonization for, 73–75; East/West divide for, 14, 63–64, 75–77, 79–84, 89, 93–95; education in, 36; globalization for, 74; Greece for, 88–89; Hellenism for, 78–80, 87; ISIS for, 147n40; Islam for, 65, 79–80; MENA people for, 12, 31–34, 46; Middle East for, 67–68; modernity for, 76; myth in, 129; non-whiteness in, 66; Orientalist-racism in, 4–5; Ottoman empire for, 83, 140n23; politics in, 25; power for, 14; punishment in, 49; racialization

in, 140n46; social policing in, 143n5; stereotypes in, 15, 42–43; violence in, 29; white supremacists for, 66

whiteness: for Anderson, C., 143n29; Blackness and, 56, 73–74; for Catholic Church, 62; for citizenship, 28–29; marginalization for, 48–49; for MENA people, 29–30, 141n51, 141n58; non-whiteness, 66; as race, 26; racialization of, 57–58, 62; in United States, 25–27

white supremacists, 61–64, 66–67, 87–88, 141n51

Whitewashed (Tehranian), 61

women, 11, 120–21, 123–25, 153n26

The Women's War (podcast), 124, 153n26

Wynter, Sylvia, 4, 39, 74, 96

xenophobia, 12, 20–21, 28–31

Yancy, George, 151n42

Yang, Andrew, 42–43

Young, Peter, 115

Young Turks, 84–85

Zehr, Howard, 40, 101

Zinn, Howard, 129

About the Author

George N. Fourlas is the SHIFT endowed associate professor of applied ethics at Hampshire College and a visiting faculty member in philosophy and government at Franklin and Marshall College. He received his Ph.D. in philosophy from the University of Oregon, completing most of his dissertation work in a predoctoral residence with the Institute for Democratic Governance, Globernance, in Donostia, Euskal Herria/Spain. His work can be situated across various disciplines, as it is problem-focused, specifically reflecting on the possibility of a world wherein presently subjugated peoples can exist in cooperatively-determined communities without fear of violence or the objectification that affords violence. To that end, his teaching and research take place at the intersection of social-political theory, applied ethics, critical race theory, conflict resolution, decolonial theory, and global studies. He has taught a range of courses related to this work, and his publications have appeared in peer-reviewed journals such as the *International Journal of Transitional Justice*, *Critical Philosophy of Race*, and *Journal for Peace and Justice Studies*. He is also a coeditor of the *Radical Philosophy Review*. When not working the academic grind, George enjoys spending time with his family, being outside, and practicing martial arts. You can learn more about Dr. Fourlas from his website: gnfourlas.com.

www.ingramcontent.com/pod-product-compliance
Lightning Source LLC
Chambersburg PA
CBHW052045300426
44117CB00012B/1977